W9-AVS-619

Women in American History

Series Editors
Mari Jo Buhle
Jacquelyn Dowd Hall
Nancy A. Hewitt
Anne Firor Scott

The Working Class in American History

Editorial Advisors
David Brody
Alice Kessler-Harris
David Montgomery
Sean Wilentz

Lists of books in both series appear at the end of this book.

Radicals of the Worst Sort

Radicals of the Worst Sort

Laboring Women
in Lawrence,
Massachusetts,
1860-1912

Ardis Cameron

UNIVERSITY OF ILLINOIS PRESS
Urbana and Chicago

Publication of this work has been supported in part by
a grant from the Museum of American Textile History,
North Andover, Massachusetts.

This book is printed on acid-free paper.

Library of Congress Cataloging-in-Publication Data

Cameron, Ardis.
    Radicals of the worst sort : laboring women in Lawrence,
Massachusetts, 1860–1912 / Ardis Cameron.
        p.   cm. — (Women in American History) (The Working class in
American history)
    Includes bibliographical references and index.
    ISBN 0-252-02013-8 (cl)
    1. Women textile workers—Massachusetts—Lawrence—History.
2. Strikes and lockouts—Textile industry—Massachusetts—
Lawrence—History.   3. Women—Massachusetts—Lawrence—Social
conditions.
I. Title.   II. Series.   III. Series: The Working Class in American
history.
HD6073.T42U518   1993
331.4'877'0097445—dc20   92-39119
                                                              CIP

To my parents, Art and Doris Cameron,
and to the memory of Elizabeth Wyon,
each in their own way
Radicals of the "Worst" Sort.

Contents

Preface   xi

Introduction   1

PART ONE

Self-supporting Women and the Struggle for the Real

1   The "Woman Question" and Self-supporting Women   17

2   Women, Consciousness, and Militancy   47

PART TWO

Immigrant Women and the Fight for Bread and Roses

3   Immigrant Women and Textile Culture   75

4   Neighborhoods in Revolt   117

Conclusion   171

Notes   187

Index   225

Preface

In August 1859, Mary Ann Hamilton brought her fourteen-year-old daughter, Margaret, and four other children to Lawrence, Massachusetts, in hopes of finding employment in one of the city's monster mills. With no husband to help support the family, her choices were few. Of her five children, only Margaret was capable of earning a wage; the others, too small for any work other than the kinds of casual scavenging always available to the strolling poor. Either she or her eldest child would have to enter a mill. Exactly how these new arrivals survived between August 1859 and January 1860 is unclear, but on January 10, 1860, Margaret began working in the spooling room at the Pemberton Mill, "the main support of the mother and four younger children."[1]

By staying at home Margaret's mother could care for the youngest family members as well as take in bits of work—laundry, sewing, and at times the children of working neighbors—in exchange for food, clothing, and only occasionally cash. In the shadow of the mills, the Hamiltons foraged and gathered, bartered and exchanged, and carefully calculated the making of something out of nothing.

Three years before the Hamiltons moved to Lawrence, Bridget Sampson left Ireland. A widow with three dependents, she and her nineteen-year-old daughter found employment in the recently opened Pemberton Mill. Illness and slack times cut into already meager wages so that by 1860 the combined wages of mother and daughter failed to provide even the necessities of life. Carefully dividing their weekly income of $5.22 into thin allotments for food, rent, and fuel, they seldom made ends meet. For most of the year, mill wages left the family with a weekly deficit of 13 cents.[2]

Poor, on the move, self-supporting, frequently widowed, and often with dependents, women like Mary Ann Hamilton and Bridget Sampson drift in and out of the historical record. Yet while their numbers swelled the ranks of an increasingly industrialized nineteenth century, self-supporting women had always been a part of the social landscape, and in a time when women's marital status largely determined their place in society, the woman without a man was a stock figure of tragedy, humor, and foreboding in the tales, ballads, rhymes, and "sayings" that made up much of rural New England's popular culture. To be "dulled," for example, was to blunder in marriage, while to be particular was to be a "tip-toe Nancy," an affected girl. "You better look out," warned a common expression, "and not have to go through the woods to pick a stick." Yankee girls understood the threat: don't pick wrong but pick. And if they chose badly, hundreds of verses, jingles, and tales served to remind them that complaints about deeds done fell on deaf ears. Like a sailor's telltales, such stories kept fixed the prescribed course of female life even as they chronicled real women's departures from it.

In a society where women's prospects for a decent life had always depended on support from men, women on their own experienced the full brunt of New England's industrial revolution. As the system of wage labor pulled more women into its orbit, their numbers constituted a growing portion of those found in the region's antebellum almshouses and jails and on the streets; and urban reformers never tired of making clear the ties between prostitution and the destitution of women without men. On the eve of the Civil War, roughly one-half of all women undertook some form of wage labor, and although most of these women would stop working after marriage, more than a third would continue to struggle in "an endless effort to earn income."[3] Differentiated by race, ethnicity, age, and occupation, self-supporting women nevertheless shared a powerful commonality: they were the working poor, inhabiting the very bottom rung of the economic ladder.

Textile manufacturing had always depended on the labor of women, typically serving as a magnet for those forced into a wage economy. In the cotton and woolen towns that dotted the New England landscape females typically outnumbered males by ratios as high as two to one. Often living outside a strictly defined "family economy," they shared rooms in boarding houses, combined households, lodged with other women, or like Mary Ann Hamilton and Bridget Sampson, headed their own struggling households.

Recruited to produce the nation's cloth, these women were rewarded with economic hardships, insecurity, and social marginality. Unlike the early "factory girls from Lowell," who, declared Nathaniel Hawthorne in 1830, "shall mate themselves with the pride of drawing rooms and literary circles, the bluebells of fashion's nosegay, the Sapphos, and Montaques and Nortons of the Age," women like Mary Ann Hamilton and Bridget Sampson occupied a meager place in the public imagination, and even to the most careful observers, they seemed like phantoms on the industrial landscape.[4] Writing about her Lawrence neighbors from her home in rural Andover, Elizabeth Stuart Phelps remembered how dimly the operatives appeared when, in the years before the war, she and her brother rode their carriage past the towering mills. "We did not think about the mill people; they seemed as far from us as the coal miners of a vague West, or the downgatherers on the crags of shores whose names we did not think it worthwhile to remember."[5]

The marginality of laboring women in the period preceding the Civil War was itself a product of the very processes that had called them into being. Even as Hawthorne wrote of his hopes for the nation's "factory girls," the demographic and economic changes that pulled women off their farms and into the mills of Lowell, Lawrence, and Manchester were rapidly transforming the landscape into which they moved. Increased expansion and intense competition sharply depressed global cotton prices by the 1840s, sending shock waves throughout the textile industry. As dividends hit all time lows, mill owners were pressured to find new ways to regain once high profits. Unable to control the external dynamics of the textile market, New England mill men turned inward, hoping to simultaneously reduce labor costs and increase productivity. The most common solution was either to "stretch-out" the work by increasing the number of looms for which a worker was responsible or to "speed-up" existing machines. At times, both methods were used, dramatically increasing the pace and rate of work. On the eve of the Civil War, machine tenders were handling three times as many spindles as they had in 1840, while their wages remained unchanged.

Throughout the thirties and forties New England operatives were quick to protest, and as Thomas Dublin and Caroline Ware have shown, women organized strikes and sponsored numerous petitions to redress their grievances. Calling themselves "daughters of freemen" and making "Mary Wollstonecroft" [sic] speeches, operatives made clear their belief that it was not the "pressures of the times" that threatened them but rather greedy manufacturers. The "oppressing hand of avarice," they argued, was extended by the "mushroom aristocracy," whose "Tories in disguise" denied operatives their rights.[6]

Despite the protests of striking women, inconstant times continued to alter both their world and public perceptions of it. Throughout New England, depressions, recessions, financial panics, and labor unrest underscored the instability of the new industrial order. In the years preceding the Civil War, fears of a pauperized proletariat contributed to a renewed series of attacks against both newer forms of production and female wage labor. "To see the mob of women that block and choke these few and narrow gates that are open to them—the struggle, the press, the agony, the trembling eagerness there displayed" was disturbing to a Republic that prided itself on its independence and self-reliance.[7]

The economic vitality that characterized Lawrence's early years and fueled its growth floundered in the unsteady conditions that preceded the Civil War. Lawrence industrialists blamed low tariffs and saw little relief without government protection for New England textile manufacturers. "How we are to get along without some new invention of this sort," wrote Amos Lawrence to his brother Abbott, "unless there be change in the times, and that very soon, we cannot now foresee."[8] The note of caution in the Amos letter, however, was a thin whisper against the cacophony of expansionism that marked the decade. Throughout the 1850s the growth of transportation networks and the development of national markets substantially increased the demand for goods, but expectations far exceeded reality. Reflecting these national trends, Lawrence's "monster" mills were built and both the Pacific and the Pemberton Mills were enthusiastically promoted, even as stable cotton goods began to flood the world's market. Massive unemployment at the Bay State Mills in 1855 underscored the problems of overproduction, yet few were prepared for the crisis that came with the panic of 1857. Within a few months, the national panic reached Lawrence and swamped the fortunes of numerous firms. Within a few weeks of each other, the Pemberton Mill, the Bay State Mills, and the Lawrence machine shop all went bankrupt with losses totaling $4.35 million. "For a time," recalled the founder of Lawrence's first newspaper, "a stranger would infer from the placards that the city was for sale."[9]

While "the extraordinary financial embarrassment" did not, as city fathers feared, cause the corporate giants to abandon the city, it did swamp the fortunes of many independent proprietors. Unlike large corporations, who used commission houses to guarantee loans extended to their leading customers, small shops, who tended to market their own goods, had no such protection against customer defaults. As the panic spread, increasingly curtailing customers' ability to pay for merchandise, the artisan entrepreneur was forced to assume debts or shut down. Bankruptcies and foreclosures forced small shops and independent merchants to pull up stakes and leave town. Out of 147 "active" businesses that started in Lawrence, only 25 remained by 1868. "Of the 122 missing links in this chain," commented one observer, "some, too eager to be rich, or too anxious for distinction . . . have moved along to new locations."[10]

Rather than puncturing the spirit of expansion and production, the panic actually reinforced Lawrence's commitment to large-scale manufacturing. Initiating a series of capital drives, city industrialists called on outside interests and personal capital to ride out the storm. Abbott Lawrence alone committed over one million dollars of his personal fortune to prop up corporations grounded on hard times. In short order both the Pemberton and the Bay State (now the Washington Mills) reopened under new management. Selling its huge machine shop, the Essex Company financed the conversion of the now silent buildings into one of the largest cotton and worsted manufacturing establishments in the city. Opening in 1860, Everett Mills soon became known worldwide for its high quality ginghams and denims.

It was the Civil War, however, more than anything else, that successfully yoked Lawrence's future with that of the monster mills. Under the exigencies of the conflict, Lawrence's corporate giants took root, expanding at a rapid rate and establishing the city's reputation as one of the world's leading textile manufacturing centers. In the process Lawrence became an international magnet for the textile operative, its economy no longer hospitable to the artisan-entrepreneur or the family shop, but increasingly dependent on those who could draw a frame, mend a split, weave a pattern, or simply tend a machine in one of Lawrence's enormous manufacturing establishments. The handloom weaver and the proprietor capitalist "moved along," receding in both size and influence while the immigrant operative swelled the ranks of Lawrence's toiling classes. What Elizabeth Stuart Phelps saw in the "new city" of Lawrence was not simply an alien landscape but a landscape filled with aliens. In the years before the war, native-born women simply stopped applying for jobs.

As they left the mills, so too did the "factory girl" leave the female operative, for what was changing was not simply a labor force but a conceptual system as well. Jolted by the shock waves of economic and demographic change, female operatives emerged both transformed and transfigured. Even before the war, the reputation of the "factory girl" was on the decline. By midcentury, the "pride of drawing rooms" would associate with factory girls only at the risk of losing their reputations. "Acquainted with *factory girls?*" asked one young man in an 1847 play, *Factory Girl.* "Do you suppose that I would disgrace my character by associating with that class?" Stigmatized by their efforts to earn a wage in the nation's mills and their willingness to protest mistreatment, factory girls were refashioned "for a little fun or a—conquest."[11] Increasingly placed outside the bounds of respectability, female operatives were pushed from public view, providing a seemingly invisible labor force even in the cities they once made famous.

From the outset, the construction of the "mill" or "factory girl" was an act of social comprehension, a representation of female labor that sought to make "sense" of rapidly changing arrangements in the family and in the world. As a kind of mental map that charted the alien terrain of industrial life, the "mill girls of Lowell" helped normalize wage labor for women, bringing into high relief both the female operative and the new order from which she sprang. The "factory girl" established sharp conceptual distinctions between a "woman" and those *women* who worked. She made familiar to a suspicious world the strange landscape of industrial wage labor even as it illuminated the boundaries within which female wage work could take place without threatening the social order. "Girls," after all, are not full fledged members of a society but belong to a transitional category, what the anthropologist Victor Turner has defined as a form of "structured liminality," an in-between state that because it is recognized by society and "contained within a culture's ritualized processes," is not in itself a threat to society. The "factory girl" did not endanger the new social order because like adolescence or the revival-conversion experience, it was a recognized liminality, one that-would come to an end, in this case when the "girl" left the mill and became a "woman."[12] Thus could Nathaniel Hawthorne, deeply troubled by "the damned mob of scribbling women," look happily upon the factory girls of Lowell.

When Elizabeth Stuart Phelps rode her carriage through Lawrence in the late 1850s, she did not see "factory girls" but rather women who worked. Disrupted by industrialization, the world of laboring women stood disordered as well by the chaos of reconceptualization. Operatives like Mary Ann Hamilton and Bridget Sampson seemed vague to genteel observers not simply because they were different from the Lowell "girls," but because as *women* who supported themselves, who lived without men but not necessarily without families, they destabilized the "logic" of their circumstances, the means by which they became socially visible. Thus what was at work as women like Hamilton and Sampson replaced Yankee operatives was not only a transformation of the workforce, but a reordering and realignment of those interpretive conventions through which the "logic" of laboring women's lives, the means by which they become socially visible or invisible, legitimate or "unreal," natural or deviant, takes on meaning in the world.

Positioned outside the conceptual categories that constituted the "woman" operative, self-supporting women emerged an economic phenomenon before they became a social "reality." Socially invisible, the new female operatives found themselves in a world that simultaneously depended upon their labor and masked the labor of women. It was a fate they would share with thousands of other women who, in the decades between 1860 and 1920, entered the paid labor force burdened not only by poverty but by "the extraordinary weight of characterization" that saturated female persons as "women" became a modern social category.[13]

My dramatis personae thus leave their own burden on the social historian who needs to enter not only the workshops and dwellings of laboring women but the context of domination; the "diverse but congruent" discourses within which women struggled as they sought to understand their world and their place in it as particular social beings: as women, and as women who worked. My own forages into the thorny landscape of words and gestures has brought not only a deeper appreciation of the constraints of gender categories but of the transforming power of "women in motion." Such interdisciplinary excursions have also deepened my debts as friends and colleagues patiently listened to inchoate ideas, read numerous revisions, willingly crossed the boundaries of their own disciplines, and in numerous other ways demonstrated the collective nature of feminist scholarship. I am especially grateful to those friends at Boston College who, as members of the "dinner and dissertation" reading group, helped me clarify and strengthen my arguments by softening each round of criticism with wit and good humor as well as generous portions of ricotta gnocchi, spanakopita, and carrot cake. For their unflagging support and sustenance, I especially thank Nancy Kavanagh, Greer Hardwick, Mark Ferrara, Jim Diskant, Sharleen Cockrene, and Robert Macieski. I owe as well a special debt to the many faculty members at Boston College whose support, encouragement, and criticism confirmed my commitment to feminist politics and historical scholarship. For their part in helping to clarify my arguments, I would especially like to thank Andrew Buni, Allen Rogers, Paul Spanoli, and Judith Smith. To Judy Smith I owe the kind of debt that comes only to the most fortunate of students. With her clearheaded comments, her wise counsel, generosity of spirit, and perceptive questions, incipient ideas took shape and vague hunches emerged into arguments. I hope that in this book she will find her efforts well served, her faith well placed.

I owe, as well, a special debt to Nancy Hewitt, whose commitment to women's history helped me to see the possibility of this study and whose unstinting support, encouragement, and friendship helped bring it to fruition. I would also like to thank Nancy Kavanagh, Phil Scanton, Peter Allen, Donna Penn, and Linda Stubblefield who kept me sane while writing my dissertation and to my students and colleagues at Harvard University and the University of Southern Maine who, with kindness and good spirit, entertained my questions, confusions, and doubts while revising it into a very different book. For their criticism, wit, and love of argument, I especially thank John Farrel, Patricia Yaeger, Joe Conforti, Julian Murphy, Leigh Gilmore, Donna Cassidy, and my students in the New England Studies department. A special thanks to Elspeth Brown, Johnette Lundy, Rita D. Disroe, and Dorothy Sayer for their assistance in preparing this manuscript, and to William Wolkowich-Valkavicius for his translations of Lithuanian newspapers and interviews and his knowledge of Lithuanian immigrant history. The Faculty Senate at USM, the Newberry Library, and the Museum of American Textile history gave me the resources and time to research and write this-book. I am especially grateful to the Museum of American Textile History for generously funding the color maps and to the staff of the museum for their ongoing help in researching this study. I would also like to thank Eartha Dangler, who as founder and director of Lawrence's Immigrant City Archives, has rescued literally thousands of documents and records from private and personal trash cans. Her efforts to preserve the words and events of ordinary men and women make local history possible. Certainly this would have been a very different book without the oral histories, scrapbooks, photos, and discarded collections of the Immigrant City Archives.

Many people have contributed to the development of this book. For their insightful comments, clarity, and patience, I am deeply indebted to Mari Jo Buhle and Jacquelyn Dowd Hall. In these pages I hope they find the fruit of their many labors. For sharing their astute comments, extensive knowledge, and perspective questions at various stages along the way, I want to also thank Alice Kessler-Harris, Carole Appel, Carole Turbin, Thomas Dublin, Sonya Rose, Susan Porter Benson, John Miller, Ruth Milkman, Eileen Boris, Donna Penn, Mary Blewett, Ava Baron, and Marcy May. For their patience and good humor and for providing me with the software, hardware, and other technical services necessary to complete this manuscript, I'm especially grateful to the Dean of the College of Arts and Sciences of U.S.M., Dave Davis, and to Dick Stebbins and Carl Helms. Disrupted by the transitions to a new place and a new life, this book also owes a special debt to the constancy and generosity of many friends, including Elizabeth Wyon, Freddie Wachsberger, Sylvia Newman, Anne MacKay, Cynthia Beer, Nancy Hewitt, Judy Smith, and especially Nancy MacKay, whose wit, good humor, and comradeship irresistibly mark the completion of this work. Thanks go as well to my parents, who always encouraged the independence of their children and never turned away from the consequences. To them I dedicate this book.

Finally, I owe perhaps the deepest debt of all to the men and women who readily shared with me their time, their stories, and their radical visions of an America transformed not simply by bread, but by roses too.

Introduction

In 1882 and again in 1912, the women of Lawrence, Massachusetts, took to the streets demanding better pay and a more equitable position in the relationship between capital and labor, what activists called a "fair" or "square" deal. Most, but not all of the women, were employed in Lawrence's "monster" cotton and woolen textile mills, and when wages were cut, they turned a deaf ear to both the "nice sweet words and flatteries of gentlemanly capitalists" who, complained one operative, "attempt to jolly us women" out of striking and to the aristocracy of labor—male craftsmen and skilled operatives—who also opposed the actions of the women.[1] Once out, women organized parades and demonstrations, built alliances with neighbors and kin, including shopkeepers, teachers, social workers, midwives, city workers, and, at times, local policemen, delivered formal and informal "stump" speeches, drafted and delivered proclamations, and in 1912 maintained soup kitchens and nurseries for strikers and their children. In the process women broadened the critique of capitalist development to include issues of daily community and household struggle. Armed with "lots of cunning and also lots of bad temper," they brought their demands to the center of national debates calling into question not only low wages but the whole of "corporate power."[2] To the industrialists in the textile manufacturing centers of New England such women represented what one mill official called "Radicals of the worst sort."[3]

While women have always occupied a central place in the history of the textile industry, their importance in worker struggles over control and authority has not. Based on thin description—what one scholar describes as "a one-dimensional view of labor conflict that fails to take culture and community into account"—studies of working-class politics seldom strayed from the point of production in the decades following World War II.[4] The complexities of female wage-force participation remained largely peripheral to analyses of class struggle, worker militancy, and consciousness. Women's efforts in the neighborhood and the community went largely unnoticed by historians convinced that the place to study workers was at work. Conceptually separated from the world of production, white working-class and immigrant women typically receded to the backwaters of labor history even in the textile communities they helped create. Those historians sensitive to the relationship between culture and politics still shared the assumption that only within the "unsteepled temples of worship" of male subculture were radical sensibilities formed, a political agenda forged.[5] Individually interesting, the female militant was portrayed as an anomaly, a curious but mute witness to the power politics of class formation.

Yet a countertale, forged by feminist scholars, has forcefully challenged such a paradigm and today an impressive body of work chronicles the rich and long-standing tradition of female activism. Recapturing the "venerable tradition of disorderly women" feminist scholars have unearthed buried sources of worker organization and militancy—those located not in the union hall, but in the web of female-centered networks that criss-crossed the neighborhood and the shop floor. No longer the domestic dustbin of labor history, the private world of proletarian women—including female friendships, sexuality, and notions of womanhood—has emerged as a central frame of reference.[6]

These scholars have also shed new light on the opaque world of laboring women. Drawing together efforts in the kitchen, the garden, and the laundry, with those of the mill worker and the maidservant, accounts of female labor accentuate the complex connections between the supposedly separate worlds of unpaid domestic labor and wage work performed outside the home.[7] In the real world of proletarian daily life, the task of "piecing together livelihoods" involved women in a complicated set of activities that were seldom understood as distinct from or independent of the home, the neighborhood, or the community. Whether in the streets of antebellum New York City, the barrios of turn-of-the-century Tampa, or in the working-class neighborhoods of Lawrence, poor women juggled wage-force participation with the ever-changing circumstances of their households, their families, and their neighbors.[8] Moreover new work on women's auxiliaries to male unions, labor leagues, co-operatives, and spontaneous boycotts demonstrates that women's buying power was also used as a weapon in class warfare.[9] It is not, in other words, at either the so-called point of production *or* consumption that we can best understand the lives of proletarian women, but rather at the myriad intersections of the two, where the bits and pieces of female labor converged in the daily struggle to make ends meet.

The strikes of 1882 and 1912 suggest the importance of these connections for worker militancy and class consciousness. Calling for a "fair days wages for a fair days work," female strikers also asserted their right to clean water, proper health care, decent housing, schools, even time "which belonged to us." In the industrial upheaval of 1912, housewives and operatives blended and mixed to form a great human chain of marching strikers, merging issues of the home with those of the workplace. Who could tell where the outrage of low wages ended and the "lash of youthful hunger" began? By what alchemy were poor health, child mortality, and filthy streets separated from shop floor issues of overwork, poor conditions, and declining wages? Linking arms and pressing their claims shoulder to shoulder, women gave a totality to worker militancy, which they themselves defined as a "fight for bread and roses." A slogan of hope rather than description, working women expressed a vision of possibility and transcendence that struck a deep and responsive chord in an America undergoing rapid and dramatic change. "What we saw in Lawrence," wrote female reformer Mary Heaton Vorse, "affected us so strongly that this moment in time in Lawrence changed life for us."[10]

As the title suggests, this study argues for the importance of community to female collective action and joins a number of recent works that seek to understand women's distinctive forms of activism by exploring the local context. Here in the thick web of neighbors, kin, and friends, the lives of ordinary women are made not only visible but meaningful as words, gestures, and acts take on the logic of shared purpose and collective wisdom. In this way, local history not only permits "the careful examination of grand and sweeping hypotheses," but allows for a notion of community more sensitive to the ways in which different groups, including women, have understood themselves as members of particular communities.[11]

Analyzing working women means exploring, therefore, not only geographic space (the neighborhood and the shop floor) but social space—those autonomous spheres of female interaction and exchange. It means asking as well not only where consciousness is raised, but how. How did women's position in the sexual division of labor in the home, the workplace, and the community shape commonsense notions of the real world? How did strategies of survival translate into street smart concepts of life and labor? How did laboring women come to understand their lives as women? As workers?

By placing women at the center of working-class struggle and collective action we can begin to tunnel beneath the wall that has traditionally separated the public and private lives of workers. Rather than diluting class antagonism, the linkage between the workplace and the "private" sphere helps untangle not only laboring women's place within the productive process but also the complex relationships between gender, class, and worker militancy. What sorts of conditions allowed ordinary women, both housewives and wage earners, collectively and militantly to protest their situation? How did women's collective efforts promote community cohesiveness and neighborhood discipline? At the same time, what can be learned about the internal dynamics of local power as disparate members of the working class forged a collective response to workers' grievances? And finally, did participation in collective action change women's sense of themselves? And to what extent did the collective acts of women transform power relations in the family, the community, and the workplace?

Based as it is on the scattered bits and pieces of working-class women's lives, this book also raises more general questions about the relationship between women, politics, and what Michel Foucault labeled "the order of things." As local rebels operating outside the realm of electoral politics and (for the most part) unions, female activists in poor and working-class neighborhoods represent what historians traditionally define as prepolitical, even premodern, actors in working-class life. Adopting liberal theories of democracy that assume the political is defined by self-interested individuals with clearly felt needs and preferences, historians have focused on those persons and groups who most clearly and cogently articulated their interests.[12] Political activity included voting, lobbying, organizing unions, and running for civic office. By way of contrast, the outbursts of so-called primitive rebels—those ordinary folk who stood outside this arena—were viewed primarily as politically insignificant expressions of momentary discontent. Seemingly spontaneous and relatively short-lived, they appeared to have little impact on the development of formal political movements and institutions. Cast as the inarticulate, participants in such skirmishes, along with the positions and visions they trumpeted, flashed across the historical landscape but with little long-term effect.

Following female activists through their own neighborhoods, especially at the height of labor-capital tensions, suggests an alternative notion of politics—one developed relationally, from neighbor to neighbor, and rooted in the material reality of everyday life. Expressed in a gestural language of female acts, it was a politics not simply thought up but thought out as women collectively confronted the world of "public" law and market forces. Forged as women sought to fulfill traditional roles as breadgivers and sustainers of life, it stood in contradistinction to the liberal paradigm. Recent studies focusing on women's activism in contemporary America suggest that for many working-class women, politics is "less [a process] of creating an allegiance to something *other* than the self-building community out of isolated individuals—than of finding ways to link the concerns, visions, and perspectives they share with neighbors and coworkers to the 'political system' that stands apart from them and seems to control their lives."[13] In working-class neighborhoods like Lawrence, networking was not about strategies for individual advancement but rather a recognition of "how things at bottom are."

Viewed in this way, politics becomes a process of daily life—a series of practical actions and strategies, carefully calculated in the context of family, kin, and neighbors. While few women would self-consciously define their activities in the neighborhood as political, their efforts in securing the welfare of families and friends often provided the emotional ties and communal networks that made change in their lives and in their communities possible. Located more widely and deeply than organized political activity, the web of informal relationships that were nourished and sustained as women performed their customary tasks of mutual help, daily exchange, breadwinning, and food preparation proved especially critical to the events that unfolded in 1882 and 1912. Both ordinary and routine, female collaborative activity was nevertheless bound up with larger issues of identity, power, and legitimacy. How this latticework of female exchange and reciprocity operated as a source of community cohesion, identity, and collective power is a central subject of this book.

Finally, this brings us to recent questions concerning the "order of things"—the establishment of hierarchies that often reveal more about the writing of things than about the things being written.[14] As questions of epistemology and methodology move to the center of scholarly debates, historians have become increasingly sensitive to the challenges imposed by the literary nature of their craft, a recognition that history is both about the past and about the telling of the past—a thing that is simultaneously "real" and made up. Committed to recovering the past and making it intelligible to the present, historians depend on narratives to make "the discontinuous facts of the past" meaningful in a world far removed from those "facts."[15] Stories help us make sense of things but they also help make "senseless" things, like violence, if not understandable, comprehensible; that is, they contain the past and provide both individuals and society a "stay against confusion." As Isak Dinesen once commented, "I could bear almost anything if I could make it into a story."[16]

For historians in general, and of the "inarticulate" in particular, narratives are both necessary and problematic, for in the struggle to understand, to see our lives as plotted and purposeful, narratives establish distinctions, create hierarchies, and formulate categories. Just as myth "makes things go without saying," stories tell us which things *go;* they give order, shape, and a trajectory to the clutter of things. Like the prickly, inedible New England spider crabs collected by lobstermen in traps intended for other more valuable prey, the comings and goings of working women thus come down to us in the present as the refuse of the past, incidental lives gathered and stored in the corners of greater narratives. As the subplots of what earlier feminists called "his-story" the lives of laboring women appeared "invisible," "hidden from history," a majority lost on the margins of a central story.[17] Yet, as theories of language and culture unravel the connections between narratives and knowledge, it becomes clear that there is no single narrative apart from those who seemingly stand outside it. As accounts that document ascendant definitions of reality, official stories—whether of countries, institutions, or individuals—are always partial tales, constructed oppositionally and almost always shaped by the alternatives against which they are asserted. They exist, in other words, in constant tension with the "other," which, for all its invisibility, remains no less "real" among the scattered fragments we tend to call history. Far from idle fictions, stories of the past take on importance as both structures of meaning and as structures of power.[18]

From this perspective, history can be seen not simply as a record of incomplete facts, but as both a producer and a product of historically constructed knowledges. Understood as a social production, the past takes on new meaning, revealed as an active participant in the "struggle for the real, the attempt to impose upon the world a particular concept of how things at bottom are and how men are therefore obliged to act."[19] No longer the product of Ranke's "innocent eye," history emerges as a process of legitimation that invests certain things—particular discourses, knowledges, events, as well as specific categories, concepts, and patterns—with power and authority while it simultaneously "disqualifies" others. As Robert Darnton wryly put it, "pigeon holing is . . . an exercise in power."[20]

Such a view of history assumes the centrality of struggle, and it problematizes what is often seen as natural or inevitable. Conventional categories, established "truths," traditional hierarchies, dominant groups are thus viewed as constructed realities produced for particular purposes in particular contexts during particular moments of transformation. As history, then, this book tells a story about people who lived in the past, but because women come down to us in the present pigeonholed by that past, it is also a study about domination, of power constructed and consolidated not simply at the level of economics and politics, but at the more general level of social perception and conceptualization. It asks, therefore, both about women and about shifting perceptions and definitions of "what a 'woman' should be."[21]

One of the central arguments of this book, then, is that laboring women, like other members of the "inarticulate," cannot be seen as somehow separate from and outside of the process of their own construction. Far from hidden or invisible, the radicals described here were the subjects of great controversy and public debate among contemporaries who viewed the "Woman Question" as one of the greatest issues of the day. In 1882 and 1912, Lawrence's female strikers drew national, even international attention. But as a distinct working-class culture took shape in the decades between 1880 and 1920, laboring women underwent a process of redefinition and conceptual transformation. In these years, the proportion of women in the labor force jumped from 15 to 25 percent, fueling conservative anxieties over the decline of the family.[22] Increasingly, women who earned a wage found themselves the subject of heated national debates, their lives interpreted in ways that further diminished their ability to support themselves or their families. Militantly rising to protest starvation wages, they were in turn branded as unnatural women, their poverty blamed on moral turpitude and maternal ignorance.

The fear of female militancy, "cherished," as Jane Addams once observed, "even by the Greeks," may have been an ancient one, but in the years between 1880 and 1930, conservative anxiety over a rapidly changing and conflicting world, transformed fears of female radicalism into an elaborate assault on gender deviancy. Embellishing earlier arguments that rested on biology, divinity, and evolution, with the "science" of sex psychology, twentieth-century sex reformers and psychoanalysts outlined the boundaries of natural and unnatural social/sexual behavior. If Freud had been tentative in his theory-building, his followers and conservative popularizers showed little restraint in formulating rigid categories of masculinity and femininity that refashioned separate spheres and the "cult of true womanhood" in the "modern" garb of psychology. By 1920, "even the unconscious was ridden with gender differences."[23]

Central to this new schematic was the fundamental principle of male economic hegemony. In this "new male discourse," writes Carroll Smith-Rosenberg, "Only the 'unnatural' woman continued to struggle with men for economic independence and political power."[24] Transforming women's struggle for economic autonomy and her historic participation in militant protest into a paradigm of "deviancy," an assortment of newly minted "experts" sought to redefine female activism as pathology and psychosis. Writing in 1929, sex reformer J. W. Meagher summed up several decades of "scientific" opinion: "The driving force in many agitators and militant women, who are always after their rights is often an unsatisfied sex impulse, with a homosexual aim. Married women with a completely satisfied libido rarely take an active interest in militant movements."[25] Declared unnatural, the female militant, the lesbian, the self-supporting woman, and the woman without a man, coalesced into a single category of deviancy. "Real" women stood in opposition to it.

Because contemporaries saw working women at the center of the strikes of 1882 and 1912, the dynamics of gender and class unfold with particular clarity in their stories. Eclipsed by both bourgeois claims to "science" and craftsmen's demands for a "family wage," the independent wage woman stood transformed—her claims to legitimacy a thin voice in a cross-class chorus of domesticity. So, too, does the strike for bread and roses reveal the centrality of gender in working-class politics as labor conflict itself conditions the reinterpretation of immigrant women in the years immediately following 1912. Both strikes, then, map out not simply the remote terrain of laboring women but, more importantly perhaps, the gendered landscape of working-class life as issues of worker poverty and low wages were reframed by the sexual politics of late nineteenth- and early twentieth-century America.

The title *Radicals of the Worst Sort* suggests therefore the role that perception and conceptualization plays in the history of worker struggles in general and of female collective action in particular. Certainly female activism cannot be understood outside the overall politics of identity, a politics often hidden in history but always at work as categories and concepts of difference—of class, race, ethnicity and gender—historically take form and shape, become fixed and are made "real." Neither arbitrary nor rooted in nature, as a number of recent scholars have shown, identities of all sorts are developed relationally, in opposition to or in contrast with elements of difference. Dominant groups define the familiar and normative "we" through inclusion and exclusion, "by suppressing the voices of those whose historical, social, and bodily experiences differ from their own."[26] The meaning of work for women has itself shifted over time but it was always the product of contest and struggle, of competing social formations and collective identities.[27] In the history of working women, categories have most often been constructed in opposition to bourgeois concepts of domesticity. Thus, self-supporting women, whether widows or single adults, have taken on historic meaning as "factory girls" or "women alone," and by the late nineteenth century as "redundant," "surplus," "odd women," and more ominously, as women "adrift." Such labels pushed working women to both the margins of existence and to the outer rims of labor history.

These official ways of labeling, sorting, and codifying, as Foucault's work has shown, were bound up throughout the nineteenth century with the formation of new social and anthropological sciences so that even today we find it difficult to identify, typologize, and categorize working women in ways that resist "naturalizing" economically dependent wives and daughters. The vocabulary of marginality which neutralizes the politics of meaning still haunts social history as scholars search in vain for labels removed from hegemonic "ways of seeing."[28] Rooted in the logic of our own social perceptions "factory girls," "women alone," "women adrift," and "at home," continue as metaphors for working women even as their descriptive power is exposed and weakened.

The strikes of 1882 and 1912, then, suggest the degree to which women could be both constrained and empowered by shifting understandings of work, womanhood, and ethnicity. As we shall see, both events bring into high relief the often hidden contests over the meaning of things as activists sought to make their words, acts, and gestures count in the struggle to change how things are. Far from passive participants in struggles over the shape and meaning of their world, Lawrence's female activists gave voice to a vision and a language that suggests much about the practical limits of hegemony in everyday life. Nevertheless, women could not, as one scholar put it, "invent themselves."[29] Severed from the "command of meaning," laboring women participated in the struggle for the real but their sense of self, of what it meant to be a woman, a worker, an immigrant, was neither absolute nor without constraint. At times women struggled against established meanings in order to participate in militant collective action while at other times women used their position as caretakers of the home and family to justify their radicalism and their use of violence.

We need, therefore, to see Lawrence's female activists as "woman," what Teresa de Lauretis defines as "a fictional construct, a distillate from diverse but congruent discourses dominant in Western cultures," and also as *women,* "the real historical beings who cannot as yet be defined outside of those discursive formations, but whose material existence is nonetheless certain," and the central subject of this book.[30] In this way Lawrence's laboring women can be seen not simply in history, but as history; they were, simultaneously, social actors whose historical situation as *women* provided the inspiration for collective action, and as historically constructed concepts that worked to both legitimize rebellion and to marginalize the rebel.

Women engaged in militant forms of resistance then, not simply because they were women, or workers, or immigrants, but rather because such acts made sense according to how they understood themselves as social beings and as members of particular collectivities. Conversely, female radicals were attacked and feared not simply because they were *women,* but because they were women who in their words and gestures challenged the parameters of what a "woman" should be, and in so doing, called into question those social and sexual hierarchies defined by conservatives as the very bases of modern civilization.

Because strikes disrupt the ordinary, they bring to the surface of official scrutiny those frequently invisible struggles over the meaning of things—of words, gestures, acts, even of the events themselves. For this reason the strikes of 1882 and 1912 are organized to stand alone. The former is not a backdrop from which to view the latter. Both are conceived as separate social dramas that destabilize the ordinary and explode—to use Joan Scott's phrase—"notions of fixity." As one of those "dramatic clashes that suddenly illuminates the plots of peoples lives," strikes also bring to the surface of official discourse those incomplete, illogical, naive, and inconsistent ideas and things found outside of and beneath established hierarchies and traditional frames of reference, what Foucault calls "subjugated knowledges."[31] The women in this book embraced no one theory or "ideas proper" and thus their positions— what Joan Kelly defined as "an outlook within which ideas develop"— have seldom been taken seriously in the annals of labor history. Yet as Scott reminds us, political movements are not "coherently unified systems of thought" but rather "melanges of interpretations and programs"; as actors in that process of interpretation laboring women were seldom "inarticulate."[32] It makes sense therefore to explore not only those things that emerged triumphant—a particular union, an established political party, a successful program, or a revered leader—but also those things that did not, and because they did not, are rendered not only inconsequential but, over the course of time, invisible as well. As a moment of disruption, the strikes of 1882 and 1912 move Lawrence's labor movement away from the orderly realm of linear continuity and posit it instead within the web of relationships from which it originally drew its meaning. Here at the ground level, where ordinary people sort out the common sense from the commonplace, the variegated nature of working-class politics is thrown into high relief and expressed in the street-smart language of women in motion. Attending to female acts, gestures, and spaces, this study explores Lawrence's labor movement as it grew and developed not in the journals and speeches of the aristocracy of labor-usually male craftsmen—but in what Natalie Davis once described as "the dangerous nooks and crannies" of women's lives.[33]

To view the house of labor from such remote and irregular corners is thus to begin where history is most denied, at the level not of economics or politics, but of social perception and cosmology. Part One, entitled "Self-Supporting Women and the Struggle for the Real," considers a number of conceptual categories and the disappearing acts occasioned by discursive practice. It explores the life of women who, brought together by the dilemma "Work or starve, were thrown onto their own resources in the industrialized world that followed the Civil War, providing the bulk of New England's textile operatives. This section explores the lives of self-supporting women and examines as well their transformation from independent wage earners to "surplus" women radically redefined as "adrift." In Part Two, "Immigrant Women and the Struggle for Bread And Roses," this theme is further developed by exploring the role of immigrant women in the famous strike of 1912. Using the techniques of nominal record linkage[34] and oral history, this section examines women's use of neighborhood spaces and traditions of mutuality and reciprocity in community efforts to collectively protest conditions in the city. The subject of widely circulated news reports and government investigations, the strike brought to the attention of a reform-minded nation the poverty and ill-health of the country's immigrant workers. It brought as well a new object of reform: the "unruly female elements" who hurled insults along with rocks, tore officers' coats, stuck hat pins in the horses of cavalry boys, and spread "anarchy everywhere." In the aftermath of the strike, efforts to educate the "ignorant foreign mother" would quickly outpace reforms committed to abolishing poverty by improving the wages of workers.

If, as Roland Barthes has argued, history is most at work when it is most denied, then it is among the marginalized where we will most likely find a past that speaks to the present. Ultimately this book is about the struggles of working women, but it is also about conceptual contests—of identities in formation and contention, of categories forged and forgotten, of possibilities transformed and eclipsed—of those moments when a label sticks, a pigeon is holed. In 1882 and 1912, women revealed the complexity of women's advancement as they sought not only to make their lives better but through their actions to *make* them, and to make them count. Certain of themselves and convinced of the justice of their cause, they staked out what they believed to be their place in a movement to change history. As one anonymous female militant put it, "I only add the record of my experience as a possible atom of force to that lever which shall one day topple the rock out of our road."[35] Such records reveal what this book assumes, that working women are not left out of history, but are rather the subjects of a history deeply at work. The ability of Lawrence's laboring women to disrupt "history"—to demand in the community, in the neighborhoods, and in the streets, a voice not only in the world but about how the world is—was what made them radicals. That they disrupted established meanings and gave motive force to alternative visions of gender is what made them radicals of the "worst sort."

PART ONE

*Self-supporting Women and
the Struggle for the Real*

1

The "Woman Question" and Self-supporting Women

It is well for us to remember this. Whatever the struggle for the elevation of women means, it means that which a sneer, a scowl, a threat, a *bon mot* can no longer blow away.

This is the "woman's hour."

—Elizabeth Stuart Phelps, 1871

In the dark, cold dawn of January 1860, just under a thousand mill operatives left their rooms and cottages in the "Plains" for the short walk down the canal and toward the Pemberton Mill. Here in the tall five-story building of red brick and exposed oak beams they would spend the light of day producing 115,000 yards of fancy cambric and cottonades that they themselves could not afford.[1] For Phelps, it was the time to see Lawrence. "So languidly the dull-colored, inexpectant crowd wind in! So briskly they come bounding out!"[2] On this particular day, however, Pemberton operatives would not leave the mill, for in the hours just before closing, the mill suddenly left the workers.

The Fall of the Pemberton and the Rising of the Women

Built in 1853, the Pemberton was one of Lawrence's largest manufacturing establishments and with its unusual width of eighty-four feet and its great number of wide expansive windows, it was also one of the city's most handsome structures. John Lowell, a staunch supporter of Lawrence, orchestrated its founding after a visit to England convinced him of the desirability to create a model mill equipped with the most modern technology. At a cost of eight hundred thousand dollars, the stately Pemberton crowned the city of Lawrence and by all accounts was one of the finest mills in New England.[3]

Seven years after its opening, just as the sun set on January 10, 1860, workers on the fifth floor of the mill suddenly felt the cast iron pillars supporting the center of the structure begin to buckle. A few seconds later, the flooring gave way, crashing through the remaining four floors and trapping most of the work force. Those who could escape joined rescuers who worked frantically to release the living from the rubble, but in the confusion of the night, a lantern suddenly fell, igniting the pools of oil and scattered cotton that covered the site. Relatives and friends watched helplessly as trapped workers waited in horror for the flames to consume them. Some slashed their own throats or begged bystanders to shoot as the fires reached them. In the end, eighty-eight lay dead and dozens more were severely injured.[4]

The collapse jolted the nation. Reporters flocked to the city and interviews with survivors, relatives of victims, even reenactments of the night, flooded the popular press. City fathers were immediately on the defensive, worried not only about the adverse publicity, but about the possibility that it might drive mill owners out of town or prevent future investment. "Lawrence officials," wrote David Nevins, a controlling partner in the Pemberton, "were hesitant to even suggest that the mill owners compensate the injured or the families of the dead in fear of causing industry to leave the city due to unfavorable and unfriendly attitudes."[5] The relief committee, composed of several mill agents including Henry Oliver and Charles Storrow, acted accordingly, minimizing corporate responsibility and extending only a minimum amount of aid to the victims and their families. The City Mission, whose motto was "Intelligent giving and intelligent withholding are alike true charity," was equally dubious about the benefits of direct aid. As funds poured in from around the country, the City Mission joined mill owners and city fathers in a successful effort to limit the fund to sixty thousand dollars. Explaining their reasons for limiting funds to the victims, officials argued that, "continued assistance might prolong their dependency by encouraging them to claim exaggerating injuries, or not to seek re-employment either in Lawrence or other New England manufacturing centers."[6]

No effort on the part of city authorities, however, could prevent the groundswell of criticism that followed in the wake of the accident. One of the worst peacetime disasters in the nation's history, the collapse of the mill temporarily redirected attention away from the "peculiar institution" of the South and onto the "system of slavery . . . in our own manufacturing establishments."[7] Like a national pageant, the "Fall of the Pemberton" dramatized the oppression of factory operatives, forcefully and graphically undermining the industrial *bon mots* of mill masters in general and of Lawrence's lords in particular. Throughout the winter and spring of 1860, the vague people of the Plains were made suddenly and poignantly visible. "One January evening," recalled a startled Elizabeth Stuart Phelps, "we were forced to think about the mills with the attending horror that no one living in that time when the tragedy happened will forget."[8] A poem in Vanity Fair underscored the mood of the times:

A Curse on ye, ye Millionaires,
    Who sit at home in your easy chairs,
    And crack your nuts and sip your wine,
    While I wail over this son of mine![9]

For Phelps, like many other women of her class and generation, the "Slaughter of the Pemberton" unearthed a new and troubling social reality. Highlighting the vast changes that had begun to eclipse their world, the fall of the Pemberton anticipated the postbellum awakening of millions of women transformed by war and by the twin processes of urbanization and industrialization.[10] As the national press initiated a series of "thrilling incidents" focusing on the lives of the Pemberton heroes and victims, the distance between middle-class women and those of the Plains became especially marked. Almost daily, "shocking revelations" along with graphic stories of "woman's heroism" saturated popular newspapers like *Frank Leslie's Illustrated, Harper's Weekly,* and *Vanity Fair* exposing a forgotten class of self-supporting women. Over 70 percent of those killed or injured in the tragedy were women and girls, and reporters dramatically reconstructed stories of sisters, mothers, and daughters struggling to support elderly parents, young children, even husbands out of work. Every day throughout the winter and spring of 1860 the national press poured out the grim details of Pemberton victims revealing to a conflicted republic the underside of the northern system of wage labor. In Lawrence, it was made clear that many New England women desperately needed to work and that most wage women labored in the knowledge that all men do not support all women.[11]

Awash in the sentimentality of the times, such tales brought to shore the marooned world of women who, like Mary Ann Hamilton and Bridget Sampson, entered the labor force "not because they choose, but because they are pushed into it by a dilemma, on whose horns are written, Work or starve."[12] It was "a world," wrote one anonymous working woman, "where men meet women on a cool, business level of dollars and cents," and where "nobody makes a discount because of sex, except in paying wages."[13]

What the Pemberton collapse began, the Civil War brought full bloom. The demands of battle siphoned off one-seventh of the city's male population while those of a booming textile industry pulled thousands of war deserted wives and daughters into Lawrence's labor-hungry mills. Throughout the nation women found themselves tugged in new directions by the war emergency. Middle-class women joined relief agencies, sanitary commissions, hospitals, and at times found themselves in leadership positions vacated by men now in uniform.[14] Others, less fortunate, entered the paid work force. Employment patterns, of course, varied by class, race, and ethnicity, but the wartime experiences of women confirmed what the Pemberton collapse had made so clear: "plans need to be devised, pursuits require to be opened, by which women can earn a respectable livelihood."[15]

To meet the challenge, women in Lawrence organized the Ladies Soldiers Aid Society, which established the city's first all-female charity and the only benevolent association initiated without mill involvement.[16] Catering at first to the needs of soldiers and their families, the organization soon broadened its scope, offering supplies and a day nursery for children "while mothers were at work."[17] In 1875, it incorporated as the Ladies Union Charitable Society (LUCS) and appealed to "all the ladies of the city whose hearts beat in unison with all efforts to relieve the needy in this season of hard times." Propelled by the belief that "the one sweet touch of nature has made them kin," they sought not only "that the mother should go contentedly to her work," but that the "sick and suffering women . . . be made comfortable."[18] Under the direction of Dr. Susan Crocker, concerned women established the city's first free "invalid" home. Other projects called for the construction of cooperative houses especially designed and built to meet the needs of working women. While the model house was never built, cooperative apartments were organized by activists and the invalid home eventually developed into the city's only public hospital, the Lawrence General.

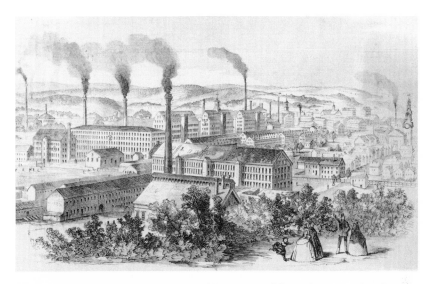

Figure 1. Pastoral view of the city of Lawrence, Massachusetts, showing the site of the Pemberton Mills (no. 1) before their fall. Courtesy of the Museum of American Textile History.

The vulnerability of Lawrence's laboring women brought home to Crocker's generation the uncertain fate of women in postbellum America. The unbridled competition and greed that ushered in the Gilded Age revealed to many middle-aged women exactly how far the nation had drifted from the values of their youth. Although Abbott Lawrence, the city's principal investor and namesake, had urged his own daughter to "prepare . . . in case of need to obtain your own living without dependence upon others," the female offspring of the new industrial elite were more likely to embrace a world of idleness and "Mammon," what Harriet Beecher Stowe described in 1871 as the "Pink and White Tyranny."[19] "We have no women now," complained an Andover editorial, "now-a-days instead of women, we have towering edifices of silk, lace, and flowers."[20] For women like Crocker, as well as her more famous neighbors, Phelps and Stowe, the devaluation of women's productive labor by those who would claim that for women "the business in life is to look pretty, and amuse us"[21] was not only a violation of Republican values but a threat to survival as well. What united middle-class reformers with the cause of laboring women was their fervent belief that a woman's ability to support herself was the only true stay against the storms

Figure 2. In stories and traveling shows like this one from the National Theatre production of *Mill Girls of Lowell,* wage-earning women entered popular culture as "Factory girls," c. 1849. Courtesy of the Lowell Public Library.

Figure 3. The rebuilt Pemberton Mill, c. 1855. Courtesy of the Museum of American Textile History.

Figure 4. One of the country's first disasters, the collapse of the Pemberton Mill in 1860 brought national attention to Lawrence's laboring women. Courtesy of the Museum of American Textile History.

Figure 5. "Women's Heroism" from Frank Leslie's *Illustrated Newspaper,* January 20, 1860. Courtesy of the Museum of American Textile History.

of industrial life. Arguing that wage women "preserved the republican heritage from those who sought to introduce the trappings of European decadence," middle-class women linked their own uncertain futures with the plight of laboring women.[22] The "right to equal pay with men, for equal expenditure of time and skill" united women in "bonds as bound."[23]

In Lawrence, as in many urban areas, the advancement of wage women thus took central stage as reformers sought to reconstruct "corrupt, filthy, American cities."[24] Denied legitimacy as public actors, and thus exposed to the abuses of male power, wage-dependent women highlighted the abuses of the industrial system and provided graphic evidence that it was time for women to put things right. "Quietly, gradually, powerfully," wrote Phelps, "an 'agitation' is becoming a consecration; a problem is solving into a creed."[25] As historians have shown, the path to "the good times coming" would be rocky as suffragists, philanthropists, temperance workers, cooperators, free lovers, and woman rightists tripped over competing visions and approaches, but in the decades after the war, a growing army of women shared a deep belief that a reconstructed America ultimately depended on the economic and personal independence of women.[26] "It is no figure of speech to say that the 'woman question' is the most tremendous question God has ever asked the world since he asked, 'What think ye of Christ on Calvary?' "[27] Linking women's efforts with the future of humanity, "the Queen of the Platform" reformer and socialist Mary Rice Livermore made clear the enormity of the "woman's hour": "As long as courage and capacity, self-poise and independence, are regarded as qualities ennobling men, but dewomanizing women—so long will low ideals of womanhood prevail, necessarily dragging down the standards of manhood. We rise or sink together, Dwarfed or Godlike, bond or free."[28] A generation shared her passion. "No reform has ever struck the stratum that this movement strikes. It lies deep in the tangled roots of things. Every false soil piled above it must crumble into it."[29]

Emphasizing the goals of female self-support and independence, supporters of Lawrence's day nursery and cooperative housing projects also brought to the forefront of city politics a radical belief in the public nature of domestic life. Defending their role in the sheltering and feeding of children, Lawrence activists countered arguments like those of the Pemberton Relief Committee with terse rebuffs declaring that their work "is like the mothers daily work" and "made our responsibility" through "the necessities of poverty." Echoing national reformers who, like Melusina Fay Peirce, Marie Stevens Howland, and Mary Rice Livermore, sought to socialize child care and household labor in order to emancipate women and "domesticate" the urban jungle, Lawrence "Union Ladies" advocated changes in the domestic environment of laboring women.[30] Campaigning for reforms in the material lives of women, they sought "to set women free and put the world right."[31]

While never abandoning their deep faith in female domesticity and the "home," middle-class reformers nevertheless staunchly defended a woman's right to equal pay and placed the blame for "fallen women" squarely on the shoulders of a system that denied women the ability to support themselves. When Margaret Jakes, "mother of thieves," was arrested for child neglect, members of the LUCS helped fund her defense, arguing that "starvation alley" and "traditionalism," which "still lingers to impose its artificial and restrictive economy for women," and not Jakes, were to blame.[32] Arguing that women operatives "who only get half the pay however good," be admitted to the city's suffrage rallies at half the price of all men and of women who didn't earn a wage,

Lawrence's female activists linked the ballot question squarely with the earnings of laboring women, "the bread and butter of their life."[33]

If the world, as Mary Rice Livermore argued, was to be made more homelike, then women had the right, even the duty, to involve themselves in the public sphere. Linking Margaret Jakes to the failure of society, not nature, and unequal pay to the evils of the nation, women reformers countered male city missionaries who saw public relief and charity as a dangerous intervention in "natural laws." "Had a kind hand" intervened, asked the President of the LUCS, "might we not have seen in place of criminals, a race of noble men and women?" This question kept the plight and the right of laboring women in the forefront of Lawrence's political culture.

So too did the actions and voices of Lawrence's laboring women. Embroiled in the Woman Question, the city was as well a hotbed of grass roots agitation. Free thinkers, socialists, and labor radicals, carrying traditions of an indigenous radicalism into the Gilded Age, joined suffragists, women's rights advocates, and a bevy of "female agitators" to promote the "good times coming." "Equal rights" was invoked to demand not only citizenship, but "comfortable dress," "equal pay for equal expenditure," and even equal access to the city's baseball fields for its girl teams.[34] In 1882, a series of lectures on the "Fallen Woman" was defended on the grounds that "unfortunate women be put on an equity with male sinners." The enthusiasm for equality surfaced as well in unexpected places. Seemingly unrepentant over her inebriated state, Mary McCabe defended her actions in court with "her assertion of a woman's right to do what she please—even to getting drunk."[35]

Between 1860 and 1885, newspapers record the presence of numerous "woman agitators" addressing the myriad needs of "the women of the mills." Whether in "huge crowds" or small "knots," they produced "stirrings" around the town. Four years after the war, Lawrence operatives staged the largest rally in the city's history. "The hall was full," noted reporters, "and in the evening every woman who was present in the afternoon, and her next door neighbor, and her next door neighbor, were on hand." Drawing on community networks, "a large majority from the disfranchised class" gathered to usher in the "time near at hand when women shall have their day and their say."[36] Demanding votes for women, labor activists like Mrs. Bower, whose husband headed the Short Time Committee, laid claim to the nineteenth century's most "radical" notion, that women be defined not solely in relation to their positions as daughters and wives, but as citizens and indi-viduals, "independent of 'mate' or 'brood.' "[37] It was an argument that struck a responsive cord in the city's operative class. Challenging the arguments of national labor leaders who sought to cast female wage women as victims in search of male protection and male wages (the "pearls of princely duty") as the "natural" support of women, partici-pants demanded their right to equal partnership in a reconstructed Union. "They held up their heads," commented one reporter, "and looked as bold as lions."[38]

The significance of the Gilded Age woman's movement then, was less in the fact that middle-class women "discovered" self-supporting women than in their conviction that wage labor was the key to woman's advancement. It was this, more than anything else, that set the Gilded Age movement apart from earlier women's reform movements and po-litical struggles.[39] Postbellum women publicly challenged the myth that all men support all women and questioned as well the dependence of women on men. Laboring women like Mary Ann Hamilton and Bridget Sampson thus emerged not merely as objects of reform but as socially legitimate subjects whose uncertain fate, popularly known as the Woman Question, symbolized for many activists the precarious position of *all* women in the new industrial order.

A City of Women

A moment of contemporary revelation, the fall of the Pemberton provides as well a glimpse of the past to present day historians. On the day it collapsed, Margaret Hamilton was starting her first day of work as a "learner" in the Pemberton's giant spooling room. She was, noted a vigilant relief committee, "the main support of the mother and four younger children."[40] Like her coworker, Mary, the nineteen-year-old daughter of Bridget Sampson, it would also be her last. "God forgive me Mary Burke," cried the mother of another victim, "for murdering you by bringing you to America."[41]

Death stole the lives of these individual workers but it also robbed Lawrence families of essential support. The Sampson household, al-ready threatened with starvation, now found itself destitute without the $2.76 earned each week by Mary. Many families, similarly reduced to greater levels of poverty, turned to the relief committee while those who could still do so looked for work in other mills and in other towns.

The Civil War would pull them back. When the conflict began, Lawrence's manufacturers, unlike those in Lowell, predicted that the war between the states would be a long battle. As soon as hostilities began, they stockpiled large quantities of raw cotton. Rather than dumping these reserves on the open market when world prices began to soar, Lawrence mill owners used them to keep machines running. While Lowell's mills stood idle, Lawrence underwent one of its greatest periods of expansion. Two new mills, the Everett and the Arlington, opened during the war, while older mills increased their productive capacity and modernized machinery. Simultaneously, the city's mills moved to protect themselves against fluctuations in the global cotton market once the war ended. Every cotton establishment in the city introduced or expanded its worsted or woolen departments, a move that would eventually guarantee Lawrence the lion's share of the world's woolen and worsted textile market.

The Pacific Mill typified the changes in Lawrence's industrial capacity. Built in 1853 along the banks of the North Canal, the Pacific specialized in cotton warp and all-wool dress goods.[42] In 1860, it had an annual product of 11 million yards of dress goods. Eight years later, the mill resembled a city within a city, operating its own transportation system, a huge power station, and consisting of forty-one acres of flooring in twelve buildings. Five years after Appomattox, it was producing 45 million yards of cotton and woolen goods and by 1878, the figure had climbed to 65 million yards.[43]

The war reinforced the region's commitment to textile manufacturing, but both expansion and technological change altered how cloth would be produced and who would produce it. The introduction of the spinning mule in 1850, a machine far heavier and more demanding than the old jennies, encouraged the hiring of male spinners whose physical strength gave them an advantage over women spinners.[44] Still other inventions reduced the amount of skill required to operate once difficult machines thereby reducing the corporations' reliance on experienced workers. Less dependent on Yankee girls and women whose labor had always stirred controversy and whose protests had jeopardized popular support for the new industrial order, employers turned to a growing supply of machine tenders eager for work. "Unnoticed and unopposed," men, women, and children from Canada and Ireland entered New England's mills and cities.[45] By 1852, "half of all factory operatives in New England mills were already foreign-born."[46]

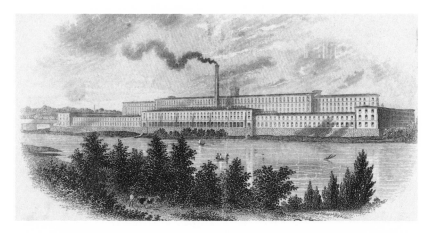

Figure 6. Built in 1853, the Pacific Mills expanded rapidly during the Civil War. By 1868, the Pacific boasted forty-one acres of flooring in twelve buildings and produced 45 million yards of cotton and woolen cloth annually. Courtesy of the Museum of American Textile History.

As Lawrence's mills clattered with activity, hungry men and women once again turned to the monster mills at Lawrence in search of work. Between 1860 and 1865, the city's population jumped by 23 percent as "a large influx of strangers" joined veteran operatives, swelling the central district to a density seven times that of five years before. By 1870, Lawrence's population stood at thirty-four thousand, almost half of whom were immigrants.[47]

By far the largest number of newcomers to take advantage of the city's wartime boom were the sons and daughters of Erin. Between 1845 and 1860, over one-third of Ireland's population emigrated, driven out of Ireland by famine, unemployment, and a series of mass evictions generated by decades of English control. Crossing the sea to England, workers like Bridget Sampson and her daughter, Mary, typically took up work in English textile mills until they were able to buy passage to America. Lured by New England's mills, they rapidly filled the region's textile towns where they provided a large bulk of the industrial proletariat. At war's end, the Irish accounted for more than 65 percent of Lawrence's foreign-born population, the second highest percentage in the state.

Again, however, the Civil War merely solidified a process already underway. The Panic that preceded secession sent hundreds of Yankee factory girls to rural homes, thus opening a toehold for the city's underemployed immigrants. When production resumed several months later, they rapidly filled the vacancies. At the Pemberton only a handful of Irish were among those operatives employed in 1857.[48] At the time of its collapse, however, almost 80 percent of the Pemberton work force was born outside the United States, the vast majority of them in Ireland. Children, once a rarity in the mill, now made up a fifth of the Pemberton payroll.[49]

The records that survive in the wake of the Pemberton tragedy support studies that chronicle the transformation of New England's operative population from native factory girls to one of immigrant men, women, and children. In Lowell, Waltham, and most other Massachusetts textile cities, tasks once performed exclusively by Yankee girls and women were, by midcentury, increasingly being assumed by a more diverse and heterogeneous population.

The waning of the Yankee "factory girl," however, should not be interpreted as representing an automatic shift to an operative class composed primarily of parents and their children. While families were increasingly recruited by mill managers eager to take advantage of dependents, the city's machine tenders remained an assortment of "independent" operatives. "In Lawrence," noted Carroll Wright, director of the State Bureau of Statistics of Labor, in 1875, "there is more of the individual in labor, and less of the family."[50]

Contributing to Wright's assessment was the inordinate number of women operatives like Mary Ann Hamilton and Bridget Sampson. These included widows, deserted wives, as well as unmarried operatives, many of whom were "quite aged." Pushed into the factory by the dilemma "work or starve," they represented a new corps of industrial workers in the Gilded Age.

As one of the few gates open to needy women, textile manufacturing attracted a large bulk of such working women, not only from abroad but from economically depressed states as well. The war, along with the economic boom that it generated, pulled thousands of war deserted wives and daughters into Lawrence's mills, deepening the city's dependence on female labor. Nor was this trend reversed when national hostilities ended. Throughout the 1870's, women swelled the ranks of the city's neighborhoods, creating a highly visible operative class who understood the precariousness of their lives as women dependent on a wage and as women frequently independent of male support. Lawrence's growing reputation as an international center for cotton, woolen, and worsted textile manufacturing also made it an especially attractive location for families with large numbers of female kin, who eagerly (often desperately) came in hopes of finding employment for all members, a survival strategy that continued well into the twentieth century.

Consequently, the transformation of Lawrence's proletariat involved large numbers of actors generally dismissed by historians as marginal or peripheral to class formation. While some were married women who worked alongside husbands, many others headed their own households, often working at night in order to care for their children by day. Numerous others, denied husbands by sex ratios overwhelmingly slanted toward women, remained single but not necessarily young.[51] Self-supporting, they also maintained others, either directly as kin or indirectly as roomers and boarders who contributed wages to households "kept" by widows or single parents. Whatever their marital status, however, few could afford to view marriage as a permanent removal from factory labor. This assumption would have been especially hazardous among the Irish, as male death and desertion made them more vulnerable to the demands of widowhood and self-support than any other ethnic group.

By war's end, what had once been a "woman-operated system," increasingly became a women-dominated city. A magnet for women "compelled to work in order to live,"[52] Lawrence drew women to its mills in far greater numbers than men so that in the Plains, where the vast majority of Lawrence's operative class lived, women outnumbered men by ratios as high as two to one.[53] New inventions, like the ring and fly spindle, contributed to this trend by gradually replacing mule spindles and the highly skilled male mule spinners, with ring frames and their less-skilled female operatives. The new Pemberton, opened in 1861, foreshadowed the movement toward an increasingly mechanized technology when it replaced 15,000 crushed mules with 6,656 new ring and fly spindles.[54] "One of the evils in this city," complained a male weaver twenty years later, "is the gradual extinction of the male operative. The female," he correctly observed, "has the preference."[55]

Speaking to a state investigator, the weaver reflected the growing concern over the "excess of females" in the commonwealth. Between 1855 and 1865 self-supporting women doubled in the Bay State, initiating a sexual imbalance that would escalate in the wake of the 1873 depression.[56] By 1875, the numbers of self-supporting women grew rapidly by "nearly 300 per cent," according to Charles Elliott.[57] Acknowledging public interest in this "often discussed question," Carroll Wright set out to discover exactly "who are the 63,146 excess women?"[58] Wright found that the vast majority were immigrants, most of whom were widows, while many others were deserted wives or unmarried women: all were desperately in need of work.

While the sexual imbalance in Massachusetts was more acute than in any other state, it was especially dramatic in textile communities long dependent on the cheap labor of women and girls. "In our cotton mills especially," noted a popular magazine, "the women and children largely exceed the men, being from 2/3's to 5/6's of the whole."[59] Lawrence was a major example of textiles "preference" for women. By 1880, women comprised as much as two-thirds of the city's working-class population in the Plains. By far the largest section of Lawrence, this central area was the hub of the city. Spread out in the shadow of the city's major mills and wedged in by the Merrimack River to the east and the Spicket River on the northwest, the Plains harbored the vast majority of the city's Gilded Age working classes.

Large numbers of Irish immigrants began to enter its neighborhoods in the late sixties gradually displacing older residents, most of whom were skilled workers, mechanics, retailers, mill overseers and entrepreneurs of various stripes.[60] These groups slowly retreated to more bucolic sections of the city including Prospect and Tower Hills, or clustered in the sections closest to the Common.[61] As tenements, shanties, and private boarding houses competed with the corporate living facilities, operative blocks grew into rambling neighborhoods. Houses in these streets increasingly stood in contrast to the carefully planned and orderly dwellings designed and built by city industrialists. Jerry-built tenements and private boarding houses containing new mixtures of populations now spilled into blocks once reserved for skilled men and their families. Mechanic Row, for example, once a spacious section of neat brick blocks available to married employees at the Lawrence machine shop, was by 1860 a series of subdivided units rented to operatives "at will."

Although, as one machine tender put it, it would have been more "politic" to live in the corporate boarding houses and thus "be assured of work," immigrant operatives overwhelmingly preferred the less-guarded streets and crowded lodgings of the Plains.[62] Boarding houses, once the principle abode for "factory girls," now housed a dwindling proportion of the operative class.[63]

Table 1. Sample of Female Mill Hands, by Neighborhoods and Marital Status, 1880

| Neighborhood | No. of Cases | Single | Marital Status | | |
			Married with husband	Married without husband	Widowed or Divorced
Everett	44[a]	31	8	1	2
%[b]		74	20	—	—
Corporate					
Reserve	90	61	20	0	9
%		68.0	22	0.0	10.0
Plains Central	96[c]	69	8	3	3
%		68.0	22.0	—	10.0
Total	230	161	40	11	16
%		70.0	17.0	6.0	7.0

a. 2 Missing values. These include those individuals for whom information is incomplete or illegible.
b. Percentages based on known cases. Columns may not add up to 100.0 percent due to rounding.
c. Thirteen missing values.
SOURCE: United States Census, Tenth Census . . . 1880, Manuscript Census Schedules, Lawrence, Massachusetts, 1880.

While immigrants, especially the Irish, rapidly populated the "Plains," it was the immigrant woman who dominated the landscape. Among the Irish, Scots, and French Canadians, who, by 1880, collectively accounted for 77 percent of the city's foreign-born population, women consistently outnumbered their male counterparts. For every one hundred women in the Plains who had been born in Ireland, Scotland, or in French Canada there were respectively only sixty-three, forty-two, and forty-nine of their countrymen.[64] Sex ratios were especially lopsided in the years most associated with female labor force participation, underlining the "pull" that Lawrence's mills had for women in need of employment.[65]

Both census data and contemporary reports provide a closer glimpse of Lawrence's "excess" population and help map the territory of Wright's "individual" operative population. As table 1 shows, single women made up the largest share of Lawrence's female machine tenders, accounting for roughly 70 percent of the neighborhood samples, but wives, many of whom were either deserted or separated from husbands employed elsewhere or in search of employment "out west," also swelled the ranks of the city's female population.[66]

Working wives appeared in the records regardless of the ethnic composition of the neighborhood (see table 2). In the Everett Neighborhood (map 1), where native-born women accounted for 80 percent of the mill hands, one in five machine tenders was married, and even in the Corporate Reserve, a district whose boarding houses traditionally catered to single women, wives made up more than one-fifth of the operative population. A comparison of table 1 with studies of the Pemberton payrolls of 1860 suggests that it was the instability of industrial labor and not temporary "Hard Times" that guaranteed married women a permanent place as a group in the textile labor force. At the time of the Pemberton collapse, just under 20 percent of the mills' work force consisted of wives and women whose husbands were no longer living.[67] While some of these women were deserted wives, others had spouses too ill to work or were unemployed at home. Mary Armstrong, whose husband was chronically ill, was the "only support for her family." She "did night work," noted inspector William Joplin, caring for her three children in the day. Seriously injured during the mill's collapse and no longer able to resume factory work, she was reduced to taking in "homework," which at this time in Lawrence included mending clothing or taking in wash at a fraction of factory wages. The plight of Mrs. Lawrence Kennedy was no doubt repeated in other families as well. Injured at the Pemberton, Lawrence "got well enough to work" and left town for Fall River. In what was apparently a common strategy among the working poor, he left "a wife and one child here who if he can get work he will support."[68] Living outside of marriage, almost one-fourth of the Pemberton victims lived in female-headed households, a figure roughly comparable to the structure of Irish families in other industrial towns at the time.[69]

Ages of mill women also challenge assumptions that wage labor was essentially a temporary stage in a women's life cycle. Mary Duffee, an "old woman" who "lived alone caring for a daughter," was, like many textile operatives, no longer young. Almost 40 percent of the sampled female mill hands were twenty-six years of age and older, while fully 18 percent were over the age of thirty-one. The existence of older women in Lawrence textile factories confirms other studies that show significantly large numbers of older women in the ranks of the labor force.[70]

Table 2. Sample of Female Millhands by Neighborhood, Age, Marital Status, Employment, and Ethnicity, 1880

Neighborhood	Age						Marital Status					Employment				Ethnicity				
	N	15–20	21–25	26–30	31–40	over 40	N	S	M	W^a	D	N	Cot.	Wool O^b		N	Native	Irish	U.K.	Can
Everett Newberry St. Orchard St.																				
Number	44	12	11	6	11	4	42	31	8	3	0	42	14	27	1	44	35	1	8	0
Percent^c		27.3	25.0	13.6	25.0	9.1		73.8	19.0	7.1			33.3	64.3	2.4		79.5	2.3	18.2	
Corporate Reserve Methuen St. Essex St. Canal St.																				
Number	90	29	20	15	19	7	90	61	20	7	2	89	52	30	7	90	35	46	9	0
Percent		32.2	22.2	16.7	21.1	7.8		67.8	22.2	7.8	2.2		58.4	33.7	7.9		38.9	51.1	10.0	
Plains Central Oak St. Short St.																				
Number	96	31	38	14	11	2	83	69	8	6	0	94	48	46	0	96	4	81	8	3
Percent		32.3	39.6	14.6	11.5	2.1		83.1	9.6	7.2	0		51.1	48.9	0		4.2	84.0	8.3	3.1
TOTAL	230	72	69	35	41	13	215	161	36	16	2	225	114	103	8	230	74	128	25	3
Percent		31.3	30.0	15.2	17.8	5.7		74.9	16.7	7.4	.9		50.7	45.8	3.6		32.2	55.7	10.9	1.3

a. Widow or married no husband listed.
b. Refers to mill other than textile manufacturing.
c. Columns may not add up to 100% due to rounding. Proportion based upon known cases. Missing cases include those individuals for whom information was either incomplete or illegible.

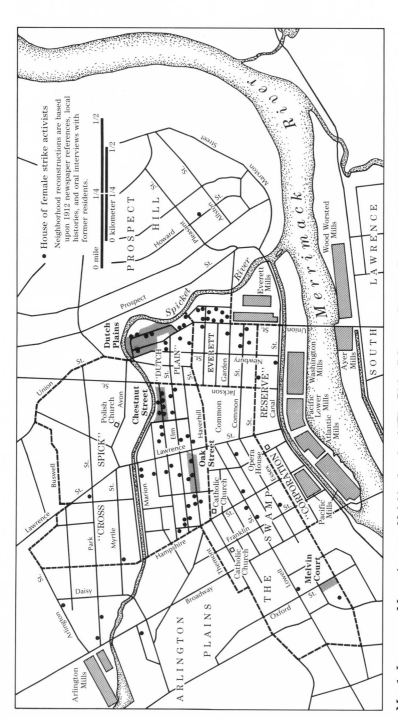

Map 1. Lawrence, Massachusetts: Neighborhoods of "The Plains." Source: Boston: Sampson & Murdock Co., 1912.

Table 3. Household Structure of Unmarried Irish Female Operatives in the Plains[a]

| | Living with Parents or Parent | Boarder | |
		Male Head	Female Head
N	48	14	44
%	45.3	13.2	41.5
Total Cases	106		

a. Plains includes all single women sampled from the Everett, Corporate Reserve, and Plains Central neighborhoods.

While deserted wives, spinsters, and widows made up a significant proportion of Lawrence's self-supporting women, single women under thirty provided the bulk of its operative class. Often portrayed as immigrant daughters living under parental roofs, these laboring hands were as likely to be independent boarders and tenants living in the numerous "private" facilities that dotted the Plains. Outside the traditional "family economy," they contributed to the growing ranks of urban natives and newcomers who lived "on the margins."[71] Of 106 unmarried Irish women living in the Plains in 1880, slightly more than 50 percent boarded in noncorporate establishments headed by nonkin, usually widows or married women whose husbands were absent (table 3).[72]

To Wright the bureaucrat, such women represented a new corps of "independent" workers, for they lived outside traditional household settings. By the turn of the century, "independent" wage-earning women would account for one out of every five urban women who worked for their living.[73] Moving away from familial settings and into the new subcultures of rooming house districts, they would provoke national concern as women perceived to be both unprotected from the hardships of urban life and susceptible to the vices of an independent one. Yet even in the anonymous environment of cities like Chicago and New York, self-supporting women maintained meaningful social ties as they formed surrogate families and found friends to help them.[74]

In Lawrence, the independence of self-supporting women was, in practice, defined by their necessary dependence on others, including kin as well as friends, housekeepers, neighbors, and coworkers. Self-reliant, they remained nevertheless within the social and emotional networks of the Plains community. Unlike metropolitan tenants, boarders, and lodgers, single women in the smaller environs of Lawrence were often near family, and sisters comprised a large percentage (19 percent) of the boarding population.[75] Private boarding houses in the Plains also imitated the family by providing an assortment of services as well as a place for informal socializing and entertainment. Residents usually shared meals and "keepers," usually older women, cooked, cleaned up after meals, mended clothes, and, no doubt, served up a sufficient supply of advice and insight. Unlike room-only "lodging houses" on Essex Street, which, by 1870, began to gain a reputation for a "cheaper class of help," these family-styled establishments were greeted with approval, for "keepers," while maintaining less control than corporate houses, exerted their influence by screening newcomers and evicting troublesome residents. A "good" house increased its desirability and in turn brought a touch of respectability to its residents.

At least one house in Lawrence experimented with more radical forms of housekeeping. Apparently inspired by Socialist and Feminist debates over the relationship between industrial development and the role of men and women in domestic labor, the house was organized collectively, with boarders "united in a club and running the thing themselves."[76] A city dependent on the labor of women, Lawrence offered an ideal location for a number of progressive experiments where wage women rationalized domestic work and, as in this house, "employed a cook and other domestics."[77]

For the most part, however, women's choices were few. Many lived with kin and not a few struggled to support themselves as well as relatives too sick or unable to find work. Theodora Morrison, an operative from Maine, whose "father was out West and not been heard from for three years," supported her Aunt and Grandmother, both of whom "were not entirely dependable." The father of another Pemberton victim, a tailor, "does not work much," reported one ward inspector, relying instead on the wages his daughter and wife earned at the mill. Similarly, Ellen Collins, whose father "does not work anywhere in particular," assumed the role of breadwinner for the family of three. In a city increasingly devoid of economic opportunity outside mill gates, underemployed men often found themselves dependent on female kin. "Within a radius of two squares in which I am living," explained one operative, "I know of a score of young men who are supported by their sisters and mothers because there is no work for them in the mills."[78] Even in families headed by working men, however, female earnings were critical, as wages were never sufficient to support dependents even during boom times. Only skilled American men could afford to keep wives and daughters out of the mill.

The twin threats of male absence and poverty encouraged women to pool scarce resources and combine households. Not untypical of Pemberton victims was the assorted home of Mary Crosby, a young operative employed at the mill when it collapsed in 1860. Mary's family consisted of a brother, a sister, and a widowed mother, all of whom worked in the Pemberton Mill. Living with them was a coworker, Mrs. Catherine Clark, whose husband worked in the Pennibec Mills in New Hampshire. Clark's three children worked in other mills out of state, her son, according to authorities, could be "found by referring to the Sonacook Mill in New Hampshire," and her two daughters who could be "found in New Market, Maine."[79]

Not surprisingly, newspapers and "gaping visitors" noted in the bleak aftermath of the Pemberton disaster the important role of friends in providing care for the victims. "Friends of victims" wrote one reporter, "care for them more often than families."[80] Typically substituting for absent kin, friends and neighbors overlapped with blood relatives connecting individual immigrants to a wider network of shared values and collective experience.[81] Personal hardships such as food shortages, illness, birth, abusive husbands, or unemployment were less likely to be experienced as private failures than as reminders of a common vulnerability and mutual adversity. Widows and deserted wives played especially important roles in cementing shared values and a common identity. As they "kept" house for operatives, these financially dependent women no doubt reminded younger women of the precarious fate that might easily await them. Washing their clothes and cooking their food, they also supported them in ways reminiscent of absent mothers and old-world "wise women." Dependent on each other for survival and bound up in a latticework of relationships, "individual" operatives in Lawrence were frequently women without men, but they were very seldom women alone.

The concentration of women on the shop floor and in the proletarian neighborhoods of the city had important implications for female identity and consciousness. As frequent household heads, as traditional caretakers of home and family, and as essential contributors to the family income, toiling women found themselves in a position that demanded skills and a character structure very different from those prescribed by supporters of "true womanhood." In the Plains, female economic prowess, strength and vigor, not passivity or submission, were the essential qualities of womanhood. The daughters of Erin proved an especially sharp spur in the sides of domesticity and separate spheres, for in Irish communities a woman's importance was often measured according to her ability to earn. Far from jeopardizing the marital appeal of women, the ability of a daughter or sister to earn a wage contributed to their status as women. Irish men valued women who could add to the family purse, for no matter the type of work, "the money a woman brought into a marriage may have been a more important asset than good looks, a charming personality, or whatever other 'empemaral' characteristics went into romantic attraction."[82]

The lack of importance given such attraction notwithstanding, the degree to which many working-class families would come to expect, as a social norm and family goal, the "woman" at home cannot be denied. Many workingmen especially envisioned "homelife" in ways that emulated the bourgeois ideal, and even radicals like Ira Steward argued for the day when "men whose wives and children are laboring in the mills will become ashamed of competing in such a manner, with those whose families do not, and allow them to remain at home, and unite with their fellow workmen in demanding pay enough to support them in their proper sphere."[83]

As an ideology that criticized industrial capitalism in the name of an idealized nuclear family, the "family wage," however, did not simply recreate genteel notions of domesticity, but neither did it merely reflect working-class strategies and aspirations.[84] Historians are correct when they write that the ideology of domesticity "was not just a set of oppressive ideals foisted on a supine female population; it was an ideology actively adopted by many working-class women as the best in a very narrow range of unhappy options."[85] Yet in practice, ideologies are never simply adopted or rejected in the same way that one votes for a favorite political candidate. They emerge as "maps of problematic social reality and matrices for the creation of collective conscience."[86] The ideology of the family wage came about as men and women, disrupted by the trauma of industrialization, sought to understand their world and their place in it. For male activists it provided a powerful metaphor that spoke to the abuses of capitalism, but it operated, as well, as a signifier of new social relationships in the transformed world of industrial wage labor. As metaphor, the family wage articulated class difference in a way that encoded economic autonomy as masculine in contrast to the feminine domestic side. Household head, the shop floor, skill, and producer emerged as signs of maleness and signifiers of masculine prerogatives. Steward saw himself, no doubt, as a political strategist, but with the rhetoric of the family wage he simultaneously reflected *and* constructed working-class identity and consciousness.

By 1900, the family wage would unite an array of strange bedfellows including workers, Progressives, employers, woman activists, and socialists, but its hegemony was always partial and contested. As power relations shifted in the unsettled sands of textile households, various "maps" competed with one another as men and women sought to make meaningful the otherwise incomprehensible social situations created by industrial life. In the years before corporate America solidified, no map was accurate, no conscience wholly creditable. Confusion, not clarity of purpose or vision, dominated communities like Lawrence, and neither the logic of the new industrial order nor the authority of tradition stilled the turbulent waters of the Gilded Age factory town.[87]

Newspapers recorded the results of such confusions. Typical was the story of one father's attempt to "inflict . . . punishment upon a younger member of the family." The mother unhesitatingly "interposed" while the eldest son "bit his father's finger, cut him in the face, and bruised his body generally with the aid of a chair." Sent to jail for sixty days, the boy returned home, and with his mother went to Illinois "for a tour."[88] Here was the topsy turvy world of disorientation; "a disorientation in whose face received images of authority, responsibility, and civic purpose seem radically inadequate."[89] It was this loss of orientation that typified factory towns and produced among those most immediately connected with their operation a tangle of ideological activity. While labor agitators like Steward articulated more clearly their demands for a family wage, others sharpened their own ideas about the expectations of women. Still others, "just took a notion" and went "for a tour."

In Lawrence, where women provided the bulk of the city's labor force, the notion that men were primary bread winners entitled to higher wages to support a wife at home entered the laboring community as something of a strange idea. When several male labor leaders from out of town suggested in 1855 that women be excluded from factory labor, an outraged activist in Lawrence asked, "Is it just to exempt one class of operatives from the performance of labor while another . . . is left to themselves?"[90] The solution, he argued, was to allow "all persons 16-60" the right to work, "but only for ten hours a day."[91] By 1870, female operatives had made clear their determination to organize themselves, joining with their male counterparts to demand a shorter work day. In petitions and rallies women sang the song of the ten-hour day. "Ten hours a day for men and women, the young and the old, to toil in our mills is quite long enough," conceded one city official.[92] If male leaders in Boston and Fall River hoped that resolutions directed at removing women and children from the mills would succeed where a total reduction had failed, they badly miscalculated the city's and the region's dependence on female labor. "Lawyers and doctors we could do without," admitted Lawrence's mayor, "but labor is indispensable to the welfare of the community."[93] While city officials generally supported the reduction of working hours, they knew full well that it was the "sisterly" association of the mills and its laboring women that generated the city's wealth. "They started life together," wrote one newspaper editor in 1882, "and spent a busy youth in helping each other into a vigorous womanhood."[94] Uncertain of the future and unable to predict it, local politicians like Duncan Wood made certain that, should the time come and woman gain the ballot, they would be favorably remembered.

Textile culture itself was an "affair of the tribe" involving those who depended on it for a livelihood in an elaborate system of reciprocity, dependence, and co-operation. At the ground level, where ordinary men and women make sense of their lives, the family wage was in perennial erosion from below as daily routines, unsteady economic conditions, and lopsided sex ratios diminished its ability to persuade. Forced to "remain idle while the women work," Lawrence men were at times also forced to assume work normally performed by women. "I know of a number of men," stated one Lawrence man, "who are compelled to stay at home, do the housework, and attend to the children."[95] No doubt at times a "source of complaint" for women as well as men, the exigencies of textile manufacturing underscored the limits of an ideology exclusively dependent on male family members. Asked to comment on the unemployment of men in Lawrence, a male weaver proposed a very different solution than that of the family wage. "I think the proper way," he explained to state officials in 1882, "would be to equalize the work for the sexes so that every member of a family can work."[96] It was one map among many, and we know little of its history. But that it did not ascend with others to positions of influence is a story less about its appeal and more about the construction and consolidation of power.

Traditions of reciprocity, neighborliness, and familial juggling of responsibilities lessened the hardships of mill life, but as one wage women reminded her audience, for the women who worked, it was always "the object of their lives to hold their heads above water and keep the sharks at bay."[97] The predators that swam in textile waters included seasonal unemployment, low wages, the premium system, speed-ups, overproduction, and high rates of accidents, all of which deepened the "sisterly" relationship between women and the mills. Time spent in the drawing room, the weaving room, the mending room, and even the less-desirable spinning room further consolidated one's identity with wage labor, for few women were ever permanently out from under its shadows. In families with married women strategies varied according to ethnicity, but in general, the precariousness of textile manufacturing forced all women, including grandmothers and those with young children, periodically back to the spindle and loom. Table 2 points out this continuity of wage labor for mill women. Regardless of their place of origin, all three neighborhoods record significant proportions of married and older women in the ranks of Lawrence's operative class.

Statistics do not tell, however, the degree to which many married women, officially recorded "at home" by census enumerators, periodically left home as temporary workers, what today is sometimes recognized as "permanent part-time." Newspapers hint of just such a shadow population of women operatives taking over jobs for sick friends, injured husbands, or for unemployed kin and neighbors. A short notice in 1882, concerning the accidental injury of a Mrs. Richard Bodkin, who, declared mill management, was "not an employee of the corporation" but had volunteered to take the place of another woman at the Pacific Mill, suggests both the uncertain nature of textile work and the fluidity of women's lives as they sought to earn their living from it.[98]

Thus, while married women comprised a quarter of the female work force at any one time, it was likely that the individuals within this group changed frequently, making factory labor a familiar experience for many more married women than fixed samples suggest. Substituting for each other, women also helped secure jobs for neighbors and kin and remained in the social network of mill life long after active participation ended. As one historian has pointed out, "Although working women may have been temporary workers as individuals, they were permanent members of the labor force as a group."[99] In the Plains, neither wedding bells nor grey hair diminished the enduring claims that textile manufacturing held on women's lives.

Artisanal traditions privileged craftsmen, but textile manufacturing diluted masculine claims to master status. In neighborhoods where cotton and woolen workers dominated the labor force, sexual hierarchies were disrupted by women whose quick hands and sharp eyes earned them reputations as skilled workers and valued employees. Contemporary reports typically lump female machine tenders together as "operatives," a label erroneously implying that jobs for women were indistinguishable one from the other. Woman operatives, however, maintained great distinctions. Neighborhood grapevines and boarding houses discussed openings not for "hands" but for menders, weavers, and drawers. These were highly skilled positions that were offered to only the most capable, and it was with a sense of pride that women accepted such employment. At the table, in the streets, and in the community, mill women were identified not only as operatives but also as operatives with particular skills or as learners of specific jobs. Margaret Hamilton, Mary Sampson, and Catherine Clarke were not simply Pemberton operatives who lost their lives when the mill collapsed: in their community and in the press they were spoolers and dressing-room operatives.[100]

As machine tenders, of course, neither men nor women had more than limited control over the productive process, but whatever skill and knowledge did exist was seldom the exclusive domain of fathers and husbands. Again the contrast with artisanal traditions was sharp. While artisans and skilled craftsmen could claim a degree of superiority based on their ability to teach family members the details of their craft, textile skills could be learned in months, not years, and these skills, with few exceptions, were dispersed throughout the household. Mothers and wives, daughters and sisters, as well as fathers and husbands, shared a position as "learners" or teachers, passing on information and experience to household members with a rough equality and a sense of pride generally considered unique to a male subculture of skilled workers, the "aristocracy of labor."[101] No matter how skilled, however, women performed their tasks in a shop floor that was organized to subordinate the work force in general and women in particular. Hierarchically structured to teach all workers the rudiments of industrial "time-work-discipline," mill authority was also sexually asymmetrical; men managed the payroll, "bossed" the floor, and supervised the "hands." With words, actions, and gestures, mill bosses infused the workplace with a set of oppositions—between men and women, household and workplace, skilled and unskilled, managers and hands. Deference, passivity, and obedience was expected from every hand but from women it was expected sooner and in greater quantity. Here, then, gender differences entered shop floor relations as a component of industrial organization. At work, the sexual division of labor reinforced an ideology of separate spheres increasingly articulated through demands for a "family wage." At the point of production, in other words, women confronted a world of value and symbol that promoted what one historian has called a "specific psychology of female subordination," enhancing men's ability to define their womanhood and to control their labor power.[102]

In Lawrence's neighborhoods, authority relations provided a constant and dramatic contrast. The female-dominated neighborhoods of the Plains carved out for women what one theorist calls a "landscape of subterfuge"—autonomous social spaces within which they could develop and sustain an independent sense of worth and self-esteem.[103] Forced to assume the role of breadwinners, many women were especially well situated to experience the contradictions between the observed reality of female economic importance and worth and shop floor policies that emphasized female marginality, subordination, and dependence. Furthermore, the exigencies of migration and the feminized character of the city stimulated the growth of female networks as widows, deserted wives, self-supporting boarders, and married providers struggled to survive in an industrial world marked by rapid change and brutish conditions. Often blurring lines between kin and friend, collective living arrangements also helped dilute distinctions between generations and between single and married women. Whether as single boarders sharing meals with widows or as married women occasionally substituting for a friend at work women honed a consciousness of themselves that emphasized their commonality as women.

In the tangled households of the Plains, individual tragedies and personal crisis spilled into the crowded lives of neighbors, friends, and kin. Childbirth, illness, childcare, wife-beatings, male desertion were not private events to be hidden away behind locked doors but rather events to be experienced and redressed collectively. Like the lines of laundry that crisscrossed the city's alleys and courtyards, women in the Plains joined together in hopes of keeping dry and holding "the sharks at bay."

It was from within this latticework of relationships that women confronted rumors of impending cut backs at the Pacific Mill, Lawrence's largest and, by 1882, most influential factory. Without oral histories, it is impossible to map precisely the spread of this news, but the actions of the strikers make clear the collective nature of their decision, which rested on a solidarity rooted in the community. Confident that they could "rouse the public sympathy," secure the support of "grocery and provision men," and "find cheaper lodgings" once evicted from corporate facilities, hundreds of women and children walked out, boldly launching Lawrence's first major confrontation between labor and capital.

2

Women,
Consciousness,
and Militancy

In conclusion I would say to treasurer Wood and his understrappers, that I think I can exist on earth, make a respectable living with the labor of my hands, have a clean heart and a clear conscience, and live just as long as if I were the daughter of a capitalist living off the labor of my fellow beings, instead of what I am more proud to be—a woman of the working-class.
  —Lawrence striker

In March 1882, frame spinners at the Pacific Main Mill received news that their wages were to be reduced from ninety cents a day for eight sides, to sixty-eight cents a day for ten sides. Calling a meeting at the noon hour ("which belonged to us"), spinners met to formulate plans and elect leaders. "A woman representative," most likely Mary E. Halley, boldly approached the department supervisor and immediately went to the heart of the spinners' complaint. "We are all women," she told him, "some are married and many are of an advanced age and it is preposterous to think of the possibility of working at sixty-eight cents a day when the operatives have not even time to comb their hair, the work requiring their entire attention."[1] While speed-ups and wage reductions were not new to the Pacific work force, especially in the wake of the 1873 depression, the spinners saw spring cutbacks, which reduced their pay at a rate far greater than those of male operatives, as part of a long list of grievances specifically affecting the "poor working girl" and the "honest women." As Halley's outburst suggests, the spring reductions would make it impossible for women to support either themselves or their families. Denied a living wage, they declared it was "better to starve outside the mill than at work."[2] When overseer Parker refused to speak with the spinners, "passing into his office and closing the door" in Halley's face, the women quickly made "arrangements." Leading a handful of spinners out, Halley marched to the Plains to regroup, gather support, and make further plans.

Inside the mill, operatives spread the word of what had happened and room five made preparations for Halley's return. A few minutes before closing, they went downstairs and as one striker told reporters, "waited for the weavers in number 4 to come out. They were preparing to come out but had no leader. They were also somewhat frightened by overseer Phillips who kept moving up and down the room, watching their movements and [by] corporation detective Philbrick, who was stationed near the door looking on." No one was sure what happened. Suddenly hundreds of shouting and waving women were heard marching up Canal Street. "Our approach was the signal," explained one striker, "for the waving of handkerchiefs, aprons, and shawls, and hats." Then operatives inside were to go to their looms, shut them down, and walk out. In a "spontaneous expression of individual feeling," over five hundred women and children triumphantly marched out declaring their fight "a struggle against oppression and tyranny."[3]

The Strike of 1882

The strike took industrialists by surprise. Two months before the spinners revolted, a state survey of three industrial towns asked, "Why is it that the working people of Fall River are in constant turmoil, when in Lowell and Lawrence they are quiet?"[4] A smug Saltenstall, treasurer of the Pacific Mills, quipped, "I believe the operatives would not strike if they were starving."[5] Some blamed the weather. "People who labor shut up during a long winter are always restive at the approach of Spring."[6] Certainly, wrote the *New York Times,* "a few kind words, a little evidence of kindness, would have ended the trouble."[7]

Jolted from their complacency, town officials quickly called a meeting at city hall to remind the striking women of the benefits Lawrence offered its operatives. "There are more people in Lawrence owning their homes than in any other city of its size on Earth," noted the first speaker, James Eaton, treasurer of the Essex Savings Bank. Duncan Wood, local agent and aspiring politician, agreed. Comparing Lawrence to other towns, he reminded the several hundred women of the Pacific Mills's international reputation as a model mill. "It had always been a source of pride to him," he told the rebellious audience, "when in other cities and mills to refer to the Pacific Corporation."[8] The meeting, however, did not turn out the way city fathers hoped. The women were unimpressed. Standing up after the line of speeches, a woman's voice filled the hall. "It is all very fine for businessmen to advise the weavers what course of action to take," she stated, "but all this talk does not amount to a row of pins."[9] Asking other women to accompany her, Halley set out to "rouse the sympathies" of others "in behalf of the operatives" and to form a union. Within three days, sixty-four thousand spindles shut down and over five thousand operatives walked out.

The immediate impetus for the strike came when it was announced that wages throughout all departments of the Pacific Mill were to be reduced and piecework was to replace the old system whereby ring spinners "were employed by the day, irrespective of capacity."[10] Mule spinners were cut from $11.50 a week to $10.25 but with no increase in work.[11] Female ring spinners and weavers, however, sustained the greatest reductions, suffering a 20 percent drop in wages, from 90 to 68 cents per day. Furthermore, weavers, most of whom were women, were still reeling from a series of speedups initiated in December. By raising the work load from six to ten picks a minute, new production levels forced weavers to suffer reductions even as they produced more cloth.[12] Newspapers and labor leaders cautioned the women not to strike, arguing that "their places would be filled." Mule spinners, traditionally rebellious male operatives, also opposed the strike. Female operatives countered, however, by pointing out that it was "the girls in the spinning room who are the hardest worked and the poorest paid of any in the mill, and they can ill-afford to suffer any reduction in wages."[13] Once out they refused to return. "Everyone was honest," reported Halley to the press, "in the determination to hold out."[14] Outraged by reductions that would deny "an honest living" to the "poor and decent working girl" and angered by a "corporate power" both "ignorant and blundering," the striking women brought a new militancy to the city's dormant labor movement as they sought to "emancipate the millions of white slaves to corporate power."[15]

A cut in pay, however, was tyranny only in its most obvious form. Declaring themselves to be "all honest" and entitled "to a fair days wages for a fair days work," female operatives confronted the mills, but they pitted themselves as well against the contradictions of a system dependent on their labor yet unwilling to pay them because of their sex. As an earlier working woman had noted, it was the female laborer who needed to know "the difficult art of making three dollars out of one," for women, she declared "have no share in that American privilege which sets in full view of the poorest white male laborer a growing income, a bank account, the possibilities of an Astor, and every office within the gift of the Republic if he have the brain and the courage to win them."[16] As female reformers had argued for decades, low wages for women worked in tandem with a "system of education which only looks to marriage, where the thinking and planning will be done for her" to deny all women the means by which to earn a livelihood.[17] For female strikers, tyranny was multilayered.

A threat to their survival, wage cuts were seen as well to be an affront to women's once valued position in the industry and in the city. Throughout the strike women voiced their resentment over management's refusal to recognize their worth and value to the industry and to the larger commonwealth. Writing under the pseudonym "Spindle," Mary E. Halley complained that "the poor working girl has to toil for daily bread and mere existence to pay for the faults of the higher paid ignorant officials."[18] In both words and acts, female strikers represented themselves as essential but "grievously mistreated" producers of Lawrence's wealth in general, and of corporate profits at the Pacific, in particular. It is "poor cloth without us," wrote Halley as she encouraged all women to use "our most potent weapon" and leave the mills. Calling themselves "first class" operatives, women weavers and ring spinners saw the strike as a means of denying the Pacific mills "that experienced and trusted help which has been the principle source of its great prosperity in the past."[19] For their part, management sought to intimidate the operatives both as workers and as women. Whether by stationing themselves "near the door" to "look on," moving "up and down the room, watching," "puffing cigar smoke" at female leadership, or through the use of "nice sweet words and flatteries to jolly" the women, management sought to reassert the sexual hierarchy of the shop floor and trivialize workers' complaints.[20] Throughout the conflict mill men adopted a condescending tone toward the women, blaming both "Dame Fashion" and the extravagant dress of female operatives, "Fine cloths" rather than "calico," for overstretched women's budgets.[21] "Many of the mill girls" complained one mill director, "dressed better than his daughters did."[22] The editor of the *Catholic Herald,* labor sympathizer Peter McCory, agreed. "Had the girls in the employ of the Pacific corporation appeared on the streets in rags" he argued, "this cut down would not have been made."[23]

Thus, gender entered working-class politics in ways that repeated the social organization of the shop floor. At work, sexual differences between men and women provided the primary means through which the system of labor was organized. Segmented according to sex, wage labor awarded men greater renumeration and authority than it did to women. During the strike, differences between men and women were elaborated in ways that extended shop floor divisions to include taste, deportment, clothing, and style. As women who refused to "dress in rags," striking ring spinners were portrayed as selfish workers whose wages went to support luxuries in contrast to male mule spinners whose "dissatisfaction although deep did not assume so demonstrative a form as with the ring spinners."[24] According to management, "natural" differences in gender rather than the unnatural organization of capitalism were held responsible for wage reductions and for the separate actions of male and female spinners.

Such skirmishes heightened gender consciousness among female strikers. Acting in the belief that women alone needed to "decide what course of action to take," strikers initially refused men, both workers and reporters, entrance to their meeting hall. Attributing this act to "feminine fickleness," city papers attempted to "smuggle" reporters into these meetings "in disguise."[25] Only when striking women became convinced that their struggles would receive serious attention in the press did they agree to admit men to their meeting, but only those men "who showed support" and "repeated the password, 'Perseverance.' " Unfriendly reporters, especially those from the Republican controlled *American,* remained excluded.[26]

From the beginning of the strike, women stood together and worked to overcome mill authority despite being "somewhat frightened by overseer Phillips" and "corporation detective Philbrick." Before walking out, they asked newspapers "not to say anything unkind of them" for they were pursuing the "only course that remained for them." To overseer Clarke, the women gave "a proper sendoff," which apparently included much shouting and at least a few rude gestures. "We liked him as an overseer but if our demands could not be adhered to we must leave his employment."[27] Similarly, when the mills announced that loyal workers would have "all necessities attended to," including food and lodgings, while strikers were to be evicted from company houses and blacklisted, female operatives remained defiant. "The matter of board" reported one tenant, "does not trouble me in the least, . . . as for food, I am not particular about luxuries."[28] "We are black-listed," admitted Halley, "but we don't care for that; we can get work outside the mills."

Calling themselves "Stone Crushers," a reference to an unpopular mill superintendent, women organized committees to raise funds, rouse the public, and prevent dissention. "Will you stand by," asked one circular, "or be content to remain slaves and scabs?"[29]

Keenly aware that no woman could survive on the new wage scale and that many of the female operatives were the sole support for families, women were fiercely loyal to the strike and worked hard to win public sympathy and support. "There is," explained one striker, "a young lady working who has been the only assistance to two sisters who have been ill for over a fortnight and they say they would almost starve before they would consent to work for 68 cents a day."[30] Women also brought their sons and younger brothers out with them so that a "juvenile strike" paralleled the main walkout. Hoping the men would join them once they had solidified their protest, the weavers and spinners concentrated on winning over women and girls not yet prepared to leave. While the ethnicity of the strikers cannot be quantified precisely, newspapers and surnames suggest that the overwhelming majority were Irish and native-born, with some Scots and English women in both rank-and-file and leadership positions. In the first three days of the strike, only "three French girls" returned. Immediately Halley and Folsom sent for French speakers who, disguised as scabs, confronted the French girls at work. "After working a short time, they were induced to quit and making [the] excuse that they wanted to go out for the purpose of changing their clothing, neglected to return."[31]

In general, however, French-Canadians eschewed labor activity, denouncing strikes in their paper *Le Progres*. Differences in language and culture clearly affected solidarity, but situational factors were perhaps more important. Patterns of settlement, which encouraged native and Irish working women to act autonomously, reinforced female dependency in French Canadian households. Generally migrating to Lawrence in family units, French parents continued to control household decision making and to enforce claims on children's wages and loyalty. Among the French workers who were reported to be scabs, most tended to be quite young, between ten and thirteen years of age. Furthermore, unlike the Irish who distrusted the church and its immigrant priests, whose reputation for absconding with parish funds was widespread, French Canadians oriented much of their community life around their church. St. Annes, established in 1873, was the largest parish in the city and it maintained several schools. A fixture in the life of the Franco-

American community, the church was a model of patriarchy and a teacher of deference and obedience to authority. From the pulpit French Canadian priests rallied against the strikers and demanded loyalty to the mill. Irish women and girls, on the other hand, faced a less-unified church hierarchy. When Rev. Regan, pastor of Irish St. Mary's, urged his female parishioners to return to work, they got up from their seats "and proceeded to the church of the Immaculate Conception," where the priest supported the strike.[32]

Strike leaders worked hard to maintain solidarity by arranging for interpreters, soliciting support and credit from grocery men, and by organizing neighborhood meetings and rallies. Within the first few weeks over seven hundred sympathizers had contributed to the strike fund, including local clergy, a number of benevolent societies, a cluster of professionals, and a number of operatives from other mills. At times, however, support came in more demonstrative ways. Town policemen, many of whom had worked in the mill or knew the strikers as friends, neighbors, and often as kin, were frequently accused of "preventing workers from going to work." Two weeks into the strike each member of the police department contributed one dollar to the strike fund, and two officers, Carey and Johnson, were accused by Pacific superintendent Stone of entering the mill in order to gather information and "report to operatives outside."[33] Charging "that officers had themselves done the acts they were ordered to prevent," superintendent Stone hired private police from out of town, further isolating the industrialists from the community.

Striking women, both operatives and nonworkers, took advantage of police sympathies and exerted a continuous campaign against scabs, calling them names, hissing at them and pushing them down. Almost two months after the strike began, Mrs. Boyd, the mother of a striker, "threw water on Mrs. King as she comes home to work." When the local officer asked why she had done this, Boyd replied, "because she went to work in the Pacific." Learning that the police had refused to arrest Boyd, Mr. King went to the corporation and got a detective to prosecute. The trial, however, quickly took on the flavor of a carnival as a "large crowd of strikers hooted 'the King' and his wife." The case was dismissed.

Sabotage within the mill was also rampant. Arson in mill property was widespread and serious fires closed the Pacific Dye House and destroyed the mill's cotton reserves. If not all workers showed their support by striking, many made known their sympathies in more clandestine ways. Throughout the spring newspapers noted slow downs, room disruptions, and, almost weekly, foreman and section hands found themselves the victims of "freak accidents" falling down stairs and tripping over machinery.

The ability of the weavers and spinners to defy male authority allowed many women to overcome fears and collectively resist management intimidation, but it was participation in the strike that transformed most women by encouraging them to question not only immediate wage cuts but the whole of "corporate power" itself. Angered over the assertion that women's dressing habits had caused the strike, women initially demanded an apology but then set up a campaign of their own to investigate the causes of the spring slow down. With letters, speeches, and interviews the women challenged management to prove their allegations. It was not the women, they argued, but mill management that was responsible for hard times in the textile industry. Asserting their own knowledge of textile production as superior to management, one female striker argued that "today the operatives don't complain so much about the cut-down as they do about the extra work they have to do from superintendents and overseers lacking knowledge."[34] Calling attention to a series of recent firings where "old and tired employees of the mills were removed to make place for theoretical, technology-school graduates," strikers sought to rouse the sympathies of both disgruntled male workers and city officials, many of whom had relatives in the mill.[35] Louis Towey, a recently appointed member of the city's Board of Health, had himself recently been fired from the Pacific for protesting "shoddy work." Holding aloft a piece of "poor cloth," he backed the women's claims, calling the material "a product of the school of technology, or of the philosophy of Harvard College." He angrily told reporters that "while Stone was wasting 10,000 of dollars on experimenting with dyes, the most ignorant employee of the department could have at once instructed them in the proper method, saving mills thousands of dollars."[36] Three months into the strike, Halley and costriker Jeannie Folsom, came to a new, more radical justification for higher wages. "Not one of the operatives," Halley told her audience, "could say that she had received any portion of the profits made by the mills. Labor produces all wealth and labor is worthy of its hire."[37] Folsom agreed, reminding both workers and industrialists that "the corporation was originally created by Lawrence and intended as a benefit to the people." Decent wages, conditions, and dignity, they concluded, were the rights of the worker.[38]

As women gained confidence, they also challenged the personal behavior of bosses on the floor. Asking women if they would return upon receiving better wages, a striker sharply replied, "We would have received our old pay two weeks ago, but there are girls here who do not dare call their souls their own in the presence of the overseers."[39] By late spring, many were convinced that "the strikers had the corporation in the corner," and agreed to bring the issue of male intimidation before the board of Pacific Directors. During one stormy meeting in April, strike leaders accused a foreman of "abusing young girls in his employ" and also charged overseer Philips "with ordering section hands to knock girls down that looked from windows and did not attend strictly to their work."[40] Unwilling to separate starvation wages from what Mary Rice Livermore called, "low ideals of womanhood," strikers brought both gender and sex to the surface of working-class politics.

The militancy and solidarity that marked the strike were unmatched in the city's history. Previous walkouts in 1867, 1875, and 1881 lacked, as one paper put it, "the cooperation of the great body of colaborers."[41] The 1882 strike, however, was a significant anomaly orchestrated against a history of repression, disunity, and accommodation. Furthermore, the strike had implications for textile workers that reached beyond the gates of the Pacific Mill. Politicians throughout the state, as well as reformers such as John Boyle O'Reilly, who rented Faneuil Hall in Boston to raise money for the strikers, saw the strike as a critical test of industrial power.[42] Management in Lawrence's other mills as well as industrialists throughout New England agreed, and they watched the strike carefully, basing their own decisions to cut wages and challenge worker prerogatives on the failure or success of Lawrence's striking women. At the Washington Mill in Fall River, noted the *Lawrence Eagle*, owners "had thought to cut but the strength of strikers changed their minds."[43] No one was more aware of this than Mary Halley, who believed the strike critical to the future cause of the labor movement. In a letter addressed to her "fellow working men and women in America," Halley argued, "This is not a struggle for the interests of the Lawrence weavers and spinners alone, but one in which the interest of the whole of the working classes are involved."[44] The solidarity of the workers and the power of their arguments convinced Halley that the time was right for a "new labor society" comprised of all mill operatives in the city regardless of skill or employer. To those ends they organized a huge mass meeting to be held on the first Fast Day of the summer and invited well-known labor agitators to address the "great issue of association."

By June, the city became host to some of the most prominent labor agitators in the nation.

"The backwardness of men in the movement."

The plans that Halley and Folsom hatched in the spring of 1882 continued what had been, throughout the strike, new directions for the labor movement in both Lawrence and in the region. From the beginning, women organized themselves in ways that would maximize their base of support, welcoming nonworkers as well as operatives into newly established associations of weavers and spinners. Men, once they had spoken the pledge of "perseverance" could also join, and within a week of the walkout each group boasted over five hundred members.[45] Even more inventive were their efforts in the neighborhood. As workers, women went on strike, but as women, strikers understood the bargaining power of grocers and landlords who controlled the necessities of life. As Halley made clear to the city's business leaders, most female operatives supported others, and without credit or rent deferments, their ability to remain on strike would be seriously eroded. Organizing female operatives into pairs, the strike committee assigned teams to various sections of the Plains, instructing them to win the sympathy of critical individuals and in turn to bring strikers' grievances to the community at large.[46] Emphasizing low wages and poor management, strikers sought to build an identity of interests that would force changes at the Pacific. Their tactics were a practical strategy designed to pressure the directors into replacing "present managers with men in whom the operatives and directors have confidence."[47] To be sure, strikers developed throughout the conflict a broader critique of industrial capitalism, but for many of the spinners and weavers, the sense of crisis did not extend beyond the everyday world of the shop floor. Unlike male spinners and craftsmen, who expressed new anxieties over a system moving far beyond their control, leaders like Halley and Folsom felt confident of their importance in the production process. Female operatives saw the strike as a means to deprive the mill of the skills needed to produce high-quality cloth; by walking out they asserted the long-standing mutuality of their relationship to the mills, a mutuality recognized by the city of Lawrence.

The militant actions of the women thus continued traditions of protest and buttressed the city's labor movement. Lawrence operatives first organized around the Ten Hour Movement, which came to Lawrence in the form of the Cotton Spinners Association founded by mule spinners in 1858.[48] Throughout the postwar period, Ten-Hour clubs flourished in Lawrence and the short-time movement drew hundreds of workers to the cause of labor reform. "Adding new fuel to the flames" were the city's female operatives who, by 1865, accounted for almost three thousand signatures despite persistent harassment from overseers and section hands. Together, male and female operatives demanded "an end to the oppression and drudgery of days too long at spindle and loom." Throughout the campaign, demands for reduced hours were argued on the basis of men's and women's shared relationship to production, and not as a concession to gender differences. While night work was attacked as "a special hardship on women," hour reductions were defended in the name of a common oppression so that when Lawrence mills dropped their hours, men and women were equally reduced first to 62.5 hours a week and then to 60 hours by 1874.[49]

Despite the successes of the short-time clubs, activists were hard-pressed to organize permanent associations. Socialists, largely from the English and German communities, split over a number of issues and followed separate paths—the Germans establishing a Socialist Labor Party in 1874 and the English working to build a more class-conscious unionism. Mule spinners, the most militant and experienced workers, also found Lawrence a difficult city to organize, and the economic fluctuations of the late sixties and seventies kept most craft organizations on the defensive. Mill repression was severe, and both blacklisting and the use of "discharge papers" was common throughout the city. Left without an "honorable" discharge, a worker had little choice but to leave town, yet even relocating did not always guarantee employment as directors exchanged names throughout New England. As one state investigator noted, "The discharge paper, like the French livret, does its work effectively and quietly."[50] Forced to operate in secret, activists had difficulty sustaining membership, and with the national depression of 1873 organizations declined dramatically in Lawrence and throughout the country. Between 1873 and 1878, labor associations fell from a national high of thirty to only nine, and membership plunged from three hundred thousand to roughly fifty thousand.[51] Reflecting national trends, Lawrence's labor movement ground to a halt, and its craft unions increasingly adopted a strict policy of "arbitration to prevent strikes."[52]

Working-class organizations, having run aground on the rocks of depression, splintered and turned increasingly defensive. The rapid pace of mechanization increased skilled workers' hostility to broad-based organizing, and their allegiance to craft traditions kept both women and unskilled men at bay. By 1882, industrialists correctly assessed the antipathy among the "aristocracy of labor" to militant collective action. The strike of 1882, then, marked a continuation of traditions of militancy, but it highlighted as well the contradictory meanings that changes in production would have for male and female workers.

The social policies of Lawrence's mill owners took advantage of the insecurity inherent in textile manufacturing by offering its most highly skilled male operatives protection against seasonal slow downs and global fluctuations. Anticipating the transition of the work force from "factory girls" to "a new class of help" comprised of immigrants and their families, postbellum mill owners initiated a series of benefit programs directly aimed at securing the loyalty and cooperation of its skilled aristocracy. Unlike blacklisting and the use of "honorable discharges" which sought to intimidate individual workers and eliminate "radicals of the worst sort," benefit programs antedated turn-of-the-century "welfare work" that sought to tie workers to the interests of the corporation.

The most effective and well-established plan was a home ownership plan designed by the owners of the Pacific Mill. All "honest and worthy workingmen" could apply to join the program and withhold savings in a special account at the Essex Bank. Mill directors also sat on the boards of all the city's major banks, so that loans could be initiated and controlled by employers. Mills also set up funds and savings programs to help favored employees obtain a mortgage. "The corporations aid them all they can," admitted one "well informed party" to a state inspector, "for they believe that when a man becomes a landowner he becomes a good citizen. Each man is then a policeman: he is quiet and does not want to see any row or strike, for if one should come it would upset work and possible result in his losing his home."[53] Responding to the uncertainty of the industry, mill men hoped to secure the loyalty of the skilled craftsmen but they did so in ways that further accentuated sexual difference and threatened the world of self-supporting women. The "worker cottages," funded by mill savings were for single "worthy" families headed by male employees of the "right stamp." Physically, they resembled the houses of English artisans. Small, square framed, and white washed, they included a yard and were spaced at a gracious distance from their neighbors. In Lawrence such houses dotted the Plains, but most were clustered on the outskirts of the Everett Mill, along the city's common, and especially around the Arlington Mill, where the English dominated the labor force. To help the "poor, temperate, and industrious" secure this "safeguard of human happiness and content-ment," Abbott Lawrence left fifty thousand dollars in his will, a trust to be distributed by the city fathers. Almost every manufacturer in town experimented with some kind of home ownership program well into the twentieth century.[54]

Lawrence's mills also adhered to a policy of promotion from within the ranks of its male employees. Loyal men could look forward to be-coming section hands, overseers, and even mill officers; loyal women could not. The mercurial rise of William Wood, who entered the Ayer Mill as an immigrant hand from the Azores and became its treasurer a decade later and eventually President of the American Woolen Com-pany, was only the most dramatic example of an otherwise routine pol-icy. Labor leaders were not immune to the benefits of a system that rewarded company allegiance. William Bower, the former head of the Lawrence Short Time Committee, resurfaced in 1882 as an overseer at the nonstriking Arlington Mills.[55] By the 1880s even Irish men could be found in supervisory positions. Horatio Alger stories, among the most popular books borrowed from the city library, were paralleled by local success stories propagated by the mill. Baseball teams, library mem-berships, a lecture series, and the familiar rituals organized around re-tirements and birthdays foreshadowed the development of corporate welfare programs in the twentieth century.

Participants in Lawrence's home ownership programs were over-whelmingly recruited from the ranks of the skilled male workers and included operatives from England, Scotland, and Germany, as well as America. The Irish, who refused to use the city's banks and deposited funds instead with the Augustinian priests, were less affected by the mill's policies until the 1880s when the Augustinians declared bank-ruptcy and Irish men began to move into skilled positions in the mills.[56] Like many home ownership programs adopted by turn-of-the-century industrialists who argued that "good homes make contented workers," Lawrence's program sought to mask the uncertainties of industrial life by offering the illusion of stability.

As mechanization and competition intensified, increasing those un-certainties for craftsmen and skilled men, the meaning of the home would take on new urgency among an embattled aristocracy. Indeed, mill owners held out a vision of domesticity that blended with a remembered family economy where women, supported by the toil of Republican artisans, occupied a "preordained position as homemaker."[57] Quoting John Ruskin, who in 1880 claimed that the term *wife* means *weaver* because women "must either weave men's fortune and embroider them, or feed upon them and cause them to decay," a city editor took note of the growing belief that "wherever a true wife comes, home is always around her."[58] By 1875, the wives of the operative elite did their "weaving" in the cottages along the main streets that radiated out of Lawrence's central Plains. Here, where the majority of the city's skilled workers and section hands lived, census takers reported that wives were women "at home" and daughters were "at school." Nicknamed "the city of homes," Lawrence manufacturers slowly made the ideal of female domesticity a matter of corporate policy.[59]

It was certainly no surprise, therefore, that James Eaton, treasure of the Essex Savings Bank, was the first person asked to address the striking weavers and spinners in 1882. Trusting management's assessment that Lawrence operatives would rather starve than go on strike, he reminded workers that there are "more people in Lawrence owning their homes than in any other city of its size on the earth."[60] Like Duncan Wood before him, Eaton's words misfired. Keenly aware that all men did not support all women and that in many homes throughout the Plains women headed underfed families, "this talk," as Mary Halley dramatically pointed out, "did not amount to a row of pins."

By walking out, women called attention to the limits of a working-class politics that echoed conservative expectations of women at home. Halley's plans for "a union of all mills" sought to bring all workers together, and by inviting labor radicals to Lawrence, the striking women hoped to link their cause to the "great issues of the day." Supporting the efforts of the women were a number of local groups, including the Greenback Labor Club, the German Lyra Glee Club, and numerous neighborhood societies ignited by the actions of the strikers. As speakers from Fall River, Lynn, and Boston gathered for labor's "Fast Day," local "Minstrel Boy Mr. Conway added to the occasion with his wild harp slung behind him."[61]

Operatives crowded the park as they listened to well-known firebrands Robert Howard, A. A. Carleton, Frank Foster, Ben Newell, and John Irving. Throughout the spring, labor leaders had come and gone, railing against the mills, but the issue of a single association was never

addressed. On the day of the rally, a few speakers declared in no uncertain terms that strikes were useless and most of the guest speakers
opposed them in principle. Then, local women took the platform and
made speeches of a different sort. Newspapers did not bother to record
them, but a Mrs. McIntire delivered a "spirited address," which "dwelt
on the backwardness of men in the movement."[62] No doubt much of the
"spiritedness" of McIntire's address stemmed from the cold reception
given to their proposal for a "union of all mills." But operatives could not
have missed, as well, men's failure to address the specific issues raised
by the female operatives. More important, the status of women as
workers remained unresolved. Mule spinners who negotiated with management on their own showed little interest in the weavers' demands
and remained convinced that women represented a dilution of skills and
a source of competition for male workers.

It was the Mayor of Lawrence, however, who most clearly articulated male fears. The first Irish mayor, John Breen, was swept into office as "a friend of labor" only three months before the strike.
Acknowledging the growing concern among Lawrence's male operatives
and labor leaders over the city's highly feminized population, he saw
emigration, not collective association as the solution to labor problems.
"It is a source of regret" he told the strikers, "that many of the young
ladies, of whom there are a surplus in this city, do not take Horace
Greely's advice and make many young men in the West happy."[63]

By June, the strike was in its fourth month and almost half of the
strikers had indeed left town. New weavers and spinners, both im-
ported from England and recruited from within the city, gradually replaced the women. After a lengthy shutdown, the Pacific itself reopened
with new machinery, provoking some to suspect that management had
welcomed the strike from the beginning. Recovering from an illness
that kept her out of action for several weeks, Halley returned in June,
however, to drum up support and to announce a picnic for all city workers. Grocers and merchants gave "many contributions," and within a
few weeks, fifteen hundred tickets were sold in an effort to organize "a
new Labor society." Halley introduced the Knights of Labor and joined
would-be politician Duncan Wood in installing fifty new members. Calling superintendent Stone "Sir Jumbo" and his scabs the "royal family,"
speakers made clear the comparisons between the equality of the
Knights and the "slavery of corporate power."[64] Halley also argued for
a broad agenda for labor. The "strikers union," wrote the sympathetic

Journal, "favors community education, a bureau of labor statistics, factory inspectors, and supervision of food and dwellings."[65] The picnic, however, was something of a last hurray as more and more strikers left town and the mills shut down for the summer slow down. Blacklisted from all Lawrence mills and unable to win the support of the craft unions, Halley and the other female leaders gradually faded from view and by August the strike was officially declared to be over.

The Eclipse of the Self-supporting Woman

For at least one Lawrence operative, the strike was a cause for celebration. A worker, writing to the editor of the city's labor organ, *The Lawrence Journal,* noted that "it was a good time to strike." After all, he reasoned, "help has been changing from one place to another," and the walkout provided a "good opportunity for jobs."[66] Indeed, as many strikers soon discovered, wage cuts were only a small part of those changes initiated at the Pacific, not the least of which was a marked shift from "first class" help to "green" or the "cheap, inexperienced class."[67] Help, as the letter writer observed, had been changing and the strike also brought new opportunities for the unemployed. They came, however, not in the traditional way as scab replacements, but rather as part of a fundamental transformation that would dramatically alter the nature of textile manufacturing throughout the region. By 1880, over production and sharp declines in coarse goods forced manufacturers to restructure the industry or retreat from the global market. Hoping to cut costs and reduce its dependence on expensive skilled operatives, the strike provided management with new opportunities to reorganize the production process. It was not the striking weavers and spinners that would be replaced, but rather the worsted cloth itself, whose "long fibres involves the most costly intricate and truly automated machinery,"[68] operated by the skilled hands of "first class" women workers. As management searched for new ways to restructure their mills and reorganize the system of production, skilled women found themselves displaced, not by scabs but by "the school of technology, or the philosophy of Harvard College."[69]

The impetus for change came as the demand for worsted, or "lustre goods," waned and profits began to dip. Two years before the strike, the product of the worsted loom was no longer wanted as the public turned to softer, nonlustre woolen goods. A few mills began to introduce more cotton machines into their factories, replacing "first class" weavers, mostly skilled women, with the untried hands of newly arrived unskilled women and boys. Within ten years, the Washington Mill would replace its entire labor force of women spinners and doffers with "New Bedford boys."[70] While mule spinners worried over the "extinction of the male operative," female spinners and weavers found themselves reduced to starvation wages and, in the wake of reorganization, repositioned on the margins of the production process.

It was the Pacific Mill that set the course for changes throughout the textile industry. Starting with the firing of over two hundred upper-level employees, including overseers who directors considered "too friendly" with workers, and department superintendents, the Pacific hoped to reduce costs by adopting newer methods of management. "The old and tried employees of the mills," recalled a former operative at the Arlington, "were removed to make place for theoretical, technological-school graduates."[71] Men like Joseph Stone, Treasurer Saltenstall, and Superintendent Robinson, represented a new breed of managers immersed in the principals of scientific management. Trained in the state's colleges and not in its mills, they sought to maximize profits by reorganizing the work process in ways that would reduce dependence on the skill and knowledge of the workers.[72] In the dye house, management replaced the old system whereby experienced workers controlled the mixing of colors with standard formulas that were premixed, thus eliminating the skilled eye and brain of the worker. Such policies threatened skilled workers throughout the mill and by 1882, standardized practices and routinized procedures had slowly replaced older forms of paternalism and face to face negotiation between workers, overseers, and top management. Strikers were not the only ones to notice the changes taking place. Denouncing the strike, a "heavy stockholder" nevertheless blamed mill management whose "poor plan" of publishing the cuts without any discussion caused the walkout. The "proper way, and one adopted heretofore at the Pacific," he told reporters, "is to notify the overseer and have him deal privately with the help on matters of this kind."[73]

Procedural changes merely reflected larger alterations at the point of production. A year before the strike, mill bosses initiated speedups by making the cloth "one pick to the inch lighter," adding "pressure on the weavers who did not take off cloth enough" by giving them "their bill."[74]

New, more stringent fines for delays were established as well, and workers caught discussing their wages were to be automatically dismissed. While changes on the shop floor accelerated operative fears and anger, the strike intensified management efforts to transform the industry. Almost as soon as the women walked out, management sent for five hundred new, more efficient looms from Bradford, England, and in April the Pacific announced a six-month shutdown in the central mill in order to change machinery. The *New York Times* suggested that the mills "refusal to give a fair hearing to the women gives . . . plausibility to the suspicion that they welcomed the strike."[75] Others agreed, arguing that with the walkout, management "gained a pretext for suspending operations which were unprofitable."[76] By the conclusion of the strike, the Pacific had thoroughly reorganized production, shifting to more fully automated machinery and reducing their dependence on the long intricate fibres that made worsted cloth labor intensive and costly.

Those who refused to strike—mule spinners, loom fixers, dyers, and wool sorters—interpreted wage cuts as part of a mounting campaign against skilled labor and craft traditions.[77] Yet while mule spinners and craftsmen were responding to an old problem—namely the mechanization and dilution of craft skills—they were defining that problem in new ways. Their hostility became focused on the female operative whose militancy they saw as ultimately undermining higher-paid male operatives. "A short time ago," explained one Lawrence weaver just before the 1882 walkout, "a small strike was gotten up and carried through to success by women, and resulted in an advance of 10%; but the men suffered for it: as quickly as it can be done, women are given men's work to do."[78] The lessons of the rebuilt Pemberton, where ring frames operated by women replaced hundreds of mules, was not lost on the Pacific mule spinners who sought to protect their positions in a system of production rapidly moving beyond their control. Dependent on the mills for work, skilled artisans increasingly held up "good" and "honest workmen" in contrast to the downtrodden female operatives who "don't know how to keep house for they are always in the mill."[79] Arguing that "Mill life has a most demoralizing effect on women and children," skilled men emphasized the interference of mill work on women's roles as wives and mothers, while at the same time concretizing their position as protectors and providers of women as well as children. Giving work to women, "when no other employment is granted the male portion of the community, is wrong," asserted one angry Lawrence weaver, "for it keeps good workmen out of the mill who otherwise would support the female portion of the family, but who, under existing circumstances, remain idle while women work."[80] Worried over the "gradual extinction of the male operative" and "this unreasonable demand for women," Lawrence's aristocracy of labor increasingly articulated their anxiety and distrust of industrial capitalism in a discourse that equated manhood with productivity and economic autonomy, and womanhood with dependence and subordination.

Craftsmen, convinced that fundamental changes were being made that threatened their entire way of life, also mobilized the past to resist the present. Craft workers and skilled men refused to join with the women strikers who advocated a union of all mills and instead activated former single-shop organizations that eventually affiliated under the banner of the Central Labor Union. Here, speakers rekindled memories of an artisanal past devoid of conflict and committed to traditions of craft solidarity, community, and family.[81] Calling themselves, "a body of fine men," the local Knights of Labor, organized in Lawrence by Mary Halley, articulated a similar theme of a remembered community where decent wages kept "our women and children out of the mills."[82] A year after the 1882 walkout, local Knights deplored the "wasteful and barbarous methods of strikers" who forgot the benefits of arbitration.[83]

Labor leaders, hoping to stabilize the present, scripted an orderly past. It was the family wage economy based on a man's ability to earn enough money to support a wife that provided the central story in the labor movement's poststrike attempts to "traditionalize" a worker heritage.[84] Rekindling Ira Steward's demands for a family wage, labor radicals called forth warm images of family life where women tended a quiet and tranquil home. "We must endeavor," announced one master workman, "to keep our women and children out of the mills." A visiting radical introduced a plan to do just that. "There should be a law" demanded labor leader Robert Howard, "prohibiting the employment of married women in manufacturing establishments which if passed, 2,500,000 men would be employed in their stead."[85] Nationally the Knights of Labor moved to bring women into the House of labor, but at the local level labor's true women were apt to find themselves rhetorically confined to the kitchen.

Criticizing industrial capitalism in the name of an idealized nuclear family, where all men support all women, the family wage articulated class difference in a powerful metaphor that encoded economic autonomy as masculine in contrast to the feminine domestic side.[86] Household head, the shop floor, skill, and producer emerged as signs of maleness and signifiers of masculine prerogatives. Sexual difference, in other words, provided a means to develop a sense of class and class action as it simultaneously delineated the parameters of both male and female possibility. Defending the actions of striking wage women, Halley and Folsom had argued that "*labor* produces all wealth" and that "*labor* is worthy of its hire," but as sexual difference increasingly provided the conceptual language for class protest, "labor" lost the gender neutrality Halley and Folsom had assumed. To "Master" workmen, many of whom lived in cottages on the rim of the Plains, the independent wage women who filled the Plains seemed an alien group as the "working woman" became increasingly defined in relation to work performed within the home and in contrast to paid labor.[87] Turn-of-the-century demands for a family wage united an array of strange bedmates, including workers, progressive reformers, woman activists, and even socialists. "If woman's place is in the home," wrote prominent radical and union advocate, Carrie Allen, in 1912, "why not pay her husband enough to keep her there?"[88]

While labor leaders moved to domesticate the female operative, city fathers and businessmen began to link economically active women in general, and self-supporting women in particular, with the moral decay and social disorder they believed to be on the rise in Lawrence. Images of female "rum holes" and "kitchen bars," of "saucy" gamins and "hoydenish" women, and of "treating," where, announced a shocked city missionary, "friendships among women are renewed and cemented by strong drink," filled City Documents and local newspapers.[89] To startled officials, "roguish female elements" seemed to be everywhere. Typical was the experience of one member of the Board of Health who told two women in the Plains to stop gossiping and clean up their yards. The women "cursed him for all to see" and "such was the general high-pitched response they made that the agent melted away like a meteor, and has been partially deaf since."[90] A glimpse of the changing role of local government in the affairs of its citizens was hidden behind the humor with which such incidents were reported in the city's newspapers. Patterns of deference that had marked Lawrence in its earliest years, no longer functioned in a city of forty thousand residents, almost half of whom were immigrants. Like many Gilded Age cities confronted with the problems of rapid urbanization, government increasingly assumed authority in areas that had once been private responsibility: the domain of charity or the home.[91] Departments of Health and Sanitation, Public Works, a General Hospital, a Public Library, and a city-sponsored theater, joined schools, asylums, and work farms in an effort to systematize and protect "public" health.

As city authorities increasingly scrutinized neighborhoods in the Plains, they also censured women's participation in the economic life of the community. Noting that there was a liquor license for every 160 inhabitants, officials, who had once turned "a blind eye to enforcement," moved with great fanfare against all but the "bone fide hotels."[92] The city's labor press maintained that "no women should be licensed" and applauded the crackdown on the profusion of "kitchen bars" and shady "dwelling houses" run by women "steeped in the ways that are dark and the tricks that are vain."[93] Despite the effort to eliminate women and bring "respectability" to the working-class saloons, twenty-two female "proprietors" defied these newer codes of feminine conduct and applied for a license to sell liquor "at home."

As government efforts focused on the Plains, laboring women found themselves the targets of reform. Within a decade after the strike of 1882, local codes challenged the right of women to operate businesses independently of husbands, and by 1900, married women throughout the state were required to file with the clerk's office a certificate declaring the nature and location of their business. Seeking to peddle her own fruit and vegetables, Minnie Fox proved her work "legit" by filing her marital status, her husband's name, and her place of business with city hall.[94]

It was the campaign to eliminate abortion, however, that most dramatically challenged women's autonomy. A woman's right to control her own fertility was under attack from the city's recently organized Medical Club, which began its campaign against abortion in 1879. Once advertized in town newspapers and city directories, abortion had became the focus of national efforts to control female sexuality and maintain male hegemony.[95] In Lawrence, where "lax views and practice in the matters [of abortion]" existed "even among intelligent people—even church members," the Medical Club led efforts to eliminate the "abortionist art." Organized to protect their profession and elaborate "medical ethics," they refused membership to any physician who "practiced as an abortionist."[96] Excluded from membership in the city's only medical association were Lawrence's five active female doctors, including

Susan Crocker, the leading spirit behind the founding of the Lawrence General Hospital. By 1890, no female medical doctor was registered in the city.

By anchoring their mutual uneasiness and insecurities in the cultural symbols of gender, city officials and craftsmen alike sought to restore order and regain authority over an economic order rapidly moving beyond their control. In this, they joined a generation of bourgeois men for whom "woman had become the quintessential symbol of social danger and disorder."[97] Victorian men—already unnerved by a generation of women activists who, like Elizabeth Stuart Phelps, Jane Cunningham Croly, and Mary Rice Livermore, demanded a public role for women—watched with horror the advancement of their college-educated daughters. These "new" women—single, educated, and economically autonomous—constituted an even greater challenge to domesticity as they eschewed marriage and fought for professional visibility.[98] Conservatives feared the social and demographic consequences of an economically independent womanhood. "If women are trained to self-support," authorities argued, "and are able to maintain themselves by their own labor, they will not marry, but will ignore their for-ordained work as wives, mothers, and nurses of children."[99] Opposing industrial training for women, another charged that, "there is a widespread neglect, indifference, or opposition to marriage, on the part of Modern women, and they refuse to marry, because they are now able to support themselves."[100] To a growing number of bourgeois professionals and bureaucrats, the "new" woman, by rejecting motherhood and men, was not only shocking, she was "unnaturally" sexed, a deviant who not only challenged domesticity but threatened the very fabric of social life. Rooting their status in the new social sciences, institutions of expertise publicly examined the economically autonomous woman and declared her a danger to the social order.

Like the "new" woman, the female militants threatened the Victorian world in ways their numbers could never realize. Militantly asserting their right to labor and demanding "a share in that American privilege which sets in full view of the poorest white male laborer a growing income, a bank account, the possibilities of an Astor," female strikers and radical women took on mythic proportions as class conflict intensified and worker revolts swept over the Victorian landscape. Casting his vote against the 1887 female suffrage bill, a United States senator played on collective fears of social upheaval by conjuring up the specter of women during the French Revolution. "Who led those blood-thirsty mobs? Who shrieked loudest in that hurricane of passions? Women. . . . In the city of Paris in those ferocious mobs . . . the controlling and principal power came from those whom God has intended to be soft and gentle angels of mercy throughout the world."[101] To those shocked by the "new" woman, the strident woman radical represented a deeper horror, what Foucault has called the "disorder of the *incongruous,* the linking together of things that are inappropriate."[102] The bourgeois male saw in the figure of the female militant the fundamental codes of nature ripped apart. In her presence, the boundaries between crisis and chaos, unrest and anarchy, social decline and social suicide, dissolved and melted away.

Hostility focused on "gender deviant" women, but if critics blamed the "new" women for the "dissolution of the American home and the ruin of femininity," they saw the roots of corruption in the passions of women from the lower orders.[103] Apparently believing that social decay moves from the bottom up, one authority explained that the "new" woman was in fact an old version of the worst sorts of womanhood. "What is new is the translation into the cultured classes of certain qualities and practices hitherto confined to the uncultured and savages."[104] The article, entitled "The Wild Woman as Social Insurgent," underscored the dangers of an unreformed class of working-class women, who, if left unchecked from above, could pull down the social pillars of civilization. A new generation of social experts and leaders argued for modern methods and ideas of social science.

In Lawrence, these "modern" methods came as city officials followed the lead of mill management and adopted "scientific" approaches to the problems of urban life. By 1890, charity and volunteer work gradually gave way to teams of experts funded and controlled by city hall. Historians of women's lives have defined this intervention between government and what were formerly "domestic" concerns remedied by volunteer, mostly female, reformers, as the "domestication of politics," for it brought not only issues of the home into the "public" domain, but a new corps of middle-class matrons, who, in the last decade of the nineteenth century, sought legislation that would prevent general problems of poverty, ignorance, and disease.[105] As "social housekeepers," it has been argued, "women had a more active part in the political changes of the Progressive period."[106]

Unlike the efforts of earlier women reformers, however, who legitimized self-supporting women by upholding the dignity of female wage labor and demanding equal pay for equal work, social housekeepers typically justified female activism by emphasizing women's role as mothers and wives. Steeped in the tenets of Social Darwinism and committed to progressive evolution, these reformers trumpeted motherhood—the bearing and rearing of the race—for they believed that by granting the female of the species the right of selectivity over her mate, nature had granted women the power to determine the shape of new generations.[107] By the turn of the century, the cult of motherhood had assumed a central position in Progressive circles. For "new" women like Jane Addams, mother power justified numerous extrafamilial activities including settlement work, social activism, and even suffrage.[108] Even radicals like Emma Goldman, whose periodical *Mother Earth* spoke to her own "love of all children," and Frances Willard, who proclaimed that socialism "was the womb out of which the coming civilization we believe will be born," resorted to maternal metaphors as they sought to transform women's lives and set them free.[109]

Increasingly concerned about future generations, modern reformers thus called attention less to the rights of self-supporting women than to the marginality of women who toiled without husbands. Independent wage women, struggling nobly against a "fate they were powerless to control, were recast as women "adrift," their lives "surplus" in a world that located women's work in the home.[110] No longer a social cause, the independent wage woman, "mobile, unchaperoned, and outside traditional contexts of moral control," entered the twentieth century redefined, a social problem and a potential threat to national unity.[111]

For laboring women like Mary Halley and Jeannie Folsom, the infusion of domesticity and politics undercut efforts to legitimize their position as wage earners and as full partners in the labor movement. The rhetoric of social housekeeping with its emphasis on the "business of the home" and "home economics" further bolstered notions of the family wage eclipsing the claims of women who lived without men. Just as the "domestication of politics" represented new efforts "to prevent poverty rather than to aid the poor," the family wage sought to legitimize working-class struggle through a politics that protected laboring women by paying higher wages to men. The image of a kind workingman seeking, through arbitration and reason, "the comforts of a home"—the refuge for women's "natural weakness"—were to replace the disturbing vision of collective action and street protests.[112]

For working women in the late nineteenth century, then, the domestication of politics came as part of a larger process that conceptually undermined the independent wage woman. By honoring, even sanctifying motherhood, woman activists like Anna Howard Shaw embraced conservative visions of "the family," lending new credibility to the "myth that all men support all women." Once the "cardinal tenet of her liberation," a woman's right to labor floundered in a movement that elevated the power of reproduction and emphasized the dignity and value of housekeeping.[113] By 1900, feminists like Emily Greene Blach and Charlotte Perkins Gilman, who continued to define the woman question as a problem of labor, found themselves an isolated minority whose opinions no longer matched the assumptions of their audience.[114]

Lacking a feminist interpretation, the woman who toiled for her own bread, who supported others, who lost husbands to accidents and wars, or who left husbands who abused them, took on new fixity as "surplus," "superfluous," and "redundant" members of society. They were the "odd" women, repositioned outside of nature and "adrift" from society. Notions of a self-supporting womanhood lost not simply respectability but conceptual plausibility as well.[115] Represented as competitors to male workers and as demographic oddities, independent wage women, as well as women who headed or supported families, lost legitimacy as actors in an arena now defined as beyond their sphere.

As the legitimacy of self-supporting women receded in the domesticated landscape of Progressive politics, so did the memory of the strike of 1882. A curious lack of reference to the conflict marks the formation of Lawrence's labor movement in the years that followed the greatest confrontation between capital and labor in the city's history. Lawrence officials and business leaders were equally, if more understandably, silent about the strike, and it is not until 1905, when a group of "New England sons," began to write their local histories, that the great walkout becomes a part of the official past. What concerns us here, however, is not the retelling of the strike itself, but rather the extent to which the memory of Lawrence's laboring women, including its most strident and militant operative, Mary E. Halley, was used as an ideological stage from which to define and interpret changes underway in Lawrence and in America at the turn of the century. With his *History of Lawrence,* native son Robert Tewksbury inspired special sections in the city newspapers on "Women of Worth." Tewksbury, noted that in Lawrence "the loud and masculine type of women has few representatives," thereby setting the tone for the remembered women.[116] While the wives of important men received the greatest coverage and were applauded for their "benevolent impulses," and "strength of purpose in charity," the "factory girl" was honored as well for her "reputable character in early local life." What Hawthorne imagined as the present, Tewksbury established as the past, declaring that "many of these early operatives became the wives of pioneer citizens." Building upon the popular genre of "factory-girl" autobiographies where former operatives like Lucy Larcom and Harriet Robinson published warm memories of antebellum Lowell, local historians established the respectability of Lawrence's female operatives by accentuating the temporary nature of female wage labor and the primacy of marriage.

Mary E. Halley, displaced as a worker by the reorganization of production and as a labor leader by "the backwardness of men in the movement," later resurfaced in the city's official history as a "most worthy woman."[117] Tewksbury reported that "Mary E. Halley" is a Lawrence lady who had practical experience as an operative in Lawrence's mills."[118] Casting her in opposition to those women who demanded political participation and economic independence, Tewksbury reframed both her radicalism and her situation as an independent wage woman. Halley, cut off from the "command of meaning," came to represent a version of womanhood that she herself had never embraced. In the struggle over facts and their meaning, over what women were and what they did, Lawrence Progressives conjured up a remembered city of respectable "ladies" and "factory girls" that served to interpret and deplore both the "new" women, who had taken up residency in Lawrence's YWCA, and the "new immigrants" whose "unruly female elements" would come to represent in its most obvious form xenophobic fears of race suicide and the extinction of the Anglo-Saxon race.[119]

Yet while Tewksbury rewrote her past, Halley continued to reshape the present. In the 1905 Lawrence City Directory, we find her listed as a factory inspector for the State of Massachusetts. Still single, the head of her own household, she appears as well in the *New York Call* where, in the winter of 1912, her name is linked to a growing discontent among textile workers in the city of Lawrence.[120] Having turned to regulate what as a worker she had sought to control, Halley apparently never lost faith in the struggle for the "good times coming."

PART TWO

*Immigrant Women and the
Fight for Bread and Roses*

3

Immigrant Women and Textile Culture

"If you want a job, go to Lawrence."

Between 1890 and 1900, Lawrence's population increased by more than 40 percent, almost twice the rate of increase for the entire state. French Canadians, once a small minority of the foreign-born, swelled to just over eight thousand habitants, rivaling the Irish for numerical dominance. Like the Irish, however, the French Canadians were quickly outpaced by the arrival of thousands of southern and eastern Europeans who doubled the city's population by 1910.[1] Refugees from the Turkish, Russian, Italian, and Austrian empires poured into Lawrence after 1900 so that on the eve of World War I, more than fifteen "new" immigrants speaking more than forty languages resided in the city.[2]

Like most newcomers to Lawrence, turn-of-the-century immigrants were drawn by the city's textile manufacturing industry. Convinced that the labor movement had seen its last hurrah in a series of short and bitterly divided walkouts between 1894 and 1902, William Wood, President of the American Woolen Company, selected Lawrence for the site of what would be one of the largest manufacturing plants in the world.[3] Completed in 1906, the Wood Mill symbolized the era's commitment to maximized production, intense competition, and corporate consolidation. Determined to make the American Woolen Company the first textile trust, Wood oversaw the merger of eight separate plants before 1900 and the purchase of another eleven by 1918. Bonus systems and competitive wages drew more than seven thousand workers to the Wood Mill alone, each of whom was conveyed to his or her workroom by time-saving "escalators" between every floor. The world's largest

Figure 7. Wood Worsted Mills. Built in 1905, the Wood Mill extended for a quarter of a mile along the Merrimack River, encompassing thirty acres of floor space and employing nine operatives. Courtesy of the Museum of American Textile History.

worsted mill, the "Wood" lined the grey banks of the Merrimac for a quarter of a mile, encompassing thirty acres of floor space, and producing enough cloth "to belt the earth and festoon the United States from New York to San Francisco."[4] At the time of the mill's opening, the textile industry was New England's largest single employer. Beginning with the boom summer of 1899, the industry rapidly expanded, and by 1903 woolen manufacturers managed to secure a virtual monopoly of the domestic market. What was to become a controversial symbol of corporate protectionism, "schedule K" of the McKinley-Dingly tariff effectively eliminated foreign competition from 90 percent of the American market. The largest woolen concerns were located in Lawrence, and with the construction of the Wood, the city nudged out Bradford, England, as the world's largest woolen and worsted textile capital. In one decade Lawrence's productive capacity more than doubled, transforming it from a middling-sized town of just over fifteen thousand operatives to a manufacturing center of more than thirty thousand cotton, woolen, and worsted employees.

No company played a more important role in developing Lawrence in the new century than the American Woolen Company. Incorporated in 1899 under the guiding hand of William Wood and his father-in-law, Frederick Ayer, owner of the city's Washington Mills, AWC represented a combination of over fifty woolen and worsted mills throughout most of New England. By 1910, the firm employed over thirty thousand workers in New England and twelve in Lawrence, making it the single largest industrial employer in the region. Home of its largest mills, Lawrence entered the twentieth century eager for cheap hands and recruited "new" immigrants both at home and abroad. By 1909, almost 75 percent of the city's woolen and worsted textile operatives were foreign-born, the vast majority from southern and eastern Europe.[5]

Typically, workers were recruited directly through advertisements and employment agents, or indirectly through the use of local ethnic leaders and shop floor "bosses." A local Italian priest (most likely Father Milanese) reported to investigators that almost all of Lawrence's largest mills used recruiting agents in his homeland to attract wage earners.[6] Advertisements, posted in Italian villages as well as in newspapers, promised at least a ten-dollar week and the chance for steady employment. By 1900, the AWC was by far the most active recruiter in New England. Having secured an open shop following the defeat of the 1902 strike, the company confidently advanced wages by 10 percent at a time when smaller mills were reducing paychecks. By promising better wages during the recession years of 1907-8, management hoped to expand the pool of wage-labor and thus assure itself an abundant and competitive supply of factory help when it opened its new mill.[7] Unlike the legendary campaigns of Lowell, which concentrated on recruiting "factory girls," efforts in Lawrence focused on immigrant families who would provide a wide range of skills. The overwhelming majority of advertisements, even for skilled help, gave preference to family operatives with at least four children.[8] One poster, painted in "brilliant colors" and located in the center of an Italian village, pictured a well-fed family of ten, marching joyfully into the Wood Mill, the father with a bag of gold in his hands. "No one goes hungry in Lawrence," it read, "here all can work, all can eat."[9]

The opening of the Wood mill and the expansion of the city's cotton and woolen industry paralleled recessions in European textile manufacturing centers. Consequently the city attracted large numbers of experienced operatives, especially from the textile districts of Saxony, Bavaria, Silesia, and Russian Poland.[10] As recessions in prewar Europe continued to depress wages and increase unemployment rates, operatives increasingly turned to American mills; and in New England "the word," as the daughter of one Russian mender put it, "was out.

Table 4. Sex Ratios for Foreign-born White Populations in the United States, New England, and Lawrence, Mass., by Age for 1890, 1900, and 1910

Age	Ratio of Males to 100 Females		
	1890	1900	1910
United States			
20-24	108.0	98.5	97.3
25-29	128.3	116.1	119.6
30-34	139.6	128.8	134.3
35-44	127.1	134.7	133.8
New England			
20-24	86.0	81.9	81.7
25-29	96.7	97.9	98.3
30-34	105.7	109.1	111.1
35-44	99.1	107.2	109.0
Lawrence			
20-24	84.4	84.7	90.3[a]
25-29	78.4	84.0	86.7[a]
30-34	83.7	89.3	86.8[a]
35-44	79.4	87.0	89.1[a]

a. Figures for Lawrence not available; those in table represent Massachusetts as a whole.

You know, everyone heard the same thing, 'If you want a job, go to Lawrence.' "[11] By 1909, immigrant operatives, the vast majority of whom were from Southern and Eastern Europe, comprised more than three-fourths of Lawrence's operative class. Of these, almost 60 percent were women and children.[12] Employment opportunities had always made Lawrence an attractive city for women, and for "new" immigrants the textile industry offered the possibility of work for every member of the family. While emigration from Southern and Eastern Europe typically evidenced large waves of male migrants acting as "pioneers" for old-world families, textile towns witnessed more evenly balanced sex ratios, and in Lawrence, where job opportunities were expanding, women continued to maintain a plurality.[13] As shown in table 4 New England, and especially Lawrence, represented an exception to national patterns and suggests the importance of female employment opportunities in determining immigrant destinations and in shaping the region's immigrant experience.[14]

Chain migrations, initiated by "pioneer" emigrants, supplemented mill recruiters and further advanced Lawrence's reputation as a city where both men and women could find work. Families selected pioneer migrants with great care, taking into primary consideration the candidate's ability to earn money and thus reunite the family in the new environment. Most often, one individual was selected and financed for the journey, and both skill and intelligence often outweighed all other factors in the selection process. In her classic study of Syrian immigrants for *Survey Magazine,* Mrs. Louise Seymore Houghton found that women were never excluded from this important selection process. "It is not infrequent," she wrote after eight months of fieldwork in B'Sherreh, "that the eldest daughters will precede parents, or brothers, and earn money to bring father and brother over."[15]

While Syrians were somewhat unusual in their willingness to allow single women to act as pioneer emigrants, women with skills were often highly valued for their ability to earn immediate cash once in the New World, and at times, they superseded other relatives whose claims did not include economic aptitude. The experience of one young immigrant woman from Russia suggests the importance of individual skill in a family's decision to finance pioneer emigrants. Born in a small village, or shtetl, just south of Kiev in the Russian Ukraine, Sara Axelrod was the daughter of Jewish artisans who, like many of their neighbors, found themselves increasingly unable to survive on the work that was available to them.[16] While the father eventually found employment in the local paper mill, his wife continued to supplement earnings as an expert "slaughterer." The daughter of a ritual schochet, or religious slaughterer, Sara's mother knew the difficult art of butchering animals so that no holes would appear in the skin. Owners could then sell the skins at much higher prices, and they paid the schochet's daughter well for directing the procedure. Children also helped when they were old enough. Sara's father eventually secured a position in the paper mill for his eldest son, Arron, and his daughter Sara. One of the few jobs available to women, and in a factory where only a few Jews were hired, fifteen-year-old Sara was considered lucky and as a wage earner enjoyed a position of respect both at home, where she "joined the men in fierce conversation," and in the community, where her reputation for being "clever" blossomed.

Conditions in the paper factory, however, were miserable. Wages, especially for Jews, were low, while hours spent in bitter cold work rooms were long and often dangerous. While both Arron, recently married, and his father, the primary breadwinner for a family of eleven, felt powerless to change the situation, Sara soon joined a group of young Kiev socialists who held secret nighttime meetings once a week in the village woods. Having learned to read and write from a neighborhood teacher who instructed her after work, Sara soon became an active participant in the radical underground, leading discussions and often lecturing on "socialism, anarchism, and women's emancipation," what her brother called her three passions in life.

During the 1904 strike at the paper mill, Sara's radicalism became public. A member of the strike committee, Sara spoke of the revolution at hand and urged the workers to stick together. After two months of bitter struggle, Tsarist troops from Kiev surrounded the mill, arrested the strikers, and broke the strike in three days. Sara's entire family was fired. Aware that the family's prospects were becoming increasingly desperate, precious savings were gathered to send Arron to America in the hope that he would be able to bring the others over some time in the future. In the meantime, the religious community successfully pleaded on behalf of the father, now the sole breadwinner, to allow him to return to the mill. Sara, on the other hand, remained out of prison but was blacklisted from every employer in town. Unable to work for others and without the financial means to leave Russia, she learned to operate a stocking-knitting machine by disentangling woven yarns and reconstructing patterns to fit her left-handedness. Setting up shop with a friend, Sara moved out of her parents' house, manufacturing and selling stockings to the community.

While Sara's radicalism continued to make her life difficult and uncertain, it was her ability to earn money that eventually won her passage to America. By 1908, her married brother had secured enough to bring one family member out of Russia. Having Sara in his household meant that more money could be accumulated in a shorter period of time, allowing more family members access to transatlantic fares, so Arron postponed the arrival of his wife and sent for the talented Sara. After she arrived in Plymouth, Massachusetts, Sara quickly put her knitting skills to work, learning the highly skilled craft of woolen mending in the Plymouth mill. A year later, when another regional slowdown shut the mill, Sara left for Lawrence, securing a mending job in the newly opened Wood Mill. From there, an agreed upon percentage of her wages went to Plymouth and then on to Russia.

Although Sara Axelrod's experience was in some ways unique, it nevertheless typified the important role of wage labor in women's lives and the importance of female efforts in familial strategies. Like Sara, many rural women experienced factory labor early in life, and among "new" immigrant families in Lawrence's mills, women were more likely than men to have experienced textile manufacturing before emigration. According to a 1909 government study of Lawrence woolen and worsted operatives, 49.6 percent of female operatives who reported their occupation before migration, had been employed previously in textile manufacturing.[17] While most men from France, England, and Belgium had also worked as operatives, the overwhelming majority of men from Lithuania, Italy, and Russia, as well as Ireland and French Canada, had worked family farms while daughters, sisters, and at times wives entered the local factory. Continuing traditional patterns of supplementing the family purse, rural women developed industrial skills in advance of men, enhancing their ability to find employment almost immediately upon arrival and thereby strengthening their status and power within the migrating family.[18]

A recent study of Italian migrant patterns further underscores the role that female employment opportunities had for families when determining destinations. Excluded from agricultural work and increasingly unable to find work in Sicily's hard pressed textile industry, Sicilian women joined departing men in far greater numbers than elsewhere in southern Italy. Tracing the destinations of these gender-mixed groups of migrants, the study concludes that destinations were chosen by the criteria of securing work for both male and female family members.[19]

Although factory experience was rare for women in Italy, traditions of labor and productivity were not. Marriage customs in southern Italy, for example, were patterned on traditions of what one historian has called, "labor reciprocity." "Women were not dowered by fathers and brothers but by themselves."[20] Brides produced their dowries through their own labor either as hand weavers or as participants in local cottage industry. Mothers traditionally evaluated prospective brides according to their diligence as industriosa. For both those who sought marriage and those who brokered for others, "true womanhood" was marked by a capacity for hard work and a history of productivity.

Emphasizing family labor, Lawrence's mills advertised extensively throughout Italy maintaining recruitment agents in numerous southern cities and towns.[21] The fact that 14 percent of southern Italian women in Lawrence's mills had prior factory experience (compared with .09 percent of the men), suggests the appeal that textile centers held for many families and the important role that female labor often played in family decision making.[22] Lawrence, expecting women to contribute to the family purse, offered poor families a way to maximize their earning power and hasten the process of emigration. Once in Lawrence, low wages and harsh conditions would continue to require that females participate in the labor force for family survival.

For married women, textile work provided a continuity with Europe by offering the means to fulfill traditional female obligations as caretakers of the home and family. A notoriously seasonal industry that caused periodic layoffs and underemployment, textile manufacturing was adaptable to women's rhythms of reproduction, accommodating changes in the female life cycle and female obligations to kin when male support was temporarily absent. A Portuguese wife explained how her employment in textile manufacturing blended with female duties. She entered the mills in August and worked through the fall and winter "in order to make money to buy winter clothing."[23] Having exchanged twelve hours of labor for warm clothing, she began the second portion of her "double day" at home caring for the family. This wife, for example, "baked a considerable proportion of the bread used by the family, sometimes baking at night while employed at the mill.[24] During the slack season, she took in children of working neighbors in the same way she boarded her three children while in the mill.

While Lawrence's mills drew job hungry migrants to the city, pioneer emigrants were not the only ones to establish a "beachhead" or "toehold" for old-world relatives and friends.[25] The city's churches were also active agents in both recruiting immigrant labor and establishing migrant chains to distant outposts. One Catholic priest reportedly worked closely with "one of the largest mills" by writing letters to colleagues in Vermont and elsewhere, urging them to send laborers to the city during shortages and during strikes.[26] Usually an additional contribution to the church followed as mills gratefully acknowledged the role of the church in directing dependable and steady help to their shop floors.

More typical, however, was the case of Rev. W. A. Wolcot, who, as the son of a Beirut minister, helped organize emigrant routes to Lawrence.[27] It was primarily through the efforts of four or five hundred returning emigrants to the villages of B'Sherreh in Mt. Lebanon that

Syrian migration patterns initially began to shift from Egypt and the East to the United States. Chiefly traders and businessmen, the repatriots apparently spread tales of "the golden possibilities." As in Russia and Southern Europe, industrial expansion created new uncertainties for Syrian families as traditional methods of livelihood fell under tremendous economic and social strain. Global commercialization of tobacco farming and increased productivity of silk cloth, especially in Japan, rapidly depressed Syria's primary sources of income. By 1900, demand for Syrian silk goods dropped sharply, slicing prices to half their normal range. By the turn of the century, a single bad year could wipe out an entire village.[28]

Economic constraints were compounded by concomitant social and cultural transformations. Moslem and Druse families had long resented Christian Syrians who, because of their minority status, were made exempt from Turkish military service and thus able to travel, trade, and farm undisturbed by the empire's capricious and often severe conscription duties. Moslems, on the other hand, could only leave the area with great risk, as they were legally regarded as deserters, whether or not they were active in the military. It was also widely believed among non-Christians that large profits were made by the Syrian Christians off Druse retainers who also depended on Christian villages for supplies and surplus labor. As economic conditions worsened, tension between these groups accelerated, provoking a series of village massacres between the 1890s and World War I. By 1907, over forty thousand Christians emigrated to the United States, 21 percent of whom settled in New England.[29]

The "Plains"

With few exceptions, Lawrence's "new" immigrants settled into the "Plains" section of the city (see map 1) where play steads, cottages, and sandy lots gave way to form densely packed cosmopolitan neighborhoods. The heart of the "Plains" consisted of five distinct communities popularly known as the Plains, the corporate Reserve, the Everett, the Dutch Plain, and the Swamp. Housing one-third of the city's population on one-thirteenth of its land, this central district contained streets that rivaled Harlem as the most thickly settled area in America. Between 1890 and 1910, the average density of the Plains rose from ten per acre to twenty while several half blocks housed between 342 to 603 people to the acre.[30] As a whole, this community of immigrant operatives was more than 5 times greater in density than any other district in the city.[31] Crowded into the central districts, "new" immigrants gradually altered the complexion of the city's working-class neighborhoods. Second-generation Irish and French Canadians began to relocate, slowly moving across the river toward Tower Hill. Streets once dominated by Irish and native were transformed into polyglot colonies of hastily built wooden tenements, stores, cafes, marketplaces, and national clubs. Home to more than fifty-one nationalities speaking forty-five languages, the Plains constituted one of America's most international ethnic communities.[32] Living on less than three hundred acres, disparate cultures and customs spilled into one another as blocks rapidly changed identities or overlapped into "foreign" neighborhoods. "The greatest difficulty," complained one government investigator in 1912, "was experienced in finding racial uniformity in the population of the blocks. . . . In some instances," he went on, "a block tentatively selected as being inhabited by members of one race proved on closer examination to be distinctly cosmopolitan."[33] Manuscript census schedules for 1910 confirm the official's observation and suggest that ethnic clustering in Lawrence was less compact than in larger cities where higher concentrations of fewer national groups generated pronounced enclaves of "our own kind." In Lawrence, areas described as exclusively Syrian or Lithuanian typically housed an Italian family on a fourth floor, an assortment of Poles in a rear house, a Portuguese tenement, as well as a scattering of Letts, Armenians, Jews, Irish, Germans, and other "outsiders." When asked if her Lithuanian home on Brook Street had been in "an ethnic ghetto," Amelia Stundza told the interviewer, "Yes, oh yes, Lithuanians lived on the first and second floor and Italians on the third."[34] (See maps 2, 3, 4, and 5)

A block analysis of Stundza's neighborhood, popularly known as "the Dutch Plain," further displays the polyglot character of Lawrence's "ethnic ghettos." Map 3, for example, shows that the Stundza family lived across the street from Germans, and in all three neighborhoods studied, mixed populations existed not only on the same street but occasionally in the same tenement as well. "We were the only Portuguese on Concord Street," recalled Ezilda (Cardoza) Murphy; "there was Jews on one side, and Irish on the other."[35]

The analysis of ethnic residences on four randomly selected blocks in three major neighborhoods within the Plains further supports Stundza's observations. The ethnic composition of residences on Oak Street,

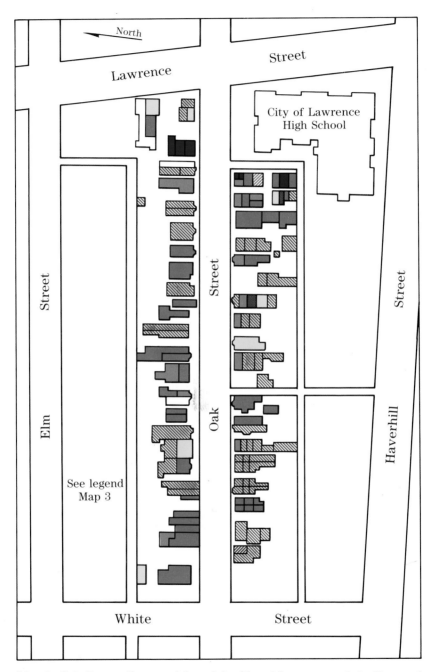

Map 2. Oak Street. Source: *Atlas of the City of Lawrence and the Towns of Methuen, Andover, and North Andover, Mass.* (Boston: L. I. Richards and Co., 1906).

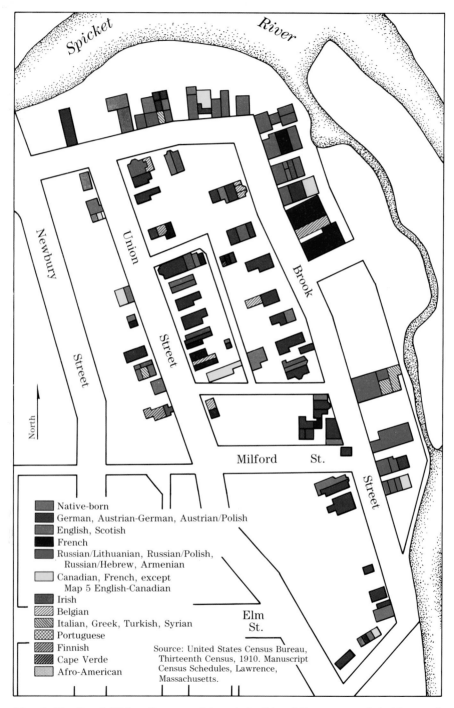

Map 3. The Dutch Plains. Source: *Atlas of the City of Lawrence and the Towns of Methuen, Andover, and North Andover, Mass.* (Boston: L. I. Richards and Co., 1906).

The following labels appear on the map:

Spicket River

Newbury Street

Union Street

Brook Street

North

Milford St.

Elm St.

Street

Legend:
- Native-born
- German, Austrian-German, Austrian/Polish
- English, Scotish
- French
- Russian/Lithuanian, Russian/Polish, Russian/Hebrew, Armenian
- Canadian, French, except Map 5 English-Canadian
- Irish
- Belgian
- Italian, Greek, Turkish, Syrian
- Portuguese
- Finnish
- Cape Verde
- Afro-American

Source: United States Census Bureau, Thirteenth Census, 1910. Manuscript Census Schedules, Lawrence, Massachusetts.

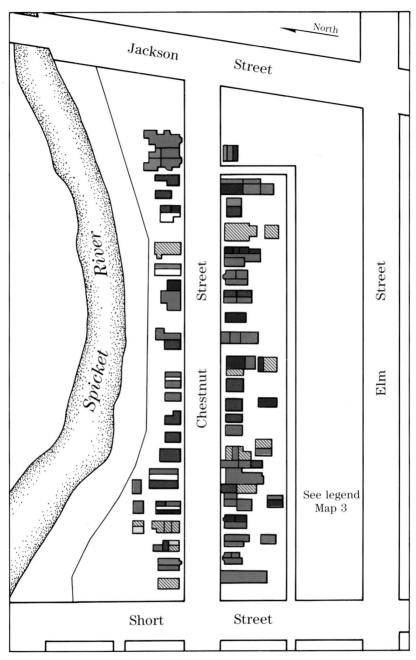

Map 4. Chestnut Street. Source: *Atlas of the City of Lawrence and the Towns of Methuen, Andover, and North Andover, Mass.* (Boston: L. I. Richards and Co., 1906).

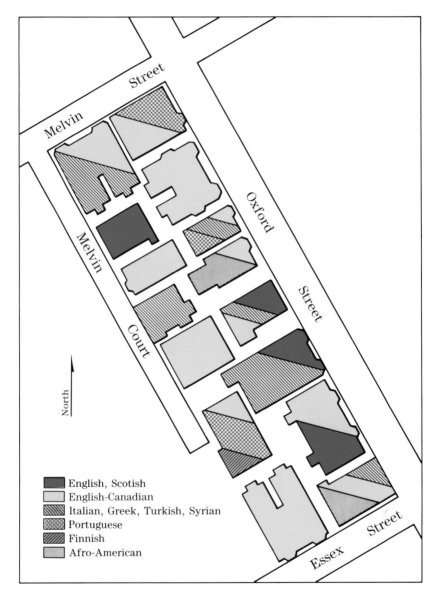

Map 5. Melven Court. Source: *Atlas of the City of Lawrence and the Towns of Methuen, Andover, and North Andover, Mass.* (Boston: L. I. Richards and Co., 1906).

Melvin Court, Chestnut, and the heart of the "Dutch Plain," Brook and Union Streets, were all mixed and cosmopolitan. In the "Dutch Plain" neighborhood, an area known for its German identity, only five houses out of forty-nine contained all-German populations. Sixty-nine percent, however, contained mixed groups of two or more ethnic groups. In Melvin Court, 33 percent of all the buildings sheltered at least three separate ethnic groups under the same roof,[36] and on Chestnut Street, where 106 apartments squeezed into 55 buildings, over half were multiethnic in composition (see table 5). Furthermore, each of these streets contained at least nine separate ethnic groups within its borders while Oak Street could claim as many as fifteen distinct nationalities. Multiethnic households completed the opaque quality of Lawrence's immigrant community.

While some groups, notably the Italians and Jews, maintained concentrations of their own kind such as on lower Common and Concord Streets, few enclaves extended beyond one block. Yet even in these unusually homogeneous clusters, "foreigners" made their presence felt as rear porches attached to Lithuanian and Syrian tenements backed into their own. Such porches were so close, real estate agents reported collecting rents by climbing to the third and fourth floors of one tenement and then reaching out into apartments on the same floors of the houses next door. In this way, observed the city's sanitary commission, "agents save a trip up more stairs."[37]

Courtyard arrangements further diluted ethnic exclusiveness as "foreign" customs, music, language, and even strange cooking odors spilled into disparate tenements. A popular arrangement among Lawrence builders who jammed as many tenements together as was possible around tiny patches of land, courtyards facilitated daily contact and provided a common space for exchange. One former Italian resident of the Plains, Rose Angelotti, also recalled the formal rituals that brought her Italian family and friends together with the Franco-Belgians. "We lived, in a courtyard so mixed up, but mostly French and French-Belge, They would have a great festival some times. Turtles would be cleaned, oh all together the women worked, all day cleaning and preparing the turtles. I met my friend Evone that way. All the time we had these kinds of activities in our yard."[38]

While Italian-born Angelotti recalled Belgian holidays, Portuguese Ezilda Murphy remembered the festive ceremonies that surrounded Italian wine making. Women from the neighborhood, including Portu-

Table 5. Block Analysis of Four Lawrence Streets by Ethnicity, 1910

| | | | | Buildings Containing | | | | | |
| | No. of Ethnic Groups in Block[a] | No. of Buildings[b] | No. of Apartments | 3 or More Ethnic Groups[c] | | 2 or More Ethnic Groups | | Single Ethnic Occupancy | |
Street Name				N	%	N	%	N	%
Oak	15	54	121	8	15	25	46	29	54
Melvin	9	15	49.5	5	33	9	60	6	40
Chestnut	10	55	106	8	15	30	55	25	45
Dutch Plains (Brook & Union)	12	49	134	12	24	34	69	15	31

a. See maps 2, 3, and 4 for exact ethnic groups.
b. Buildings based on Manuscript Census Schedules of 1910 and *Atlas of the City of Lawrence, and the Towns of Methuen, Andover, and North Andover, Massachusetts* (Boston: L. J. Richards & Co. 1906).
c. Includes multiple ethnic households as well as apartments located at each address.

guese and Armenians would join Italian women to gather the grapes and then "we'd all go down to Common Street and they'd help each other make their wine."[39]

The development of close neighborhood networks was also facilitated by the building boom that ushered in the new century. To house an expanding work force, the city hastily erected multiple-story dwellings containing as many as fourteen apartments in the districts that rimmed the city's mills. Within the first decade of the twentieth century these dumbbell-style tenements, described by the city's building inspector as "indifferently built" and "not of the expensive class," had completely replaced the nineteenth-century cottage residence, or single family home, as the workers' major source of shelter.[40] While only fifteen tenements existed in 1895, by 1911, 52 percent of Lawrence's families lived in houses of three apartments or more.[41] By 1912, Lawrence had 268 four-story wooden frame houses, more than any other city in New England.[42]

Closeness to neighbors made interior family life often public and visible. One former resident recalled how few household routines, including family meals, were kept beyond neighborly notice. "I used to hear my mother call me from the kitchen and the smell of food told me it was time to eat. But when I'd get there sometimes, it wasn't my mother, but a voice from next door, through the window! I could reach out and eat off my neighbors table we were so close."[43] In another case, investigators for the city found kitchen utensils "regularly hung on neighbors houses, clearly situated in such a way as to be of service to more than one household."[44]

Neighborhood festivals and close living conditions provided opportunities for immigrants to cross ethnic lines, but it was in the performance of daily tasks that lasting bonds and close neighborhood networks formed and solidified. Whereas mill management systematically sought to use ethnic loyalty to separate workers, crowded living conditions and domestic routine provided a means to overcome ethnic antagonisms and link disparate communities. As we shall see, such connections proved critical in forging a consciousness of kind and solidifying class consciousness during the strike of 1912.

Cemented in the neighborhood, connections between immigrant groups were most frequently the result of female efforts. Cross-ethnic networks, often an outgrowth of "women's work," emerged as women sought to fulfill traditional female obligations and responsibilities, such

Figure 8. "The Rim of the Plains, 1897." Courtesy of the Museum of American Textile History.

Figure 9. "The Heart of the Plains, 1911." Courtesy of Immigrant City Archives.

Figure 10. Tenements in the Plains. Courtesy of Immigrant City Archives.

as childcare, food preparation, laundry, and nursing. Sharing only broken English, women washed and hung clothes together over spreading porches, hauled water from common wells, watched and disciplined children from stoops and rear doors, and occasionally shared food, recipes, and kitchen utensils. Speaking of her mother's frequent exchanges with Syrian neighbors, Lithuanian-born Elizebeth Vilkaite explained: "You know how workers lived then, like slaves, but we all helped each other out, that's just the way it was back then, you did for others."[45]

Although men lived in as close contact with other ethnic groups as women, their socializing tended to take place in ethnically segregated fraternal associations, barbershops, saloons, and political clubs. Even neighborhood garden plots were divided along ethnic lines with Italians controlling the plants on upper Valley Street and Jews at the lower.[46] Italian men, for example, joined neighborhood drum corps that restricted membership not only by ethnicity, but by village as well. Barbers solicited old village clientele and Syrian cobblers and restaurateurs welcomed Mt. Lebanon men and "only a few Turks."[47]

As caretakers of the family, women frequently found themselves involved in complex patterns of exchange. "Shops," recalled one resident, "were all mixed up." Stores on Amesbury included "a barber shop run by Italian men, a cobbler—he was Armenian, and then a big Portuguese store."[48] Lithuanian, Jewish, and Syrian women, often accompanied by

Figure 11. An alleyway in the Plains. Note the basket being dropped to a neighbor below. Women used baskets to carry up goods and to exchange food and utensils with neighbors. Courtesy of Immigrant City Archives.

their daughters, shopped on the busy Elm Street and bargained with Italian shop owners. On Concord Street, Russian and German women mingled with Irish and Portuguese in Faris Brox's popular Syrian fruit store. "Everyone was there," recalled one former resident of Concord Street, "and the stores stayed open 'til late at night." During the strike of 1912, an outside observer noted that, "Italians are bargain hunters, and do not make a practice of trading exclusively with the firm with which they have an account."[49] Exchanging local gossip and comparing prices, women established what E. P. Thompson has called the "moral economy" of the neighborhood, that is, a "commonsense" notion of a fair and just price as opposed to a market value established by the forces of supply and demand. In the same way, standards of behavior and codes of conduct were honed as women exchanged gossip and assessed the world around them. Shopping with her mother, Anna Marino remembered market nights as a time when women would "take the chance to catch up." News was dissected, newcomers introduced, local "no accounts" unmasked, community delinquents railed against, misfortunes shared, and misfeasance tried and judged. Always, however, prices were discussed with great animation and knowledge, as "good deals" and the names of "cheats" circulated. Another long-time resident remembered the continuous rounds she and her mother would make from store to store. "We compared prices with our neighborhood and the other Italian markets, then we'd go to the other grocery stores and do the same."[50]

Such experiences were both ordinary and habitual, but they played a central role in developing neighborhood networks and in concretizing a consciousness of kind. Joining kin and neighbors on grocery nights and pursuing bargains in adjacent communities, women shared experiences and built alliances around common needs, problems, and injustices. As negotiators for scarce resources, women also came into contact with the distributors and dealers of those goods, reinforcing their importance in regulating and adjudicating the community's moral economy. Furthermore, contacts with store clerks, grocers, and shop keepers, brought shop floor issues of wages and payment schedules into a wider community discourse. As we shall see in the strike of 1912, both the store owner and the nonworking wife, understood the connections between their own survival and industrial wages.

While grocery stores provided women with critical contact points that cut across class and ethnicity, "women's work" provided additional pathways to cooperation and mutual exchange. Growing up close to the heart of the Plains, on the corner of Lawrence and Chestnut Streets, Antonietta Carpinone recalled the mingling of ethnic customs and cultures that often resulted from the exchange of food and recipes. "A German girl taught me how to make doughnuts, the smells from her house, you see, were well, you know, you wanted to know what they make inside."[51] Food was also the wedge that overcame Mrs. Rocco's shyness of her German neighbors. "Our yard had a cherry tree and groups of German women would come to gather the fruits. They taught us good ways to make the fruit."[52] Similarly, Consiglia Teutonica became friends with Jewish neighbors in the course of bread making. "It was when my mother made her weekly bread that neighbors put their heads out and came over. 'What you going to do today?' And we all would giggle. 'You make bread? You make bread for me too!' So my mamma makes bread for her German neighbors!"[53]

At times, such contacts led to long lasting and occasionally secret friendships. "My father," explained Anna Marino, "never knew our mother had Syrian friends. They would visit each other in the day and eventually my mother could cook like a Syrian and my father never knew how she did it!"[54]

Midwife practices suggest less casual ways in which gender definitions could loosen ethnic barriers. Foreign-born women relied on traditional midwife assisted childbirth in Lawrence as they had in the Old Country. Midwives attended just under 20 percent of all Lawrence births at the turn of the century, increasing to almost half as "new" immigrants settled into the Plains.[55] Understanding the heterogeneous character of the city's neighborhoods, one established midwife actively pursued "foreign" clients. Calling herself Henrietta Grella when delivering Italian babies, Honorata Groele demonstrated both her enterprising spirit and the necessity of multiethnic appeal by advertising names flavored especially for each group.[56] According to one recent study of Lawrence midwives, twelve of Lawrence's sixteen busiest practitioners delivered children of ethnic origin differing from their own.[57] Beginning her practice in 1899, German-born Minnie Riehm served a variety of immigrant families attending births in thirty-four of the city's precincts. Confining her talents to only two precincts, Louise Loppes nevertheless retained a multiethnic reputation so that only 48 percent of her clients were fellow Portuguese.[58]

Payment also reflected traditional forms of exchange and reciprocity as cash poor families substituted fresh vegetables for the five-dollar fee.[59] The close physical proximity of neighbors and tenements made it possible for women to share domestic tasks and exchange goods, services, and advice, but it was the exigencies of poverty that bound women together in a web of mutual cooperation and daily exchange. As declining conditions eroded women's ability to fulfill traditional female obligations, female networks concretized in an ever widening circle of reciprocity and exchange.

The Working Poor

Always the hardest working part of the city, the Plains had always worn the deepest scars of industrialization. By 1910, readers of Charles Dickens would have found Lawrence's dull streets and cluttered alleys, its black canals and purple ill-smelling river, its vast piles of soot-covered brick buildings, its flimsy, damp privies whose waste oozed down open sewers and meandered through the city's shaded backyards a familiar landscape. Over the years, the Plains, like Dickens's fictitious Coketown, had grown into an "ugly citadel," a bleak fortress of towering chimneys and pounding machinery where "nature was as strongly bricked out as killing airs and gasses were bricked in."[60]

So too would veteran residents, who might note with alarm the rapid transformation of the city's ethnic population, find, as a matter of course, inadequate public services, poor and often primitive housing, unsanitary streets and overflowing privies, contaminated water, declining wages and ever rising mortality rates. Since the collapse of the Pemberton, these landmarks of wage labor had grown familiar to Lawrence's working poor.

Nevertheless, in the years before the First World War, the familiar intensified. Steady work, newly promised with the expansion of the city's mills, was used against immigrant operatives as managers argued that "steady employment justified low wages." According to this argument, workers wouldn't need to worry about putting aside spare wages for emergency slowdowns, so that reduced, but steady, wages would provide families more consistent patterns of income. "In this way," recalled one worker, "we could starve and work at the same time." While mill wages declined, however, more and more of the city's working class became dependent on the textile industry for their livelihood. By 1910, fully three-fourths of Lawrence's eighty-five thousand people directly relied on mill wages for survival.[61]

At the same time that expansion in textile manufacturing provided newcomers with much needed jobs, depressed wages and soaring prices yielded only a meager existence for the vast majority of operatives and their families. Although wages had been slowly rising for several years, the peak weekly average of $8.75, attained in 1909, merely represented a return to 1875 levels. At the close of the century's first decade, the average wage among Lawrence woolen workers was a mere sixteen cents an hour, although 23 percent earned less than twelve cents and only a fifth of the operatives managed to exceed twenty cents for every hour expended.[62] Furthermore, unstable conditions prevented full employment, and more than half of the city's operatives were unable to maintain a full fifty-six-hour work week.

Compounding the difficulties that faced workers, was the inflationary cycle that had been building since the late nineteenth century. Prices throughout the United States increased sharply after 1910, putting additional strains on already tight budgets. Bitter complaints by workers produced a special act of the Massachusetts State Legislature creating a commission on the cost of living, but it did little more than confirm what workers already knew. Of all commodities studied, the commission found that none had risen in price more quickly or sharply than food stuffs, which, by 1908, outdistanced the 1890-99 averages by 20 percent. Staples, such as eggs, bread, and milk, increased by as much as from 25 to 45 percent in a single decade, while meat prices escalated to more than 90 percent above turn-of-the-century costs. At seven cents a quart, most families in Lawrence could only afford condensed or evaporated milks and many reported trying "to fool [their] stomachs with a kind of molasses" in place of butter.[63]

Soaring prices and declining wages necessitated the employment of women and children, if families were to survive. Even skilled workers, the "aristocracy of labor," found themselves hard pressed to earn a living without the labor of wives and daughters. Throughout the decade before the war, the Central Labor Union, a craft oriented organization, railed against starvation wages that "take our wives out of the home" and into the mills.[64] Despite a 1912 finding by the Massachusetts Commission on minimum wages that "the lowest total for human living conditions for an individual . . . was $8.28 per week," a third of Lawrence's operatives earned less than $7.00, so that few families in the city could secure even "the bare necessaries" without at least two full-time wage-earners.[65] Consequently, of Lawrence's thirty-five thousand who actually toiled inside the factory gates, over half were women and children.[66]

Immigrant women were especially critical members of Lawrence households providing domestic labor as well as mill wages or cash earned while keeping house for boarders. Of 292 foreign homes surveyed in Lawrence in 1909, just under 20 percent (18 percent) consisted of households in which the husband alone provided the families' entire income. While Lithuanian and Polish immigrants used female labor to cook, clean, launder, and sew for boarders in order to supplement income, the French (77 percent), Syrians (42 percent), and Southern Italians (38 percent), relied directly on the mill earnings of children and wives.[67] "In Lawrence," observed the *New York Call*, "all the family must work if the family is to live."[68]

Poverty and the increasing immiseration of the working classes, affected all members of Lawrence's working classes, but not in equal ways. Immigrant and unskilled workers, especially female wage earners who generally made half the wages of their male counterparts, were particularly hard-pressed as they calculated familial needs against new-world wages. "It is in evidence," noted one observer of immigrant conditions, "that a few of the English factory hands who emigrated to Lawrence declared it harder to live under wages of Lawrence than under the wages of Lancashire."[69] As managers of meager family budgets, women felt especially fooled by their new earnings. "They thought they were rich," recalled Elizabeth Gurley Flynn, "till they had to pay rent, buy groceries, clothes, and shoes. Then they knew they were poor."[70]

Poor women's responsibilities for familial health and welfare were likewise undermined by the crippling effects of contaminated city water, leaking privies, garbage-strewn streets, and dangerous, often life-threatening workplaces. In the decade before the First World War, the mean age at death in Lawrence fell from eighteen to fifteen years, as poor nutrition and unsanitary conditions left children defenseless against disease.[71] By 1900, just over two-fifths of all deaths were among infants under two years old. Occupational diseases, however, also contributed to adult illnesses and low life expectations among operatives and their families. Spinners, for example, who worked in damp and humid rooms, were especially vulnerable to the tuberculosis, the "white plague," and pneumonia. In the years before the 1912 strike, one third of Lawrence's spinners would die before they had worked ten years, and half of these would never reach the age of 25.[72] "The mortality in the crowded tenement districts," declared a shocked city editor, "especially in the summer . . . reads like battle statistics."[73]

Exposed in the neighborhoods to filth and disease, immigrant workers faced additional risks at work. Of the one thousand accidents reported by the Pacific Mill between 1900-1905, 788 of them were sustained by foreign-born workers and their children. "I got hurt in the Washington [Mill]," reported 14-year-old Camella Teoli to government investigators. "The machine pulled the scalp off."[74] In what must be one of the great understatements in the chronicles of Lawrence history, an historian writes, "the steady succession of injuries was depressing to the immigrants."[75]

A disease of another sort, "speculation fever," further compounded the difficulties of industrial life, raising rents to dizzying heights. Beginning in the late 1890's, "tenement sharps" eagerly purchased available land in the Plains, throwing up flimsy structures on every open lot. While corporations continued to build houses for its help, almost all were planned for skilled workers and occupied sites outside the Plains. After 1890, arriving immigrants depended on local developers and entrepreneurs including foreign-born shop keepers and businessmen, native investors, professional developers, and even local churchmen. "The saints upon whom the clergymen depend for their living," noted one wry observer, "are developing a decided disinclination to speculate in real estate in any other world but this one."[76] By 1911, speculators, both the holy and not so holy pushed rents to extraordinary levels. In the central districts of the Plains, rents were higher than in Chicago, Buffalo, Milwaukee, or Cleveland. At a time when yearly wages in Lawrence ranged from three to four hundred dollars, the cost of securing a cold water flat climbed to between two to four hundred dollars annually.[77]

Sharps further aggravated immigrant budgets by eliminating spaces once used as gardens and storage areas. Rapidly purchasing workers' cottages in the Plains, owners moved these smaller houses to the rear of residential lots, then attached new and larger structures which virtually eliminated surrounding spaces. Like the exhausted mill towns of Dickens' England with their "labyrinth of narrow courts upon courts, and close streets upon close streets, which had come into existence piecemeal, every piece in a violent hurry for some one man's purpose, and the whole an unnatural family, shouldering, and trampling, and pressing one another to death," Lawrence adopted the wiggly-piggly method of housing development.[78] In the Everett and the "Ol' Swamp" neighborhoods, only nine lots out of thirty-seven studied had less than 70 percent of its area occupied by buildings. The remaining parcels had from three-quarters to just under the entire land area covered by residential structures.[79] Pigs, goats, chickens and family gardens gradually disappeared in these neighborhoods, eliminating a small but valuable supplement to the family economy. In their place stood the stunted and crooked shapes of sheds, stalls, rookeries, shacks, and whatever else could be called a flat and charged a rent.

Structural overcrowding also eliminated spaces once used to store coal or wood, thereby forcing new tenants to buy in small, more expensive quantities. By the ton, coal in Lawrence was already more expensive than in any other city in the state, and without storage, operatives paid from 40 to 80 percent more for fuel than if bought by the ton.[80] By the end of the first decade of the twentieth century, Lawrence operatives could easily agree with the Slavic priest who remarked, "My people are not in America; they are under it."[81]

At the same time that mill wages and living spaces became increasingly inadequate to provide a decent living, Progressive legislation further narrowed work options for immigrant families. In the growing effort to "clean up Lawrence," it was the immigrant more than his or her surroundings that became the focus of concerned attention. Joining national efforts which sought to tame the "city wilderness," Lawrence's educated classes, organized to reform the "hardworking but ignorant" foreigner "whose standard for themselves and their families is often miserable."[82] Especially worried that "the home is fast passing away," local Republican and Progressive clubs sought to domesticate the immigrant neighborhood, initiating a series of legal actions against what they believed to be the corrupting habits of immigrants unfamiliar with American ways.[83] The annual outburst that regularly erupted each Fourth of July, dramatically brought to the surface the tensions that increasingly informed relationships between older residents and more recently arrived immigrants. Just as kitchen bars, street games, peddling, and other forms of public socializing among residents of the Plains threatened middle class notions of private life and domestic tranquility, immigrant celebrations—noisy, collective, and often lasting late into the night—clashed with reformers who feared the excesses of public displays. "Bands of foreigners and trouble makers," according to city newspapers, knew nothing of the way to celebrate the national holiday. Rather than listening to patriotic music, provided in the common, these revelers, "filled with the spirit of the day and armed with trumpets, cowbells, augmented by their own shrill voices," marched down Common Street onto Essex, where they ignited "huge piles of wood . . . and at midnight broke their bonds and pandemonium reigned."[84] Store owners along the downtown streets along with bankers, city official, policemen, and property-owners, who "paced the streets driven almost frantic," nervously watched as "hundreds of people shouted and danced around bon-fires on the banks of the Spicket." Following the strike of 1912, such activities would be outlawed and replaced by town sponsored events where audiences would observe, not participate, in elaborate pageants, concerts, and firework displays.

Reform efforts began in earnest, however, between 1900 and 1912 when members of the professional and business classes, as well as a wide variety of city officials and skilled workers, organized to ban Sunday hunting, "kitchen bars," pool rooms, group or multiple lodgings, child labor, and numerous street activities that especially offended middle-class notions of privatized family life.[85] While reformers were seldom united in their efforts to improve the city and often fell short of their goals, their campaigns increasingly penetrated immigrant neighborhoods, eroding customary sources of income and threatening the ability of the laboring poor to supplement mill wages and fulfill traditional obligations.[86]

Disrupting immigrant survival strategies, Progressive crusades threatened poor families as a whole, but they affected individual members in very different ways. Fish and game laws, for example, which required hunters to be licensed at exorbitant fees, substantially reduced men's ability to provide additional food for families. Once a common method of supplementing the family diet, hunting squirrel and other small game was disallowed unnaturalized persons unless they obtained a license from the city. Passed in 1905 after Syrians and other immigrants protested previous restrictions preventing any foreigner from hunting, the new regulations, although seemingly broader, were more strictly enforced and fees were increased. Few workers could afford the annual rate of fifteen dollars, the equivalent of three or four full weeks of work, and even if prospective hunters combined their resources to "pool the license," new city laws prevented Sunday shooting, the sole day "owned by us."[87]

Cut off from free supplies of fresh meat and fish, and caught in a downward spiral of escalating prices and declining wages, poor families deepened their dependence on women's traditional aptitude for obtaining a "just price" in the marketplace and a "penny for a pennies worth." Women combed neighborhood stores in search of bargains. As overseers of the family purse who controlled and allocated scarce resources, women's status and power was continuously reinforced in the daily struggle to stretch precious dollars. "It is the mother," observed one New York social worker, "around whom the whole machinery of family life revolves. The family economy depends on her interests, skills, and sense of order. Her economic importance is far greater than that of her wealthier sisters for as income increases . . . the amount of it controlled by the wife diminishes . . . "[88] A Jewish wife recounted her responsibility for ensuring the families lodgings. "He earned $6.00 this week, doing a small job for the owner of this house. He did it in two evenings and he gave me the money, which I put away toward the rent which will be due in a month again."[89] An Italian proverb suggests the traditionally critical role of women in peasant societies, "If the husband dies a family suffers; if a wife dies the family cannot exist."

Married women also laid claim to husband's and children's paychecks as soon as they were picked up. "No one doubted her right," recalled Antonietta Capriola. "In marriage, women held the money. My mother was the chief here and always, always she was aware of our family accounts, at the grocery, the butcher, the landlord, she watched them like hawks."[90] While such control was seldom disputed, it could lead to conflict and even violence as decisions over the distribution of income often pitted husbands against wives. According to Lawrence newspapers, the defense "she refused me my 50 cents" was not an infrequent one among wife beaters.[91]

Faced with increasingly restrictive laws, immigrants also found themselves less able to influence city hall. Launched in 1903, the new city charter movement unsettled the patronage system that gave immigrants whatever meager representation they had in city hall. Typically, ethnic communities pressured city hall with coalitions built around the Democratic Party whose Irish leadership retained strong ties with the working class neighborhoods of the Plains. With promises to Germans that their social clubs would receive the necessary licenses to serve liquor, reform Mayor Lynch won election in 1903-4, and immediately launched his new offensive against "waste" by canceling the appointments of 16 patrolmen, two of whom originated from Russia and Syria. Forming a "reserve" police force, Lynch argued for "officers of some experience but pay for their services only when they are thus employed."[92] Licensing established ethnic clubs kept older immigrant voters in the Democratic fold, but it was an alliance that came at the expense of recent arrivals whose societies were less formalized and whose membership could ill-afford the $2,500.00 annual license fee.[93]

Increases in licensing fees put smaller immigrant saloons out of business and eliminated an important neighborhood establishment. Liquor dealers and larger saloon owners, as well as established ethnic clubs such as the Hibernians and the German Turn Hall who could more readily afford the new fees, continuously pushed for expanded enforcement of licensing laws, ironically combining with Republican efforts to regulate and eventually prevent the flow of alcohol. While the laws were never able to effectively close down all the bars, they succeeded in harassing and disrupting smaller bars, especially the ubiquitous kitchen barrooms which dotted neighborhoods in the Plains.[94] Frequented almost exclusively by men, these establishments were typically run by women, who, like Mrs. Saphire Maritelio and Kate Smith, sold liquor in their homes and provided a comfortable place where men could play cards, get warm, and escape from the pressures of the day. If Kate Smith, arrested with $150.00 on her, was representative, they also offered women a rare and lucrative alternative to the drudgery of mill life.[95]

Fueled by public anxiety over white slavery and encouraged by national movements for social purity, Progressive attacks on kitchen bars paralleled a series of local campaigns to regulate and control the activities of autonomous women. Women's participation in the public sphere grew increasingly suspect, a sign of promiscuity and gender deviance which Lawrence officials hoped to eradicate by controlling the use of public spaces. Even wives who assumed the responsibilities of a family business following the death of a husband fell under official suspicion. New codes established in the late 1890's, required widows intending to operate their husband's business, to submit written statements of "respectability." Furthermore, all married women, who intended to operate a business on their own, were also required to obtain a certificate to be kept on file in the clerk's office.[96] Similarly, peddling, a popular occupation for women, especially among Syrians who traditionally utilized female labor as door to door sellers, was increasingly curtailed by high licensing fees and stiff fines. And finally, Lawrence joined state efforts to eliminate midwives, further circumscribing female roles and undermining traditional sources of both financial and emotional support.

Regulating women's public activity coincided with national efforts to recast the private lives of the urban immigrant. In settlement houses, youth clubs, evening classes, and numerous other associations, immigrant women confronted the "respectable" world of domesticity and American homemaking. Taking up classes in home economics, immigrant mothers and daughters were taught the importance of family life and the home. "Homes," as one historian points out, "that were built on a particular middle-class configuration of possessions and housekeeping practices and a particular structure of family relations."[97]

Lawrence reformers, distrustful of autonomous women who, as wives and daughters, overstepped the gender boundaries of the middle-class, were even more distressed by the neglectful mother who conspired to keep children out of school and in the mill. According to local newspapers, Syrian and Italian families were especially noted for the "many schemes" they devised to frustrate child labor laws. Passports and official certificates were widely falsified. "Papers," complained one city father, "are usually of a relative, a neighbor, or an older brother or sister working in some other mill or out of town or perhaps at home ill!"[98] Women played especially important roles in regulating children's lives, and both immigrant families and city authorities held women responsible for childcare practices. "How little value can be placed upon the mother's oath in this respect is notorious among social workers."[99]

Contradicting reformers' notions of childhood, immigrant women responded to household needs and traditions which emphasized the contributions of children to the family economy. As recent historians have shown, children of the urban poor were treated as "little adults, unable as yet to take up all the duties of their elders, but nonetheless bound to do as much as they could."[100] Keenly aware that survival depended upon the combined efforts of each family member, mothers expected young members of the household to participate in the daily struggle to make ends meet. Scheming to get children mill jobs, women merely refashioned traditional concepts to fit the new circumstances of industrial life.

Nevertheless, the conflict over child labor sharpened the lines that separated poor women from their middle-class sisters. Speaking to the Andover women's club, a gathering place for Lawrence's elite, Florance Kelly, organizer of the newly created National Child Labor Committee and General Secretary of the National Consumer's League, advocated the adoption of stricter guidelines for identifying children. Kelly argued that weight, height, age, and literacy should be taken into account and that identification papers should have physical descriptions to prevent falsifying work papers. The so-called summer discoveries of 1904, in which dozens of underaged children were found working in Lawrence's mills, were used to support Kelly's contentions and provided a catalyst for renewed efforts to eliminate children from the mills. Mayor Lynch, responding to the combined voices of reformers and skilled workers who sought to eliminate both women and children from the mills, moved to tighten city enforcement and strengthen local codes. Within a year, new ordinances placed responsibility for detection on the parents as well as on the mill and school department which also established new codes of literacy for minors between the ages of fourteen and sixteen.[101] Previously, persons age fourteen or over could work in the mills regardless of literacy and parents were not held accountable. With the new act, however, working minors now needed certificates signed by school superintendents testifying to their ability to read and write English. Illiterate minors were further required by law to attend evening school or else their families were subject to fines. By 1905, city missionary Clark Carter, the school committee, and the mills began a "careful watch" program to detect underage children employed in the mills, simultaneously increasing fines and penalties for parents and manufacturers alike.[102]

Efforts to eliminate children from the mills placed new strains on already tight budgets. As supervisors of the family purse, women were especially well situated to understand the burdens that such public acts, what one neighborhood woman called "the deeds of the guzikmanas" or "men in brass buttons," placed on immigrant households.[103] For women in the Plains, each discovery was a time of uncertainty and crisis, for it threatened to sever the precarious threads that women had spun to sustain life. Describing the emotional turmoil that surrounded her removal from the mill as "underaged," a former twister remembered the experience as "a kind of disaster" and "a terrible blow." News of the calamity spread rapidly so that by nightfall, "All the women came to my mother and told her not to worry, everyone was angry and in a few days I got a new name, new papers, a new job."[104]

Relying on old-world practices and principles of collectivity, the immigrant community routinely "swapped" names and falsified documents in an effort to evade "impossible" laws and ensure mutual survival. "In Russia," explained Lillian Rosenberg, "many took different names to evade the draft—over here [they] took the name of the person who got you the job."[105] To those who lived on Common Street, Anna LoPizzo, a slain mill worker during the strike of 1912, was Anna LaMonica, once too young to work. Similarly, Antonietta Carpinone, became Anna Ricci when presenting her working papers. At times, families exchanged papers with friends and relatives from different cities and not infrequently, local priests aided desperate families in falsifying official documents.[106]

As primary caretakers of the family and as adjudicators of the community's moral economy, women often acted as negotiators and trouble shooters, putting into use contacts made while performing traditional female obligations. In most cases, women's duties included saving income as well as distributing it to landlords, butchers, shop keepers and grocers. Evading child labor laws frequently depended on female skills and contacts as women spread the news along established networks and squeezed precious pennies to pay the costs. "Father Milanese refused to believe I had been confirmed in Italy," recalled a former operative. "He kept telling my mother 'not old enough, not old enough!' So my work paper could not get stamped. Then my mother gets, you know, the word about what to do and so some man comes round and she pays him money to update my papers. Of course I was underage but we needed the work. We all did it."[107]

Threatened by declining economic conditions, women found themselves increasingly called upon to "make ends meet." "The lash of youthful hunger," forced many of the city's women into the mills and, as conditions worsened, the burdens of a double day deepened dependency on neighbors and kin. Compelled to share cramped and crowded physical surroundings, women utilized the proximity of neighbors, friends, and kin to mutual advantage by socializing a variety of domestic tasks. Sharing traditional female responsibilities such as laundry, food preparation, cooking, and childcare, women tightened their dependence on each other as informal relationships solidified into a widening circle of neighborhood cooperation and mutual support.

On street corners and stoops, in kitchens and markets, at bath houses and public laundries, on walks to and from factories, laboring women shared experiences, offered aid, nursed kin and neighbors, made friends and built alliances. Out of such daily exchange, concrete personal networks emerged entwining the skilled and unskilled, the homeworker and widow, the midwife and the grocer's wife, the peddler and the consumer, the young and the old.

Facilitating the growth and expansion of female networks was the unique character of immigrant family life. As recent historians of immigration have made clear, the family was the core around which immigration revolved. But families changed as old-world ties were broken and only gradually and partially reformed in new-world circumstances.[108] In Lawrence, as in other industrial cities before the First World War, village sons and daughters entered new households in a

complex assortment of relationships. Typically following chain migrations and linking up with cousins, sisters, brothers, fathers, and husbands, immigrants also entered new-world households as friends, old
village neighbors, and as friends of friends. Sara Axelrod, "bitter about
her marriage" and unable to find work in Plymouth, left her husband and
brother in Plymouth while she went to Lawrence. Once there, she located a friend of her brother's best friend and found lodgings in a boarding house of Lithuanians, Poles, and Russian Jews.[109] Similarly, Annie
Roguise, who came to Lawrence as a widow in 1906, moved into an
apartment headed by Josephine Stuka, a Polish operative whose two
daughters also worked in the mills. Annie and her two children shared
rooms with this family and with 3 other boarders.[110]

Government investigators found that defining these numerous entan-
glements was often a tortuous experience and eventually settled on describing a household in Lawrence's immigrant neighborhoods as any
arrangement "consisting of one or more families, with or without boarders or lodgers as well as all groups of persons living together, no family
included, or various combinations of family, groups, and boarders and
lodgers."[111] Unable to afford soaring rents, recent arrivals typically
shared apartments, rooms, even beds. "When I woke of a morning,"
recalled Michael Gold of his Lower East Side neighborhood, "I was
never greatly surprised to find in my bed a new family of immigrants, in
their foreign baggy underwear."[112] Like Gold's tenement home, which
"was a Plymouth Rock" for fellow countrymen and women, communal
living was a fact of immigrant life in the Plains. In two half blocks in
Lawrence's Everett neighborhood, city investigators found collective
living a common and "dangerous" practice. In three of five tenements in
these two half blocks, multiple families lived side by side, and 20 percent
of these consisted of three or more households.[113] Bedrooms in these
apartments generally encircled the kitchen, providing each family with
heat as well as a common area for daily activity. The average number of
people sharing rooms in this section exceeded two persons, a figure
that was probably low as investigators visited during a slack season
when operatives not infrequently left town, temporarily seeking employment. Even so, Lawrence as a whole ranked in the top 10 percent
among American cities for residents per house, slightly exceeding eight
persons for every dwelling and 1 1/2 residents for every room.[114]

Residents of the Plains, as one government researcher put it, preferred to "live as they please," thereby shaping family life in ways that

reproduced the emotional and financial function, if not the form, of old-world households.[115] Substituting for absent kin, neighbors and friends frequently assumed roles as surrogate or "fictive" relatives. Local "grandmamas" and "Senorias," disciplining children and "keeping an eye out" for the offspring of working neighbors, assumed parental authority and saw mothering as a collective responsibility. The youngest of five and the only family member "too young to fool the bosses," Portuguese-born Ezilda Murphy found the boundaries that separated family and friends ill-defined and vague. "We felt as if they were our family, until today as old as I am, I still feel these women, these older women, are my family. I call them dear, which is Aunt, or Senora, I still do that and it was nothing for another woman to give you a nice big slap on your fanny if you were doing something wrong. It was 17 apartments in that tenement, and everyone looked after everyone else."[116]

Providing essential and free care for children while mothers worked in the mills, older women occupied an important and respected place in the immigrant community. "Everyone called my mother, Grandmama," remembered Consiglia Teutonica, "no matter who lived in the neighborhood. We called older ladies always this, it was of respect for them, like a family."[117] At times, the bonds that united fictive family members extended across ethnic boundaries. When Dora Swartz burned her hands on spinning bobbins, she went to work for the Mahoney family, one of the few Irish households that remained in the neighborhood. "My mother just ran into her, you know. Everyone knew Mrs. Mahoney. They "adopted" me, Mrs. Mahoney called me Dora Casey Swartz!"[118]

Dictated by necessity, patterns of collectivity embraced traditional notions of cooperation and reflected old-world practices that utilized the group to solve individual problems. In Lithuania, farm families commonly operated collectively owned barns and houses, thereby reducing the cost and risk of uncertain harvests. In these rural communities the *kletis,* or communal storehouse, was also where the girls of families traditionally slept, and as one Lithuanian scholar notes, it was also "the locus of the sentimental life of the family."[119]

Although newcomers to the Plains perceived of these households as temporary arrangements, they often provided the basis of long-lasting friendships, and for at least some women, they afforded a chance to develop an identity outside the parameters of wifehood and motherhood. One Lithuanian woman recalled the flexibility of her living arrangements and the freedom they sometimes furnished. "I had been living with my cousin and his married friends in Haverhill but he wanted to marry me, to settle down like at home. We lived with Greeks, French and Poles, all men, and I missed Lithuanian women friends. Besides, I didn't come all the way to America to get married! So I moved out and went to Lawrence, yes alone and I found rooms with a married couple, two boys, a Pole woman and three Lithuanian women. We all became great friends and did what we wanted."[120]

These households, although varied in composition, also bred a certain kind of intimacy as women shared both physical space and the domestic tasks of womanhood. "One of my life-long friends and I," explained a former Jewish resident of the Plains, "first met as bedsisters in a friends place, you know, what they called a tenement. There was a saying, 'the beds were never cold.' Well sure, back then you see this is how you lived—you slept in shifts, we all lived like one then. One kitchen we all used and we all knew each other."[121]

The daughters of Sara Axelrod also remembered their mother's best friend as Sara's "bedsister." "She was introduced in that way and she was very close to our mother, you know in a way of great understanding and deep sympathy. You don't see that so much nowadays."[122] Intimacy, sympathy, and lasting female friendships, forged by exigency, took root and strengthened as women sought to provide for families and mitigate against the harsh realities of industrial life. A latticework of relationships, friends and neighbors, as well as disparate kin, sought to train and protect children, care for the sick, feed the hungry, "keep" house, and provide for families and neighbors.

What began as informal associations often developed into more systematic patterns of exchange as women were increasingly forced to perform a double day as both industrial wage earners and traditional caretakers of home and family. Frequently, working mothers would place their children in the apartment of a woman who, because of a recent birth or because she had too many young children herself, could not work in the mill. For a modest fee, or in exchange for food, these "children's boarding houses" formalized female traditions of reciprocity and provided an additional female space where women shared information and collective grievances. "We'd go there early in the morning," recalled a former boarder, "where a woman, a neighbor would take care of us. She'd send us out to school and back, have our lunch—very common. It would always be a woman that was in the building—you were brought up as if you were her child."[123]

At night, women returned from work and collected children but not without making contact with other mothers. Often the day's events were shared, future meetings were arranged, and mutual concerns aired.

Childcare practices also linked city immigrants with old-world compatriots who lived in the surrounding countryside just outside of Lawrence. Parents who were unable to support small children sent their young into the countryside where they performed farm tasks and could "earn their keep." Country boarding—a common practice in many rural southern and eastern communities where parents often hired out children to more prosperous families or to agents who sponsored migrant laborers—not only alleviated a financial burden but it also provided a valuable contact between mill workers and the local farming community, many of whom were former factory workers now eking out a living as dairy farmers, egg producers, and poultry growers. In the same way that female patterns of exchange promoted cooperation between disparate ethnic groups, childcare practices frequently brought those who shared different relations of production together. As we shall see, such links, formed as women sought to provide for their families and hold life together, would provide the foundation for community solidarity during the strike of 1912.[124]

Pathways to Protest

Women's networks and traditions of exchange were never enough to completely protect women and their families from the realities of Lawrence's industrial life. Women moved in an often brutish world circumscribed by economic hardship and gender asymmetry. Informal networks could not provide long-term assistance to needy women and their families nor supplement lost earnings when desertion, death, disease, or industrial accidents incapacitated male wage earners. Yet female networks and patterns of exchange cushioned the abuses of industrial life, providing both material aid and physical protection during times of need. More importantly, perhaps, female collaborative activities offered neighborhood women an autonomous space wherein which women could, under certain circumstances, collectively assess power relations and organize in opposition to them.

Recent scholarship, for example, has shown that poor women frequently participated in food riots, rent strikes, and other collective demonstrations surrounding what today are called quality of life issues.[125] The actions, often spontaneous, are almost always dominated by women and distinguished by a fierce and passionate militancy. At times they serve as a narrow defense of female prerogatives and community self-interest, but at other times female collective action has worked to radicalize neighbors and kin, thus broadening the extent and focus of dissent. Anger directed at the greedy landlord, the cheating grocer, or the unjust employer can, in the process of female exchange and mobilization, generate into a coherent attack upon an entire system of exploitation, what one former Lawrence striker called "the powers that prey."

Much like the mining communities described by anthropologist June Nash, textile culture was an "affair of the tribe," involving those who depended upon it for a livelihood in an elaborate system of reciprocity, dependence, and cooperation.[126] The concentration of woolen and cotton manufacturing in Lawrence tied members of the community not only to each other, but also to the day to day operations of the mills. Few events on the shop floor, no matter how small, went unnoticed in households where members were "permanent" workers, what Louise Tilly defines as operatives who "worked for most of their lives, though not necessarily continuously."[127] Responsible for the household and its members, women also worked along side men, moving in and out of wage labor as necessity dictated. Yet, the sexual division of labor in the household, also meant that, unlike husbands, brothers, and sons, women tended to understand their situation in ways that linked the external world of production with the intimate circumstances of the home. Conscious of their obligations as "breadgivers" and sustainers of life, poor women did not see themselves as limited to one sphere of activity, for it was precisely their ability to monitor, regulate, and manipulate the "public" world of rents, prices, wages, and alien laws, that allowed laboring women to fulfill female roles and obligations. Unending efforts to secure the "bare necessaries" for their family, necessarily brought women into the public arena of the market, not only as consumers of commodities, but also as negotiators for scare resources and advocates for familial and community needs. Whether haggling at the market, falsifying papers, or out-maneuvering landlords, women acted in ways that assumed an inherent unity between "private" and the "public," and they perceived of themselves as intimately involved in the comings and goings of each.

Rooted in the sexual division of labor, female social spaces also allowed women to develop sharp and exacting notions of both female duty and female rights, what one historian has called a "female consciousness."[128] Female consciousness, honed as women performed domestic labors and strained to provide a decent life for themselves and their families, emerged as a product of collective female efforts and spoke to the shared experiences of immigrant women. By participating in a daily round of reciprocity and mutual exchange, women defined on their own terms the boundaries of womanhood and in the process confirmed the collective or "public" nature of individual and personal misfortunes. Working women, sensitive to fluctuations in the cost of food, rent, and fuel, understood that "changes in the cost of living felt by one would be felt by all."[129]

As Temma Kaplan has shown, such a "female consciousness" went far in providing "motive force" for women's collective action. Yet participation in militancy was itself a radicalizing process, and whether it involved coming to the aid of a friend and neighbor or protesting food increases, collective efforts often led women to an expanded and increasingly critical awareness of the world around them. Daily events and "disasters," including illness, poor food, high prices, rent hikes, as well as unemployment, could be placed in a larger context as women found their roles as primary caretakers of the home and family undercut by the "public" world of prices and wages, of alien laws and hostile market forces.

Sharing information and extending support as women fulfilled female obligations at the marketplace, the courtyard wash place, the kitchen, the stoops, and in the streets also placed women in a position to coordinate collective and spontaneous action. While the action varied with each crisis, women's belief in the public nature of individual misfortune consistently informed group response and helped women mold grievances into specific targets of protest. Neighborhood women identified violators of the commonweal, and, depending on the nature of offense, those so identified were subjected to community derision, ridicule, and in extreme cases, violence. Similarly, when police attempted to arrest a neighborhood woman, crowds gathered, "applauding and laughing" when an "unruly" female neighbor kicked the arresting officer. "Guzikmanas," stated one Lithuanian woman, "have no place, these our streets."

The informal associations that crisscrossed women's lives were also nonhierarchical, enabling large numbers of neighborhood women typically excluded from formal institutions of authority to participate in community affairs and public debates. With upturned arms, sharp tongues, hoots and hisses, women acted out their revolt against a profit oriented economy in ways that utilized the resources available to them. In this way, they resembled other groups of women activists who, like the radical female Quakers in mid-nineteenth-century Rochester, New York, wore Turkish trousers, spoke to mixed audiences, and in general outraged officials as they dramatized their commitment to equal rights. As Nancy Hewitt points out, such acts were "the most accessible forms of social commentary for those with limited resources. The choice then was both pragmatic and ideological."[130] Outside formal structures of power, women claimed their right to a voice in the affairs of the community through participation in daily acts of defiance and protest where legitimacy preceded from deeper conceptions of the source of authority: those found in the decentralized and nonhierarchical webs of female collaboration.

Locally based and organized around women's traditional responsibilities, neighborhood networks could also work with lightning speed. Offending parties were frequently taken by surprise by the swift actions of women who, like the mother of Anna Marino, "could smell trouble coming." Her neighbors knew when "something was up," and they usually knew, as well, those responsible. "My mother's friends would talk. They would always be heads together. Sure no one got away with anything, not in this neighborhood."[131] Seldom spontaneous, the outbursts of immigrant women had shape, logic, and a trajectory of their own. They made sense not as clashes of vague mentalities but as intelligible forces rooted in a shared experience and concretized by the immediacy of political struggle.

In the first decades of the twentieth century, neighborhood skirmishes, described in the press as "small riots," accelerated. Initiated by women who "have drunk of the cup to the very dregs," they typically revolved around securing food, fuel, and housing.[132] Between 1900 and 1912, applications for city relief tripled as women "railed" against and "bullied" city officials for aid they deemed to be their right. Determined to feed their families, women pleaded, bargained, falsified papers, and collaborated together to fill empty stomachs. One woman described a "hungry afternoon" following her failed attempts to get milk for her children. "A small group of us, you know, just a few from our block, we were, oh boy, were we angry, and them with all the money. You bet I marched down there with the others. They don't own the earth. We gave that, what you call it, that relief guy hell. Why not, they had the money and we had the hunger. I spit I was so mad."[133]

Convinced that women were deliberately exaggerating their plight, city officials remained reluctant to grant aid, and what relief did come was pitifully small. City Missionary Clark Carter, upset over the "many schemes" of immigrants, denounced the "undeserving poor" who, he declared, "go to extreme means to outwit our officers." Public officials were not the only ones to note the aggressive "scheming" of women. Priests were often horrified to find their female parishioners entering the local YWCA for the sole purpose of "free lunches and hot showers." One cleric was especially well remembered for his notorious "peeping" through the windows in order to catch all wayward Catholic girls whom he would publicly expose as "agents of the devil." Despite threats, neighborhood women continued to send their daughters to the "Y" where, much to the disappointment of its Protestant directors, "mealers" made up as many twenty-five hundred participants while only a handful showed up for Sunday services.[134] For women, many of whom worked as both wage laborers in the city's mills and as nonpaid workers in the home, exploitation was multiformed and omnipresent. Participation in collective schemes and sporadic skirmishes with city officials, clerics, store owners, and landlords brought women into closer contact with the origins of their exploitation and fostered an understanding of "class" that frequently cut across categories of ownership. For many women, the common enemy could include unsympathetic priests and nuns, greedy merchants, abusive husbands, uncooperative neighbors, and even members of "bullheaded" unions. Wage labor alone, neither bound neighbors together nor kept them apart. Cohesion and conflict typically revolved around notions of the public good, as understood by women, and in contrast to "the powers that prey." Politicized by poverty and exploitation, and situated to experience the connections between their lives and the external forces of oppression, proletarian women developed a consciousness of kind that not only held alien powers accountable but embraced a broad swath of visions and alliances.

In no way was this more dramatically expressed than in the strike of 1912. Women, both young and old, married and single, angrily refused a wage reduction and defied union leaders and section hands to ignite one of the nation's most militant and class conscious strikes. Organized in their neighborhoods and dominated by women, it took the name of its most popular banner, "We want," declared the strikers, "bread and roses too."

4

Neighborhoods in Revolt

The Mob, the mightiest judge of all,
To hear the rights of man came out,
And every word became a shout,
And every shout a cannon ball.
  —Arturo Giovannitti

We not only wanted labor laws and bread, we wanted roses, too.
  —Rose Schneiderman

In the economically depressed neighborhoods of the Plains no season was without its burdens, but for the poor, winter always represented a time of additional hardship and anxiety.[1] As working women saw it, it was above all else a period of uncertainty in their already precarious lives. Would coal supplies, "bought cheap" in the summer and carefully stored in tenement bathtubs, outlast the bitter months ahead? Would luck bring a mild winter so that precious dollars could be spent elsewhere? And what if food prices outpaced wages as they had last year? While women picked and preserved berries, nuts, vegetables, and fruits every fall, they faced each winter since 1907 with the memory of "trying to fool . . . [their] stomachs" as slowdowns, wage decreases, rising food prices, and unusually harsh weather depleted supplies and forced them to adopt substitute products such as a "kind of molasses" for butter, and water or evaporated milk instead of fresh milk.[2] Commenting on the testimony given by Lawrence operatives before a congressional committee in 1912, one government official noted that "there are two very desirable luxuries in the city of Lawrence, Mass., among the mill operatives, that is, molasses on their bread, and water."[3]

In the fall of 1911, however, the fears of winter were further compounded by threatening rumors that the city's mills intended to reduce
wages when, at the end of the year, new laws regulating the employment of women and children took effect. Embracing protective legislation, the Massachusetts legislature reduced the hours of labor for
women and children from fifty-six to fifty-four hours a week, without
providing compensatory wage minimums. Governor Foss, hoping to
gain support from organized labor in his bid for the presidential nomi-
nation, signed the measure, and it was generally assumed that manufacturers would proportionately adjust their rates as they had in 1909
when the sixty-six-hour law was passed. Few workers, however, shared
the optimistic outlook of the legislators, fearing instead that management would be "up to no good." Throughout the autumn rumors confirmed the gloomiest forecasts as mill men refused to meet with workers or discuss their plans with the press. By late November food prices
began their seasonal climb, and even city officials talked of setting up
food stores for the large numbers of needy.[4]

As the days grew shorter and the cold began to penetrate thin walls,
the city's poor no doubt faced the new year aware that it was likely to
be the most appalling winter in a series of already intolerable seasons.
On the shop floor, rumors of wage cuts circulated as production levels
reached "break-neck" proportions. Demanding maximum output per
worker, both new machinery and new methods of organization sought to
mold operatives into efficient "interchangeable parts of the production
process."[5] "These people of Lawrence," observed one contemporary,
were treated "not as human beings but as mere worker machines."[6] By
1912, Lawrence spindles produced more cloth per employee than in any
other textile town in the nation.[7] "In the mills," recalled a retired operative, "they used to drive you like a hoss. That's [what] the whole
trouble was, you know."[8]

In almost all cases operatives worked according to the pace and
rhythm of the machine that required workers to adjust to the demands
of production requirements. "At the time I was just about fourteen
years old. We were changin' the empty bobbins, take the full ones off
and put the empty ones in and then starta filler up again. When they
were filler up in about ten minutes, fifteen minutes, the machine was
going up and down, up and down, it would be fuller up. And you know
what we had to do? Keep on going and going till night, keep on doffing
all the time, fast and fast. 'Come on, the boss is to come.' 'Come on, are

you still there?' 'Come! We gotta keep the thing goin'."[9] Seemingly controlled by swirling belts, vibrating wooden frames, and thundering looms and spindles, workers felt intensely alienated from the work process. "They call them 'devils' and not machinery," remarked a member of the strike committee.[10] A female investigator working "undercover" in a textile mill recorded the constant strain that the work required and observed that not a few of the women operatives "used to cry every night, from sheer fatigue."[11]

Workers who could not keep up the pace, such as older operatives, children, or workers injured by disease or accident, were quickly replaced. "Bosses do not want menders who cannot earn under the old schedule at least $6.00 a week, as those making less take up room they think could be better employed."[12] Piecework was especially grueling as workers' wages often depended on the productivity of others. Weavers, for example, were at the mercy of loom fixers who earned additional rates based upon the output of weavers in their care. This led to frequent charges that fixers systematically increased the speed of their looms thereby extracting greater output from weavers and promoting greater competition among them.[13] Women were especially vulnerable in such a situation, as fixers and other "bosses" were always men. During the strike women expressed resentment at the "bullying" and "improper conduct" of "those above them." In Lawrence the largest proportion of workers were pieceworkers, and of those, the majority were women.[14] Women also received lower rates than men so that although their output was typically higher, their income was not.[15] Other pieceworkers, such as the female menders, burlers, low spoolers, and dressers, were equally dependent upon speed so that wages suffered as output declined, and jobs remained in constant jeopardy if quotas fell below standards. "Well, if it was slack," reported Victoria Wennaryzk, "and I didn't get yarn I couldn't make more pay. I had to wait half an hour for the work I was waiting for."[16]

While wages were low for all immigrant workers, women, in every national group, consistently received lower compensation than men.[17] As one recent study documents, 40.4 percent of women "aged 18 and older received less than $7.00 per week and no more than 15% earned $10.00."[18] As table 6 shows, however, both male and female immigrants from southern and eastern Europe were especially underpaid.[19]

Such policies sought not only to extract maximum efficiency from each worker but to create intense competition among individual work-

Table 6. Wages Paid Foreign-born Adult Operatives by Lawrence Worsted Mills, 1909

Nationality	N	Average Weekly Wage	Percentage Earning More Than $7.50 per Week
Males			
English	1563	$11.39	95.8
German	538	11.17	95.0
French	234	11.07	96.6
Irish	551	10.21	94.9
Russian	170	8.59	77.1
Polish	375	8.01	50.7
Lithuanian	550	7.82	58.2
Syrian	334	7.33	31.1
S. Italian	1371	6.84	27.9
Females			
German	211	9.53	82.0
French	165	9.32	67.9
Scottish	115	9.06	90.4
Canadian	523	8.64	72.5
English	687	8.39	57.1
Irish	495	8.24	52.7
Russian	123	7.24	25.2
Lithuanian	263	7.14	31.6
Polish	182	7.10	29.1
S. Italian	902	6.39	6.9

ers and promote divisions among various "classes" and groups of workers. One of the major weapons in this arsenal of worker control was the Premium system, which in effect set quotas for operatives who worked on an hourly or piece rate basis. Once the required amount was earned, operatives received varying additional wages but only if the work was performed in an unbroken four-week period; even a day's absence cancelled their "premium."[20] Few were immune from tears "when difficult work was given to them when they were so near to winning a premium that they thought they would surely get it."[21] In this way, the premium system "killed" as one weaver put it, "by inches every day."[22] Linking individual effort to increased earnings, employers emphasized self-improvement and individual competition over collective bargaining and mutual reciprocity.

Such conditions did not go unresisted, and workers developed a number of informal strategies aimed at reducing the demands of bosses and "devil" machinery. At times, however, operatives simply quit, hoping to find better conditions elsewhere. Others utilized neighborhood friendships of nonmill workers to intimidate section hands who lived in town. When threatened by his boss for showing up two minutes late, Louis Laudani returned the threat promising his superior a visit "from Louis and his pals." "You kick my ass, I'll throw you in the river."[23] The possibility for collective efforts, however, was often undermined by both the grueling production schedules and strict shop floor discipline. The technical nature of workers' disputes and grievances also worked against potential militants, as strikes were often confined to individual departments and floors and were notoriously unsuccessful. Overseers made only enough concessions to undermine solidarity, typically making minor concessions such as shifting unpopular second hands or verbally disciplining abusive section bosses and hands. Mills also sought to exacerbate ethnic divisions in an attempt to undercut unity on the shop floor and prevent unionization. "Management," noted one reporter, "saw to it that no one nationality composed more than 15 percent of the workforce in any one mill."[24] Another recalled that "one of the bosses told me with some pride, how he once threatened the Poles who were employed almost exclusively in one of his departments . . . with displacement by Italians if they did not do as he ordered in some particular matter."[25]

Furthermore, the divisions that characterized Lawrence's working classes following the strike of 1902 supported the belief among mill management that any resistance to wage reductions that might result from the new reduced hours would be isolated, sporadic, and easily diffused. Recent organizing attempts by the Industrial Workers of the World, the United Textile Workers, and the Women's Trade Union League had been well publicized failures, and most mills maintained sophisticated policies aimed at maximizing worker divisions and undercutting collective bargaining. Widely perceived as "unorganizable," immigrants from southern and eastern Europe eschewed union membership, and mill management interpreted their preference for ethnic organizations as a sign of apathy and social fragmentation. Even the Wobblies, who found a warm welcome among the Franco-Belgian and Lithuanian communities, found the national form of organization especially problematic in Lawrence. IWW–inspired slowdowns and walkouts of 1910 and 1911 were feeble affairs involving only a handful of workers. On the eve of the strike of 1912, what contemporaries would call the "Great Industrial War," IWW Local 20 consisted of approximately three hundred members, while no more than twenty-eight hundred workers out of an industrial work force of almost thirty-five thousand paid any union dues.[26]

It was with great confidence, therefore, that Lawrence's mills joined other Bay State textile manufacturers in reducing hours and providing no proportionate increase in rates or wages. On New Year's Day, 1912, the American Woolen Company quietly informed the local press that workers should expect reduced pay envelopes when they came to collect their wages in the following weeks. Almost all textile manufacturing mills in Massachusetts followed Lawrence's lead. Workers employed at the Wampanoag Mill in Fall River were some of the first operatives to receive wages under the new rates, and their short-lived strike, initiated on payday, lasted only a few days, further reassuring Massachusetts mill men that resistance would be disorganized and ineffective.[27] Consequently, management throughout the state prepared to negotiate individually with each department and, where skilled crafts were involved, to make minor adjustments, thus hoping to prevent a united front between skilled and unskilled workers.

Following the Wampanoag strike, most radicals and trade unionists in Lawrence approached the January wage issue with caution. The IWW, headquartered in the Franco-Belgian Hall at 9 Mason Street, was already providing support and organizational aid for striking operatives at the Atlantic Mill, who, by New Years Day, were in the nineteenth week of a wage dispute that showed no signs of success. In nearby Lowell, weavers walked out over reduced wages but split ranks almost immediately after their strike, some quitting rather than returning with their coworkers at the old wage scale. Local 20 was pessimistic about workers' chances for a successful strike, especially in the bitter winter months and made plans instead for a spring walkout.[28]

Recent economic slumps also made the Central Labor Union wary of strike actions, and their fears increased when, on January 1, city hall announced that Lawrence's government was on the verge of bankruptcy. On the first morning of 1912, city workers awoke to pay reductions in the mills and "throngs of the unemployed" milling around street corners and city hall corridors. On January 2, the new city council immediately began to "prune" the departments of Health, Water, Police, and Fire, throwing hundreds of laborers and other city workers out

and threatening neighborhoods with inadequate services. Many unskilled operatives could easily understand the reluctance of organized
labor to walk out when hundreds of the recently unemployed roamed
city streets.[29]

Craft unionists, separated from the unskilled by ethnicity as well
as occupational status, felt both superior to the new immigrants and
threatened by them. To these workers, many of whom were affiliated
with the American Federation of Labor, "greenhorn" laborers represented attempts by management to undermine the trades. In large mills
like the Wood, Arlington, and Pacific, scientific management and new
technology had long been used to gain control over the work process
thereby eliminating management's dependence on the knowledge and
skill of highly trained workers. As control moved from the hands of
skilled workers to management, craftsmen lost their traditional ability
to influence the flow of labor and materials.[30] They also lost jobs. Mule
spinners, once a proud and influential part of Lawrence's "aristocracy of
labor," were finding themselves cut out of the production process as the
city's mills adopted new machines and managerial procedures. One of
the largest textile manufacturing plants in the world, the Wood Mill employed only 176 mule spinners, and when innovations were complete at
the Washington, a scant 16 spinners found jobs.[31] Many believed that
strikes would only further erode their position by providing new opportunities to modernize.

Consequently, Lawrence's mule spinners and loom fixers cooperated
with management over the new wage scales. "Mule spinners," declared
the local papers, "have no grievances." Just as skilled workers in 1882
had disassociated themselves from the efforts of female spinners to resist wage cuts, the Central Labor Union made clear its disagreement
with those who argued for a shortened work week. "The men are willing to work the 56 hours," explained one spokesman for the crafts department, "but are hampered by the 54 hour law which applies only to
factories where women and girls are employed."[32] With few exceptions,
however, this meant every mill in the city.

Confident that forms of resistance flow from the formalized structures of social life, mill management believed that workers would accept, with only minor opposition, pay reductions that would accompany
legal reductions in the hours of work. Patterns of official life—the con-
ciliatory attitude of the Central Labor Union, the weakness of the IWW,
the ethnic self-consciousness of workers—suggested to city officials, a

fragmented working class incapable of effective political expression. Surveying the political landscape from above, public officials saw a community in disarray. Yet as anthropologists have shown, "The political processes of all nations are wider and deeper than the formal institutions designed to regulate them."[33] In the unformalized realms of Lawrence's immigrant neighborhoods, far beneath the surface of official scrutiny, neighbors and kin formulated plans and organized opposition to the impossible laws of an alien authority.

Angelo Rocco, an Italian activist committed to the syndicalist movement, talked things over with his equally militant sister Consiglia. Twenty-six years old, Angelo was both an operative and a high school student who had experienced industrial labor as a skilled worker in Italy and southern France before coming to America in 1904. One of the few Italian members of Local 20, an offshoot of the Franco-Belgian club, Rocco saw himself as a link between the Wobblies and the immigrant neighborhood along Common Street. Convinced that the city's foreign-born workers would unite, he argued that the leaders from the IWW, national organizers like Joe Ettor and Big Bill Haywood, should be invited to Lawrence as soon as possible. The local, however, was less certain of support and wrote instead to William Wood, president of the American Woolen Company, requesting a meeting to discuss the wage question and find out the exact nature of the cuts. When Wood failed to reply, the Wobblies planned a public meeting at Ford Hall in order to put pressure on the mills and begin strike plans. Loomfixers responded by setting up committees in all mills that employed fixers and made plans to strike as a group, but to stagger their protest from mill to mill so that "all members could cooperate but remain working until their turn came." On the 9th, two hundred back boys walked out but they quickly returned when the traditionally rebellious mule spinners, who depended on the quick hands and feet of the boys to operate their machines, rounded them up and angrily pointed out that it wasn't the right time of year for a strike. "Besides," shouted one spinner, "we are married men and do not take kindly to the action of boys."[34]

These independently coordinated strategies, however, were quickly forgotten when, on January 11, a group of Polish women in the Everett Mill discovered their pay was short.[35] Throwing down their aprons and grabbing picker sticks (hardwood sticks about two feet in length used in the weaving process), the women shut down their machines, marched out of the mill, and called for others to follow them. The following morning, massive waves of strikers wove their way up and then down Canal

Street. Standing on each other's shoulders and shouting orders, men and women made "stump speeches" sending "flying squadrons" of operatives through all the other mills to recruit supporters and shut down machines. Hundreds of marchers, carrying American and Italian flags, linked arms and stormed the city's major mills, slashing power belts, smashing windows, and breaking down gates to release other workers. By midday, the "bread and roses" strike of 1912, was underway.[36]

The actions of the women on that Thursday in the Everett Mill dramatically altered the situation in all of Lawrence's factories. Reduced paychecks in the Everett confirmed the suspicions of other workers—whose paydays were still one or two days away—that the mill masters intended to ignore their petitions and reduce their earnings. The militant stance of the Everett weavers and their defiant shouts along Canal Street set the tone for resistance. That evening, Italians, Poles, and Lithuanians crowded into Ford Hall and decided to strike the following afternoon.[37] Rocco got permission to cable Joe Ettor, who agreed to come immediately. By Friday, twenty-two hundred additional operatives from the Everett Mill joined the female weavers, and by 9:00 that morning, the riot bells sounded from the tower of city hall.

In the Plains, the clanging of bells and the screeching of factory whistles told residents what they already knew. Throughout the morning neighborhood shops and streets were filled with people as "petty leaders" called out friends and kin. Everywhere "stump speeches" reported recent events and organized collective responses. Down Essex and Canal Streets crowds of men and women, boys and girls linked arms in "endless human chains" calling for unity and jeering mill watchmen. Others gathered in small groups and formulated plans. Everywhere small riots broke out. One week after the women went out, almost every ethnic group in the city had organized a local strike committee.[38] "A thousand years of Christianity," wrote one radical leader from out of town, "has never driven the different peoples of the earth together in so united a body as has this strike."[39] By the middle of January, twenty-five thousand operatives from almost forty different nationalities had gone out. It was an expression of solidarity previously unmatched in the history of American labor.

Historians, whether in an attempt to blame the strike on outside agitators or, alternately, to celebrate the strength and vitality of the Wobblies, have tended to posit the IWW at the center of the strike. Consequently, institutional factors, notably the establishment of a stable and effective industrial union, have provided the yardstick against which the events of 1912 have been measured. From this perspective, collective action appears less a product of local circumstances than of policies and strategies formulated by particular organizations at particular times. It is not surprising, then, that historians have turned to the IWW in order to explain the intense militancy of the strike and the extraordinary solidarity of the strikers. "The national IWW figures," argues one scholar of labor history, "and local [IWW] strike leaders together provided organizational order out of anarchy."[40]

It was not an anarchy of disorder, however, that greeted Joe Ettor when he arrived in Lawrence Saturday night. Lawrence's neighborhoods were anarchic only in the sense that they were unruled but, as Ettor was to discover, they were not unordered.[41] The outlines of an effective grass roots organization had already begun to take shape in the turbulent days before Rocco's request for help, and as Ettor stepped off the train throngs of people gathered in familiar places to mold strategy and form plans. Clearly, leaders like the fiery Ettor and popular Big Bill Haywood added powerful voices to strike activity, and the important role of the IWW has been well documented.[42] Yet the genius of the Wobblies who came to Lawrence lay in their ability to assimilate local leadership into the decision-making process and to build upon the scattered bases of local power that already existed in the community.

Here, at the ground level of daily life, neighbors and kin converted the familiar and the routine into powerful weapons of protest and resistance. As veterans of local skirmishes with landlords, school officials, city relief agents, and local merchants immigrant women relied on familiar patterns of collaborative action and organization that radiated along female centered networks. An outgrowth of traditions of female reciprocity and mutual exchange, female networks were especially effective in calling out neighbors and kin, for they accentuated the interconnectedness of individual lives in ways unavailable to unions or political parties. Based on relationships rather than memberships, female networks spun alliances that also breached the divide that might otherwise have separated workers from nonworkers, store owners from strikers, and shopkeepers from consumers. Cross-ethnic cooperation between women in the grocery stores, the streets, the children's boarding houses, at courtyard festivals, and in the swapping of food and recipes combined with a rich associational life to concretize solidarity and forge a unity of purpose.[43] "The women," wrote Bill Haywood several years later, "won the strike."

Saturday was a critical day for the strikers. Would the weekend diffuse workers' passions? Snow and freezing winds were hard reminders of their meager resources; both coal and bread were at their peak prices. The mayor wrote to all ethnic leaders warning them against the strike. In St. Joseph's Hall, John Breen, son of the former mayor and thriving town undertaker, joined with the local Syrian priest to condemn Friday's actions and exhorted his parishioners to return to work on Monday. City solicitor Cornelias Lynch made plans to close the city's saloons.[44] Hoping to offset the influence of the local IWW, Lynch also dashed off a telegram to John Golden, president of the United Textile Workers, asking him to come to Lawrence. On Sunday, the clergy condemned the strike and cautioned all workers to beware of "smart talkers" and return to work.[45]

Again, however, neighborhood activists and community networks worked to counter these influences. Worker strategies such as parades, shutdowns, and "scab muggings" were launched from neighborhood discussions and meetings that took place in ethnic halls, street corners, and parish rooms. "Directly out of the social life of a diversified, foreign-born community," noted a Boston reporter, "has sprung the trouble which makes itself felt now in sudden bubblings of riot and again in sullen ominous waiting."[46] Nonreligious Jews entered synagogues to help organize workers, Italian churches were converted to information centers, and tenement basements became headquarters and hideouts for activists.

Throughout the strike, ethnic organizations worked to promote solidarity and organize the "unorganizable." Many of the city's immigrant societies subscribed to leftist political visions, and their members were often strong advocates of direct action and strong unions. The Franco-Belgians, Lithuanians, and Italians were especially strong supporters of the left and each maintained a variety of associations organized around socialist and collectivist principals.[47] Committed to social democracy, all three groups were, as one striker put it, "actively anticlerical," and their communities provided the bulk of the radical leadership during the long struggle. The Franco-Belgians also gave the strike its headquarters, offering its hall in the heart of the Plains for meetings of the general strike committee.

The walkout galvanized these communities and pulled other immigrant organizations into the struggle. Regional disputes were put in abeyance; inactive members officiated at meetings; political activists came to the fore; and women made their voices heard as they jeered, shouted, and got elected as local representatives.

But the well-known national form of organization, "by which each ethnic group met separately and elected its own representatives to the general strike committee," was only the most formalized way in which immigrant societies operated.[48] At meetings in halls and ethnic corner clubs, businessmen and their customers checked up on their country-men, making sure that only strikers and their sympathizers were served. Barbers refused to shave "scab heads"; a "rogues gallery," naming scabs, was created in every national hall; relief stations were set up and international drum corps from immigrant societies opened meetings and marched along side singing strikers. "Only good Italians—the strikers—ever got into my fathers store," remembered the son of one activist. "At meetings over on Common Street, we'd hear about those Italians making trouble, not scabbin', but wanting to. We'd get their names and spread the word." Language and a common goal drew north and south Italians, Poles, Lithuanians, Jews, Irish, and Anglo to-gether in ethnic halls and institutions, and in the process, political sol-idarity, not ethnicity defined the boundaries of membership.

The first weekend established patterns for the next three months. National halls were packed as speakers from various points of view ad-dressed the workers. Even before the arrival of fiery Joe Ettor, one of the Wobblies' most gifted speakers, neighborhood meetings formulated plans and organized support. Many such plans were shrewdly practical and everyone was encouraged to participate. Fifteen-year-old Jose-phine Lis, an Austrian-Pole who had lived in Lawrence for many years and was familiar with a variety of languages, was enlisted to serve as a "spy" by offering her services to the town court as an interpreter. Here, she mediated for the police but only in order to counsel arrested strik-ers, gather information, and arrange bail for Italians, Lithuanians, Poles, and other strikers. By the end of the first week of the strike, Lis was elected to the local strike committee joining the IWW soon after.[49]

Others involved themselves in more aggressive schemes. Through-out the strike, as well as in the first pivotal weekend, potential scabs were often identified through discussions held in stores, stoops, streets, and corners. Among the first to be arrested, Mary Martlauski "and others had a woman against the wall at the Everett . . . and was pummeling her." When operatives refused to join strikers, she "threw missiles and chased them up Union street." Martlauski, charged with assault on the officer who tried to restrain her, "had nothing to say."[50]

Figure 12. Tenements with Everett Mill in background. Housing was so close, landlords could collect the rent of neighbors from the porch of one family. Note also that it was in this mill, situituated in the heart of the immigrant neighborhood, where the 1912 strike began. Courtesy of Immigrant City Archives.

Figure 13. "Baby Hammock," c. 1910. Older children often took care of babies for mothers who worked in the mill. Women also dropped children off with neighbors in children's boarding houses. Courtesy of Immigrant City Archives.

Her actions had already spoken for her. Nellie Rurak also patrolled the Everett gate where several of her neighbors worked. According to the paper, she stopped operatives who would not leave their work and insulted them. When words failed to convince two other Polish women, Rurak assaulted her fellow country women.[51]

In the first weekend such actions were crucial in turning the tide toward the cause of the strikers. Any show of disunity would have supported management's contention that the strike lacked the support of most workers and was the result of outside agitators who preyed on the "ignorant foreigner." Focusing on Italian men wielding "race weapons" such as stilettos and razors, the press encouraged readers to distinguish between the emotionalism of certain elements of extremists and those operatives who would return to work if unrestrained by fellow strikers. Indeed, from the very beginning of the outbreak, mill rhetoric sought to frame the strike as a struggle between contrasting forms of protest—irrational and violent, as opposed to rational and dispassionate. By linking the former with ethnic ignorance and gender deviance, and the latter with the American way, categories of difference were kept at the center of debate where they provided an interpretive strat-

Figure 14. Lawrence Strikers, 1912. Women often started small skirmishes after discussions in stores. Courtesy of Immigrant City Archives.

egy that emphasized style over substance. According to this script, wage cuts, premium systems, and inequality were reduced to questions of manner and proper forms of behavior. "We are all treated on 'the fair deal,' " explained one mender who refused to join the strikers, "and when we have trouble we go to our overseer like ladies and try to show the breeding that we have received, not like Turks, smashing and destroying everything in our way."[52] By situating the strike in a discourse that equated militant acts of protest with gender and ethnic confusion, ("ill-breeding") arguments such as this marginalized strikers by placing them outside of and in opposition to norms of respectability. Opponents of the strike may have seen themselves as merely recording their opposition to the walkout; but by emphasizing those things that separated "ladies" from "Turks," they were also constructing the parameters of both female respectability and ethnic probity. Acts of violence, in other words, could both sustain rebellion and work to marginalize rebels.

Figure 15. "Women Strikers Were Active," noted the *International Socialist Review*, March 1912. Courtesy of the Museum of American Textile History.

Wobbly leaders noted with bitterness but shrewd comprehension that in Lawrence violence was more a question of who did it?—"the Harvard athletes" who served in the militia or workers in revolt—than of what was done?[53] To Ettor and Haywood, militant action on the part of activists could thus only hurt the cause by distracting attention away from immediate goals of the strike committee. Just as both men sought to de-emphasize ethnicity by stressing class interests, they also advocated nonviolence, shifting to the tactics of passive resistance immediately upon their arrival in Lawrence. Struggling to generate public support and keep attention focused on the inequities of wage labor, the IWW used its position at the center of the general strike committee to control random acts of violence and promote nonviolent boycotts, parades, and demonstrations. As wobbly sympathizer Mary K. O'Sullivan noted, the riots emerged from other sources of authority. "After the 'blood-stained anarchists' arrived on the scene, a policy of nonresistance to the aggressions of the police and the militia prevailed."[54] At the level of representation, it was critical to keep the eyes on the "why" of revolt, accentuating the distance, not the difference, between immigrant lives and the promise of America.

To these ends workers marched with large American flags and children were displayed with red, white and blue clothing. Yet immigrant neighborhoods were themselves populations in flux both demographically, as household composition changed upon the arrival of migrating kin, and emotionally, as old-world babies matured in the new. In such a context, solidarity was a complicated process of cooperation among friends and kin and negotiation between generations. While city newspapers provided dramatic reports of stilettos and razors, face-to-face relationships and personal networks were far more important in the maintenance of a common front. As wives and mothers, women played an especially critical role bringing pressure not only on recalcitrant neighbors but on those members of the working class community dependent on workers' wages. Grocers, shopkeepers, landlords, and others tied to the neighborhood economy were targets of women keenly aware of the connections between cuts in wages and holes in the stomach. Described as the community's "scab muggers," wives, sisters, and daughters dominated neighborhood skirmishes patrolling their blocks and backing their demands for strike discipline with red pepper, scalding water, gas pipes, and ten pins whenever "reason" failed.[55] But, as we shall see, women also called attention to the vagaries of violence, protesting with words and gestures a world that condoned the "violence" of hunger but condemned as violent those who denounced starvation.

To outside observers, however, the efforts of strikers seemed disorganized and haphazard. Describing the walkout as a "spontaneous" affair, papers predicted a quiet return to work on Monday. Official leaders of ethnic groups, including priests and well-known "prominenti," urged caution and assured the press that the operatives would be cooperative. Throughout the weekend, however, resistance and solidarity were becoming increasingly concretized in the informal networks that sustained ethnic daily life. By Sunday, popular support for the strike swelled beneath the surface of official bon mots. Although agreeing "not to cause any disturbances," Syrians in St. Joseph's Church dismissed clerical advice to return to work, deciding instead "to stay out until concessions were made." Similarly, Italian immigrants, listening to prominent countrymen who told them "not to break the law by stopping those who wanted to work," responded with "hisses and jeers."[56]

The following day the city exploded as "active demonstrations," organized after Mass in church basements and streets, attempted to close the mills. Workers marched from factory to factory throwing ice and calling out others. When City Marshall O'Sullivan arrived in his chauffeur-driven car, strikers slashed his tires. At the Boston and Lowell crossing, strikers captured the hoses mill watchmen had used on them Friday and redirected the icy stream of water against the mill and its defenders. "Defiant in attitude" and "fiercer" than the men," female activists were the constant source of both official complaint and Wobbly acclaim. "Man Intimidated by Woman Picket," wrote the local press in March. "Shouting and continually waving their arms, the women," reported both local and national newspapers, "were worse than the men."[57]

Here were the unruled but ordered masses that greeted Ettor and would later inspire "two-fisted" Big Bill Haywood upon his arrival in early February. From the beginning their concern was that such an ethnically fragmented group would prove hard to organize. Rooted in the traditions of revolutionary syndicalism, Wobblies were understandably suspicious of the nationality form of organization, which they saw as an explosive barrier to cooperation and united action. Both Ettor and Haywood began their work in Lawrence by warning strikers that "there should be no thought of nationality." Called into Lawrence by an Italian member of an IWW local composed of Franco-Belgians and Lithuanians,

Ettor cautioned strikers to "forget that you are Hebrews, forget that you are Poles, Germans, or Russians."[58] Strikers, however, had already established patterns of authority that crisscrossed ethnic communities, and Ettor wisely adhered to the decentralized format that had been established in the few days following the Everett walkout.[59] Locally organized and attuned to the ear of the neighborhoods, the language federations allowed for the widest possible participation among a population comprised of over forty national groups.

Outside observers frequently blamed the Wobblies for both the militancy and the solidarity that characterized the 1912 strike, and historians have generally accepted this view, arguing that leaders like Joe Ettor "infused the immigrants with his own militancy."[60]

Yet by accepting the national form of organization, the IWW was acknowledging its own lack of control over the neighborhoods, where the real bases of power firmly rested. This situation often frustrated Wobbly leaders who frequently found themselves pressing strikers to curb their emotions, to practice nonviolence, and, as we shall see, to accept the March 13 settlement, an act that infuriated large segments of the neighborhoods, especially its most militant women.[61]

Female Space and Strike Organization

Central to neighborhood organization were the ubiquitous yet often invisible networks that emerged from women's collaborative activities. "Whenever we needed to know what to do, we just went to our street corner, you know, there the women gathered and us girls were determined to help out."[62] Strike communication was notoriously rapid along these networks as women shared news and gossip as well as child care, shopping, and laundry duty. Even before Friday pay envelops had been opened at the Wood, operatives repeated the actions of the Everett women. Blowing horns and waving flags, workers marched from mill to mill yelling the now familiar cry, "All Out. Short Pay." Once inside the mills, activists mobilized undecided operatives by smashing escalators, slashing power belts, and tearing down iron gates to permit striking workers to exit. "It was a preconcerted arrangement, absolutely," stated Mr. Sherman, overseer of the Wood mills.[63] Intertwined throughout the heterogeneous blocks of the Plains, these informal associations allowed for the rapid spread of news and information, the expansion of strike participation and political discussion, the coordination of strategies, and the possibility of a heightened sense of common purpose.

Table 7. Female Activists by Occupation

Occupation	N	Percentage
At home	20	23.0
Skilled operatives (menders, weavers)	15	18.0
Semiskilled and unskilled	41	50.0
Clerk (grocery, clothing)	4	5.0
Profession (midwife, bookkeepers)	3	4.0

In no way were female efforts more crucial to strike success than in the effective mobilization of neighbors and kin. As we have seen, women had politicized daily life in ways often beyond the reach of formal institutions. Intense sharing of experience and the ritual performance of female duties and obligations in the densely packed neighborhoods of the Plains had helped to forge social bonds among women that provided a strong basis for mass mobilization during the strike. Newspapers frequently noted that "knots of women" formed in doorways, on church steps, and on streets and stoops. In these familiar spaces women formed plans, often concluding such meetings by linking their arms and strolling up and down the block yelling to third-floor neighbors and others on sidewalks and in stores. Parades, a distinctive feature of the strike, were typically launched when such clusters formed on Elm, Short, or Chestnut Streets. Gathering support as they marched, strikers, as the *New York Call* put it, "urged the windows"[64] to join them and everywhere people hooted and cheered. At times these marches grew to ten thousand in number as they wove through every neighborhood in the Plains calling to high school students, city officials, store clerks, priests and nuns, friends and family.

Because female networks were organized on the basis of relationships, they drew their strength from consociates—people who came together, no matter how superficially, in the course of daily life. Unlike party officials or union leaders, who may or may not have any real contact with neighborhood women, the appeals of strikers were from those "involved in one another's biography."[65] Tangled in the webs of daily life, neighbors responded to the appeal of neighbors. Among the activists whose occupations are known, roughly one-fourth were listed "at home" and just under ten percent earned a wage outside the mills as clerks, bookkeepers, midwives, and teachers.[66] (See table 7).[67]

For many women, sharing picket duty seemed a natural extension of female traditions of mutual exchange and reciprocity. Because proletarian women moved in webs of association, they often depended on neighborhood networks during times of crisis to formulate opinion and articulate grievances. Bonds that were formed along these informal pathways were strengthened and reinforced in the constant struggle for survival so that sharing responsibilities, both at the home and the workplace, helped provide a communal and holistic context for individual action. At times, allegiance to the community overrode family desires. Such was the case of one mother who, although not a mill worker herself, joined strike activities and to the dismay of her operative son, "dragged Louis and his siblings to the picket lines and mass meetings."[68]

Collaborative activities among women provided a daily context within which political consciousness could be developed and sharpened. In the performance of traditional female obligations, women shared economic hardship and understood the collective nature of their poverty and exploitation. Loss of income, economic deterioration, sickness, and poverty were not understood as individual failures but rather as the outcome of forces beyond their control. Sharing information about neighbors, bosses, and shopkeepers, women came to understand the "public" nature of "private" tragedies and failures, and because female networks were nonhierarchical and organized around female responsibilities, they allowed both paid and unpaid working women to take part in the framing of popular sentiment. Here in the comings and goings of everyday life, standards of behavior, codes of conduct, notions of right and wrong, concepts of fairness and justice, of manhood and womanhood took shape. When town officials accused IWW leadership of manipulating the city's women by making them picket (a strategy rumored to have come from the general strike committee in a desperate effort to reduce acts of police violence by substituting women for men on picket lines), an indignant female striker declared, "We are not egged on by anyone or forced to go upon a picket line. We go there because we feel that it is but duty."[69] Far from pawns in a wobbly war, neighborhood women displayed a willingness to act out what they had collectively thought up. "We stick together now," explained one female mender, "all of us, to bring about a settlement according to our ideals, our ideas of what is right."[70]

Such efforts went far in promoting a shared sense of identity that often crossed ethnic boundaries, for close living and common domestic responsibilities brought immigrant women into frequent contact with each other. While mill management sought to use ethnic loyalty to separate workers, female networks provided women occasional opportunities to surmount interethnic antagonisms and distrust. During the strike, when men and women needed to cooperate as a united force, such friendships helped to link disparate communities and offered an effective basis for multiethnic solidarity. Arrest records compiled during the strike reveal the mingling of immigrant women as well as the effective uses they made of ethnic difference. Unnoticed before their arrest in a throng "heavy with women pickets," a Mexican and a Brazilian woman stood with Lithuanians and Poles in front of the judge in the early morning special sessions.[71] Word of arrests spread quickly in the polyglot neighborhoods of Lawrence, and women took turns as interpreters and observers during sentencing proceedings. Streets, too, were often patrolled by groups of girls from different immigrant backgrounds, so that when they found someone carrying the telltale lunch box of a strikebreaker, similar language and culture could be brought to bear on the worker in an attempt to turn him or her back. If words failed, women united to brandish red pepper, rocks, clubs, and other means at their disposal to maximize worker unity and promote the common goal.[72]

Organized at local level, associational ties encouraged ethnic cooperation but they worked as well to promote a popular base for Wobbly ideology. In a heterogeneous city like Lawrence, support systems were primarily organized around ethnicity as national clubs and associations provided those goods and services otherwise unavailable through agencies of government or charity. Ethnic self-assertion was thus affirmed and validated in the organization of daily life, so that national loyalties, whatever their status in the Old Country, sharpened in the New. In this context, IWW admonitions to "forget that you are Poles, Germans, or Russians" jostled with the everyday realities of immigrant life. The ability of women, however, to convert interethnic domestic networks into vehicles of cooperation, helped make Wobbly notions of internationalism more continuous with familiar patterns of daily life. In this way, solidarity was not simply "thought up" but "thought out" as women utilized the resources at hand to express their revolt against the "impossible" ways of official life.

Crossing ethnic boundaries to unite as "scab muggers," women also relied on female spaces to organize and rally neighborhood crowds. Almost all observers noted the "sudden gathering and swelling" of "throngs" of "defiant women," which almost as "suddenly melt away."[73] Arrested for swearing at patrolling officers, Margot Sonian "refused to give her name." As the officers led her to the patrol box, Sonian "danced," and was "defiant in attitude." Her behavior immediately attracted attention, and other women came to investigate. The crowds increased until cavalry finally arrived to disperse the angry mobs.[74] No one was exempt from public ridicule and neighborhood discipline. Having identified a local priest who tried to "hide his scabbing in a cloak of religion," strikers threatened to pull down his house and church a brick at a time. Singing "revolutionary hymns in various languages," marching chains always passed his residence, and women were often seen on "duty" outside.[75]

Women also affirmed their sisterhood and commonality by assisting each other against those they believed to be in league with the "powers that prey," including scabbing friends and neighbors, unsympathetic policeman, city officials, store clerks, and as one female striker described the militiamen, "those things in Khaki suits."[76] Like Josephine Lis, women also acted as "spies," at times "befriending soldiers" and court officials and then supplying information to strike leaders. In early January, Celia Prezenski traveled to Boston to find out what plans were being made by the American Woolen Company. Forcing open their letter box, she removed fifteen letters before being arrested.[77]

More commonly, women tried to help each other escape when being arrested, often crowding into police vans demanding that "everyone," or "no one" be hauled off to jail. Julia Yulla, a Syrian woman, was arrested for helping Irish-born Maggie Smith, "a notorious scab-mugger," escape from officer O'Brien. Both women had been shopping in the Italian section and possessed large quantities of red pepper under their cloaks. A third striker, Josephine Dimmock, who was from Poland, was also charged in the incident and relieved of a large piece of gas pipe she carried in her shawl. Women also tried to disguise personal liability during group actions. Instruments such as pipes, ten-pins, and scissors, were quickly passed among assembled women just before arrest, making it almost impossible for the officer to prove who had used the weapons.[78]

As the strike stretched into mid-February, such efforts became increasingly systematized. Nervously impatient with strikers and mill management alike, city officials banned mass public meetings while mill owners rented out the city's largest private space, the town ball park.[79]

The Starr Theater, a popular vaudeville house in the plains, similarly refused to allow workers to meet inside.[80] In the absence of formal gathering places, operatives grew increasingly dependent on women's unauthorized networks to get out the news, gather information, coordinate activities, and sustain unity. Observers began to note with regularity the omnipresence of women. "They're everywhere," complained one town official, "and it seems to be getting worse and worse all the time."[81] Throughout the city newspapers reported "milling and ceaseless activity." Meeting with Pearl McGill, socialist organizer for the button workers in Muscatine, Iowa, Polish women planned early morning vigils, and in the afternoons women congregated at the old well in the Common.[82] At the same time, German women began a "scab watch" using cameras borrowed from the IWW, and numerous other women lined the mills, grabbing for lunch pails and harassing scabs.[83]

Organization of this kind—woven from the threads of daily life—was especially critical as a source of cohesion and strength to those unaffiliated workers who stood outside the house of labor. "Unorganized" by formal institutions, the threads of everyday life reinforced a sense of commonality among disparate members of the community, providing an effective counter weight to dissent organized from above. Several weeks into the strike mill management intensified efforts to divide workers by offering concessions solely to skilled male operatives. On February 16 loom fixers abandoned the strike, voting unanimously to return to work.[84] Throughout the next two weeks craft unionists in almost every mill worked hard to convince German weavers and other skilled men to return.[85] Nationally, the AFL condemned the strike.

Mill management and craft conservatism were not the only threats to worker unity. State and local officials worked hand in hand to end the strike and undermine radical sources of authority. Their opportunity came in the last week of January when on January 29, a young Italian woman named Annie Lo Pizzo was killed in a disturbance on her block. While witnesses testified that a policeman had fired the shots that killed Lo Pizzo, the incident provided officials with an excuse to arrest Joe Ettor and fellow revolutionary Arturo Giovannitti who, along with local activist Joseph Caruso, were charged with "inciting and provoking the violence."[86] Like Ettor, Giovannitti had come to Lawrence as a syndicalist committed to the "propaganda of the deed," but as poet and mystic, Giovannitti was also the "heart and soul" of the movement. Hoping to discredit the left and sever the leadership from daily operations, officials jailed the three and accelerated the campaign to link the strike to outside agitators and "foreign ignorance."

Far from muffling the voices of radicalism, the arrest of Ettor and Giovannitti brought national attention to the city as "flying squadrons" of reporters flocked to Lawrence in order to cover the arrest and trial. They also came to report the arrival of a cadre of radicals, including Wobbly organizers Bill Haywood and William Trautman, and socialists Elizabeth Gurley Flynn, "the Rebel Girl," Pearl McGill, and Carlo Tresca. Haywood had already earned a national reputation as "Big Bill," the tall, broad in the shoulders, two-fisted organizer who, with his scarred face and patched right eye, electrified audiences and "bullied" the bosses.[87] His arrival in early February brought fifteen thousand workers down to the train station and then, with Haywood on their shoulders, they wove a human chain back up Essex Street, winding through the center of the city singing the *Internationale* in a multitude of languages.[88] Once again strikers put Lawrence at the center of national attention.

Denounced by city officials as a "thug," Haywood symbolized to the workers the power of their efforts. "They were American 'Big Shots,'" explained one former striker, "they knew the language, important people took notice, and the papers, always 'Big Bill this' and 'Big Bill that'—they follow him like hounds."[89] To Anna Marino they were like celebrities who "made you feel proud to, you know, be there, be involved in it [the strike]." Sara Axelrod's daughter recalled how her mother spoke with pride at having heard the speeches of Haywood and Emma Goldman. "My mother could never get enough of these discussions, she went to every meeting, every speech. Her voice always got excited recalling those, well 'reds' you'd say today."[90] Trudging from one hall to another, addressing "ten meetings in a day," carrying reports from the general strike committee to local clubs, the "big shots" coordinated negotiations but they also brought to Lawrence's immigrant strikers a sense of empowerment—a belief that their struggle was neither alone nor in vain.

Yet the dramatic presence of the IWW also drove a new wedge between members of the working-class community. Alarmed by the arrival of leaders like Haywood, Flynn, and Tresca, a number of businessmen joined local leaders in an effort to discredit the left and end the strike. Father O'Reilly, a powerful figure in the city and a staunch opponent of the strike, returned from a two-month Florida vacation and immediately began organizing community opposition. By mid-February, the Courts were increasing penalties and "cracking down on intimidation," quoting recent laws prohibiting a person from interfering with another's "right to work." Movie houses, railways, and street car companies refused admittance to anyone wearing an IWW badge.[91]

The most deeply resented actions of the authorities, however, concerned the "children's exodus," which took place on February 10. To prevent the "lash of youthful hunger" from driving men and women back to work, operatives devised a plan to send their children to sympathizers who lived outside of town. Like so many other aspects of the strike, this too was a strategy spun from practices already woven into workers' lives. For years working mothers in Lawrence had turned to neighbors who would take in their children at modest fees or in exchange of goods or services. Many others sent their young into the countryside to be cared for during the work week and collected again on Sundays. Plans to send the children of strikers to socialist and anarchist sympathizers in New York city, Philadelphia, and Barre, Vermont, was thus in many ways an extension of this method of child care, successfully merging radical political strategy with customary practice.[92]

Margaret Sanger, a nurse and socialist, headed the first "exodus" of 119 children. Not only was the exodus a practical response to strike conditions, it generated as well an enormous amount of positive publicity for the workers. Society luminaries including the wealthy suffragettes Mrs. O. P. H. Belmont and Inez Milholland, took up the workers' cause calling national attention to the plight of children whose parents made the world's cloth but could not themselves clothe their children.[93] The adverse publicity rattled city officials who saw the exodus as a mere publicity stunt. They accused the IWW of spiriting children out of their homes and denying them proper clothing simply to further their cause. Seeking a quick solution to such a "scandal," authorities ordered Colonel Sweat, Commander of the National Guard quartered in Lawrence, to prevent future evacuations of city children. Everywhere, police threatened immigrants with arrests and one-year prison sentences if they agreed to participate in any more "children's schemes."[94]

The crisis came on February 24 when 150 young people, accompanied mostly by their mothers, entered the Lawrence train station, where their parents made preparations to send their offspring to New York City and Philadelphia. More than 200 militia and police, many of them on horseback, surrounded the crowd and, despite the large numbers of women and children, charged with weapons raised. An organizer from Philadelphia later described the scene:

> When the time came to depart, the children arranged in a long line, two by two in an orderly procession with the parents near at hand, were about to make their way to the train when the police . . . closed in on us with their clubs, beating right and left with no thought of the children who then were in desperate danger of being trampled to death. The mothers and children were thus hurled in a mass and bodily dragged to a military truck and even then clubbed. . . . We can scarcely find words with which to describe this display of brutality.[95]

Women were furious over the "Russianized" actions of Lawrence officials. Organizing a boycott of the Starr, women and girls succeeded in opening the theater so that larger meetings could be called to discuss the new situation. City leaders were held accountable for the attacks on women, several of whom were pregnant, but women also used the event to highlight the plight of mothers and children. When social workers from Boston, including the well-known Robert Woods of the South End Settlement House, denounced the strikers for "dragging offspring into the matter," women retorted by calling such reformers "maudlin millionaires," who would rather allow children to silently starve than be fed in noisy protest. Elizabeth Gurley Flynn especially struck home when she pointed out that "when mothers had to go into the mills and work hard and leave their children to other people's care, there was no outcry and no offers of sympathy for her or her kids."[96] Far from "dragging offspring into the matter," women found it impossible to disentangle children from their struggle. Starvation wages impoverished families.

As the heavy snows came and public places became less accessible to strikers, the reformed Starr became a popular spot for neighborhood gatherings, especially among young girls whose parents disapproved of their strike activities. Telling parents that they were "going to a show," girls met instead to discuss plans and find out the news from older militants and strike leaders. Meeting together either in the Starr or in scattered groups throughout the Plains, women continued to organize demonstrations, pickets, collective "scab watches," and the distribution of information. Following the actions of February 24, women stepped up their activities, orchestrating daily events from every street corner and tenement stoop. Almost every major demonstration began after

Figure 16. "A Striker's Family." Whatever their affiiliation—radical, liberal, or conservative—the national press typically pictured women strikers with children. Entitled "A Striker's Family" and not "A Striker *and* Her Family," this photo brought women and children into national focus but it also emphasized women's identity as wives and mothers, masking their position as wage workers. *International Socialist Review.* Courtesy of the Museum of American Textile History.

early morning "vigils" of women gathered on the common or on the church steps (private property and therefore outside the reach of the law) where they were "constantly augmented by similar groups . . . and by those who came in twos and threes along the streets."[97]

Such was the case on February 19, when an endless human chain wove through the town. Within fifteen minutes after meeting on the stairs of St. Anthony's, papers reported over two hundred women standing by the church. Police and cavalry, attempting to disperse the crowds quickly, discovered the logic of the women's collective behavior. "As soon as they succeeded in separating one group," admitted a reporter, "another group would drift back toward the church—the cops

Figure 17. A member of the "children's exodus" with a New York sympathizer.
Courtesy of Immigrant City Archives.

Figure 18. "Extra Guards at Noon Hours." February 8, 1912. Rather than re-treating to home for lunch, strikers joined neighbors to gather information at soup kitchen, grocery stores, and in "knots" along the streets. Courtesy of Immigrant City Archives.

Figure 19. "Battery A." Militia troups included undergraduates from Harvard University who signed up as volunteers to protect private property and "prevent anarchy." Courtesy of Immigrant City Archives.

were continually drawn away back to then face a new group."[98] "The crowds flowed before them," noted another paper, "and shrank into doorways."[99] Soon a monster parade had developed.

Many such actions were organized at night when "the streets become alive again with a kaleidoscope of men and women."[100] Under the cover of dark, neighborhood activity increased and soldiers seldom entered the lampless streets and alleys that crisscrossed the Plains. Only the factories were illuminated, but the scanning searchlights, mounted on the top of the mills, failed to reach beyond the corporate reserve. Like a city under siege, dusk was a time of intense but silent planning. One reporter described the anxiety that accompanied nightfall: "As the sun moves westward and the shadows of evening lengthen, as the lights in the mills gleam through the windows and the search-lights penetrate the darkness, sending blinding rays into dusty corners, faces harden, the soldiers grip their rifles firmly and the scattered groups swell to crowds."[101]

Most soup kitchens remained open day and night, providing warmth and food, as well as safe meeting places for activists.[102] When the sun came up, nighttime plans were converted into dozens of small riots that, as one judge shrewdly observed, "often lead to something more."[103]

The success of these actions often stemmed from women's effective use of female spaces. "In every doorway," noted the press, "the flight of steps was jammed with people."[104] When police entered neighborhoods, mobs of women would follow them "then hoot" and finally disappear into stores or houses. "Officers," reported one paper, "actually begged the women to leave but they loitered about the locality." Another described a common scene: "When soldiers moved up the street every house sprouted people, and in a second the street was black with them."[105]

Whether entering and exiting doorways in a rush of activity or purposefully blocking streets, women used physical space to act out their revolt against the mills. Like many women with limited resources, Lawrence's female activists converted the things of everyday life—from mundane pots and pans that poured water on scabs or signaled distress, to familiar places where ordinary routines and daily events were carried out—into public statements of outrage and condemnation. As a source of social commentary about community life, female spaces were especially effective, for they situated political struggle at the center of everyday life, blurring arbitrary divisions between the "political" and the "personal."[106]

Participation in such forms of political expression was equally accessible to all, for unlike the ballot box it emerged from decentralized networks of female reciprocity and collaboration. Typically, women would meet in small bands often as early as 5 A.M. where, "unmolested," they would begin their watch and discuss events. Plans to attack scabs were frequently hatched here while more ambitious projects such as mass picketing and the spring assault on the Arlington Mill, were formulated in larger gatherings either at Mass or in grocery stores.

Increasingly known as the "scab mill," the Arlington was a special target of neighborhood women. Long known for its reluctance to hire "new" immigrants, the Arlington was also one of the city's few mills that continued to operate at almost full capacity. It was also one of the main housing facilities for the national guard, and many felt it was time to shut it down. Throughout the early spring, women coordinated attacks aimed at the Arlington as well as other mills, and moving chains of women became a frequent sight in the city. Such demonstrations always followed meetings held in streets, shops, and especially in church basements. Monday mornings were especially explosive as Sunday Mass provided women of different ages and ethnicity a chance to meet together and share strategies.

Every day, however, brought new actions launched from female enclaves. Routinely activists carried out the mornings' plans of scab prevention, solidarity, and publicity. The militia, many of them "Harvard boys," mounted horses and wielded billies while others frequently jostled the women on the ground and grabbed at their IWW buttons. "If people can't walk peacefully along streets and not be made to pull badges of their organizations off their clothes, it is time to revolt. We must protest to somebody higher up!"[107] One fifteen-year-old scab mugger and her sister learned how to fight back. "My mother told me she would hide long hat pins in her hair, then wait just until the horse was on top of you, then a good shove and the guy on top would go flying." Josephine Resnick, "who acted as an interpreter for the Lithuanian witnesses," found herself in court when she "struck" a soldier. Standing with other women on picket duty, she "took a gun from the soldier" and hit him in the face after he "remonstrated" the women for their behavior.[108] Several years after the strike, Haywood recalled the spirited and effective actions of female militants: "One cold morning, after the strikers had been drenched on the bridge with the fire hose of the mills, the women caught a policeman in the middle of the bridge and stripped off his uniform, pants and all. They were about to throw him in the icy river, when other policemen rushed in and saved him from a chilly ducking."[109]

Despite the praise accorded to women by radical leaders in the years that followed the strike, female activists often had to fight with male leadership to win acceptance and respect as equal participants in the struggle for industrial democracy. During one meeting of strike committee members, "a woman delegate" was greeted with condescending laughter from the men when she suggested that pickets pay special attention to South Lawrence and stated that "she was going over there herself." Hoping to shut down the USWOCO mill, a paper mill and the bleachery that continued to operate just outside the Plains, she was instead the object of "a good deal of joking." Trivializing her suggestion with an allusion to prostitution, Haywood quipped, "It wasn't every morning they were invited to meet a pretty girl on the street this way."[110] Undaunted, the "pretty girl" led fifty women, including Lithuanians, Poles, Syrians, and one Mexican, across the Duck Bridge into South Lawrence, where according to the press, "they showed up at an unexpected quarter, the Farwell Bleachery, on South Canal." As no police had been assigned to this area, the women met with little resistance and the workers were turned back. When the assistant marshal finally showed up, he was hopelessly outnumbered, and according to the press, either "falls on the ice or is thrown" down by the women. Whatever the means of his descent, women made the most of it. Jumping on top of him, they continued to pull at his clothes until soldiers arrived from a nearby mill. Such skirmishes continued all day as women extended the strike to mills in South Lawrence. In turn, officials relocated several troops from the Plains and sent them south to patrol even those industries unrelated to textile manufacturing.[111] The actions of the women put new territory into jeopardy and greatly bolstered strike morale, but their position in the general strike committee remained marginal. Several years after the strike, Helen Marot, former secretary of the New York Women's Trade Union League, recalled the frustration that many Lawrence activists felt at being denied the same power and authority accorded to male organizers:

> While the leaders of the Industrial Workers of the World show confidence in the part women have taken and will take in the industrial struggle, the women of Lawrence, Mass., observed that the officers of the local organization in that city have given them no better opportunity for taking part in the administration of union affairs than have the men of the American Federation.[112]

If soldiers were sometimes stripped, scabs and the "Black legs" at the Central Labor Union were almost always hooted, heckled, and jeered at by women who would follow them relentlessly throughout the city. One group of women, mostly from the Elm Street area, took up their daily position on Appleton Street in the heart of the "corporation reserve" and began their daily watch. In crowds of eight or ten, they would approach scabs and plead with them to return home. When operatives refused to do so, the ritual of humiliation and harassment began. Such was the case of Humphry Kennedy, who set out down Appleton Street intending to go to work. Failing to "listen to reason," his female neighbors surrounded him, grabbing at his lunch pail and loudly telling him that he could not go to work. Still resisting, Jeannie Radziwilowicz finally dealt him the blow that left him howling and got her arrested.[113] A block away, neighbors Annie Rogerz and Antonina Kobers were similarly arrested for "molesting soldiers." Again and again the newspapers reported women accosting scabs. The "women frisked men for lunch pails" and when one was discovered, they would throw "the pails into the streets and slap his [the scab's] face."[114]

City authorities were both amazed and appalled by such behavior. "It takes ten men to handle one woman," complained one Judge Advocate. Initially, newspapers headlined female activism, noting their determination and participation in the most militant strike activities. "Women to be on Picket line every morning," declared one local tabloid while another concluded in bold letters, "and will be until they are all arrested." Whether in pairs or in packs, women mounted a fierce campaign to win the strike. By mid-March female militancy, while still newsworthy, was no longer a matter for front page headlines. Reports of "Two girls hold up a man" were commonplace as were descriptions of man who was "accosted on the Common [and] only his yelling and screaming won his release."[115]

Collective living arrangements, typical of the Plains, facilitated daily exchange and the sharing of goods, services, and mutual concerns. For women, traditional domestic responsibilities such as child care, laundry, food preparation, sewing, and nursing also encouraged mutual support among female neighbors and kin, and secured the household as well as other communal spaces as women's prerogatives. Both before and during the strike, those local centers of female activity—grocery stores, streets, bath houses, kitchens—also enhanced women's concepts of material rights and sustained efforts to negotiate and agitate for economic justice. "We met a few months before the strike," commented a former weaver who shared rooms with a girlfriend and her uncle, "but both worked at different mills. We'd (all of us girls) be together, sure in the kitchen, wherever, and we talked. Of course, we all knew our pay, we compared all the time. Better pay, we go get it."[116]

Comparing wages and prices was also a common ritual for women and girls who shared their daily commute to and from the factory gates. "We'd all meet at a certain corner on our block in the morning, it was very dark, you know. We worked very early, come home in the dark, too. Well we'd get our girlfriends together and we'd walk each other to the mills. We'd talk about everything, but always too, about our pay, oh sure."[117] Several women recalled shopping with their mothers or friends in neighborhood grocery stores that served as social centers as well as forums for discussions of prices and wages. "The shops" remarked one activist, "had chairs and we'd take the chance to catch up. We compared prices with our neighborhood and the other Italian markets, then we'd go to the other grocery stores and do the same. Everyone was there, and the stores stayed opened 'til late at night."[118]

Such spaces had important implications for popular organization during the strike. Street corners and stores were transformed into daily information and decision-making centers, for despite the disruption in wage patterns, women and girls continued domestic routines. As one striker put it, "We'd all want to know, 'what to do, what to do?' Everyone was out, so we'd meet, at our corner, and oh, everywhere."[119] Traditional caretakers of the family, these women held sharp and exacting notions of what one was entitled to, and both prices and wages were discussed with keen and almost daily interest. Finances were calculated to the penny and converted into hard-headed notions of worth. Several women recalled the Lawrence strike as "the strike for three loaves," and most remember not only that the pay was short, but that it was precisely thirty-two cents short. The streets, which allowed for public scrutiny of scabs and supporters as well as space for personal contact and confrontation; the tenement stoops, where mothers patrolled their blocks and supervised community activity; and kitchens, where nurturance and communal cooperation occurred daily—all sustained close-knit, female-centered networks.[120] Popular organization for the strike was decentralized, and much of the decision making concerning collective action took place along these networks that crisscrossed local centers of activity. When town officials closed down the saloons and the city hall and when mill management rented out all available private spaces including the town ballpark, male strikers found themselves increasingly confined to small shops or crowded ethnic halls. To reach the neighborhoods and mobilize more effectively, IWW leadership and male activists often had to depend on women's use of female spaces to maintain order, get out the news, transport and distribute circulars, prevent defeatist rumors, and organize neighborhood demonstrations and parades. Stores, houses, stairwells, back porches, streets, clubs, the "monument" on the common,[121] even Jewish bath houses were used to distribute information.[122]

Women also decided daily strategy, holding elections on street corners deep within the immigrant communities, where "soldier boys" were loathe to go. On the corner of Oak and Short Streets women decided to stage a "monster" parade the following Monday and agreed to discuss the idea at Mass on Sunday.[123] It was at such a meeting that Zurwell saw a policeman shoot and kill thirty-two-year-old Annie LoPizzo, an event which alerted officials to the importance of controlling the neighborhoods, and military orders that women and children keep off the streets quickly followed. Arrests dramatically increased but shopping visits, social gatherings, communal meals, and frequent street assemblies continued to function as organizational meetings where women compared notes on scabs, which families were needy, and who could organize fund-raisers or take care of children, stand on picket duty or help out at one of the many neighborhood soup kitchens.[124]

Local leadership during the strike was seldom spontaneous, and both workers and radicals relied heavily on existing neighborhood resources. Known female activists, who the press dismissed as "petty leaders," were often either newly created militants, like Lis, or women who, as a result of their shrewdness, intelligence, strength, and generosity of spirit, had long before earned a position of leadership in the local community. "Such women," complained the local press, "spring up from time to time and brief rallies follow in the middle of the streets."[125] Typical was the anonymous woman arrested for "holding up a man on" the common. "This woman," complained Judge Campbell, "goes around and talked with other women and asked what progress they were making."[126] On dozens of blocks in the Plains, such local leaders gathered information, strengthened morale, provided the latest news, shared strategies, and helped identify those in need of help.

Others played more visible roles and their names are scattered throughout the press as arrests increased. When a "soldier boy" approached a crowd of women "doing picket duty" on Jackson Street, Josephine Lis "struck" him, then in front of the other women, took his gun away. A mender in a local worsted mill, Lis had already earned the community's respect for acting as their interpreter during arrests. Soldiers seemed well aware of Lis's position in the neighborhood, for despite the public humiliation she caused the guardsman and even though other soldiers came to help him out, they refused to arrest her at the time, waiting instead until she was alone. "The soldiers knew that she could not be moved," reported the one paper, "without serious force being used."[127] Lis refused bail, declaring that she was "in the right." Exasperated by women's willingness to be arrested and convinced that male strikers encouraged female militancy in the belief that the police would use less force, one judge wailed, "Let them put the men back on the streets; we can look after them all right."[128] Most such leaders, however, were not arrested, and their names are remembered only to those who received their help or followed their lead. Sara Axelrod, for example, left no official record of her involvement, yet her reputation as the "egg woman" was widespread during the strike. A skilled mender and by 1911, an inspector in the Wood Mill, Sara had moved outside Lawrence just before the strike and, along with her husband, operated a small poultry farm. But her advice and support were eagerly sought by the strikers, and she visited the city almost daily during the struggle—bringing food, news, and comfort. Her farm also became known as a safe hiding place for agitators, a tradition that would continue long after the strike ended. Born in Russia, Sara had been responsible for organizing her small village's only factory, a paper manufacturing firm employing about two hundred men and women, during the revolution of 1905. While a teenager she had gone to nighttime meetings held secretly in the surrounding forests, and there she had come into contact with the socialist movement as it spread throughout the Ukraine. Sara learned the rudiments of socialism and the value of united action from meeting with urban radicals who had come to make contact with local activists. Her own efforts in closing down the factory in Malvin came to an abrupt halt when cossacks surrounded the village and forced the strikers to submit. Although the religious community appealed on her father's behalf, the daughter was blacklisted, and Sara became an "actively antireligious" radical.

Setting up her own knitting business, Sara left home, became a committed anarchist, and eventually escaped Tsarist arrest by emigrating to

America. Few understood the importance of solidarity more than Sara Axelrod, and as a women with children to feed, she also knew the threat that starvation held for strikers. Just as French and Italian strikers relied on national traditions that relocated children to out of town sympathizers, Sara utilized traditions of rural support common in many Russian villages during strikes. Hauling wagons of provisions to strikers and their families, peasants in the Ukraine helped local factory workers defend themselves from the government. Like the Russian shtetl, Lawrence was surrounded by farm land containing dozens of dairies and small produce farms. Her farm served as a focal point for activity as supplies were counted and needs assessed. "I saw a great load of provisions—potatoes, sugar, bread, chickens, a pig and fresh beef—driven in by farmers of the outlying country to help the strikers," wrote one of the "flying observers" to Lawrence. "Without this outside help," he continued, "the strikers would soon have been starved into submission."[129]

The most well known female leader, of course, was the strong-minded Annie Welsenback, who was, according to Mary Kenny O'Sullivan of the Women's Trade Union League, a leader "of the most surprising caliber and personality."[130] The only female member of the executive committee, Annie had already at the age of twenty-four earned a reputation for strength and courage on the shop floor where she earned more money than even the higher-paid male operatives. Born in Canada, Annie was brought to the United States at the age of two years along with her older sister. The daughter of Polish mill workers, she spoke Polish as well as Yiddish and English. Throughout the strike Welzenbach seemed always to be everywhere: at court, at meetings, at train stations, in houses, on the streets and at every major arbitration meeting. "Consider the poorly paid girls," she told the delegation of managers at the Wood Mill. Pointing out the hated premium or "slave" system, Welzenbach argued that it was responsible for reducing women to meals of "bread and water." "She stood out," wrote Mary O'Sullivan, "for the despised foreigner."[131] Always a stirring figure whether on the speakers platform or in the street, women adored her and felt a "special pride" in her presence. At one point following a "monster" parade, Annie attempted to walk down Common Street on her way home. Recognizing the "tall and upright" stride of the ubiquitous leader, neighbors "fell in behind her" and "by the end of the street," reported the papers, "almost 2,000 strikers" marched her home.[132]

Table 8. Female Activists, Family Structure, and Household Head

	N	Percentage
Family Structure[a]		
Nuclear: husband, wife, kids	16	26.6
Nuclear family plus boarders	19	31.6
Extended family plus boarders	5	8.3
Multiple families, including male heads without		
spouse, mixed groups of families, plus boarders	9	15.0
Female headed	11	18.3
Household Heads[b]		
Female	18	24.3
Male	56	75.6

a. Based on sixty names traced through 1910 Manuscript Census Schedules for Lawrence, Massachusetts.
b. Based on Manuscript Census Schedules as well as newspaper accounts, government testimony, and trial transcripts where strikers identify themselves and their relation to the head of house. With these additional records, known cases of female strikers' household position increases to seventy-four women strikers.

Such popularity made Annie a difficult person to arrest. Following a ritualistic session of "intimidation" in which Annie and her two sisters joined in the efforts to prevent scabbing, police decided to wait until almost midnight before bringing the strident leader to court. Rather than risk a riot, they "dragg[ed] her out of her bed," along with her "two lieutenants," and hurried them into waiting vans. Women were furious and protested such "cossack" acts almost immediately. Local middle-class women's groups joined strikers to demonstrate their outrage by writing letters of strongly worded protest and organizing meetings with outside women's speakers.[133]

Female Activists

Unencumbered by traditional sources of restraint—such as older siblings, grandparents, village life, or in the case of the Lithuanians and Poles, an established church—immigrant women and girls found themselves freer to participate in strike activities than was often possible in more established communities.[134] Only one fourth of the female activists lived in nuclear families, while most lived in households with boarders or with other families in the household. (table 8) Furthermore, a significant minority of militants (24 percent) lived in households headed by women, eliminating potentially restrictive authority of husbands and fathers. The arrest of Sadie Zamon, a Syrian pioneer, who shared her tenement with a daughter and several other female-headed families, suggests the collaborative nature of such households. During the day, Zamon kept watch for prospective scabs while her daughter joined younger household members in picket duty. Scanning the streets from her upper-story windows, Sadie demanded passersby to identify themselves as scabs or picketers. Workers loyal to the strike were greeted with news and well wishes, but for scabs like Marie Nasser, a next door neighbor, Zamon reserved pots of garbage or scalding water that she hurled down on "betrayers."[135] Sharing their resources now as they had in their daily struggle for survival, mother and daughter joined their housemates in collective battle. As one of their comrades put it, "We made up our minds we might as well starve together as to take still less than we got before."[136] Households like the Zamon's helped others whose minds had not reached the same conclusion to understand the force, if not the logic, of such an ideology.

Although parental authority and patriarchal traditions among ethnic groups varied in degree and force, daughters and wives were active participants in strike activity. Thirty-four percent of female militants whose conjugal condition was known were married and living with their spouses. While others lived as daughters in family situations, parental authority in these households was seldom rigid or easily enforced. When Josephine Lis's father "told her to stay at home" on the morning of her arrest, "as she would be better off in bed," she replied that "she wanted to go out to see what was going on."[137] No doubt young Lis's stature during the strike combined with her role as a wage earner to undermine parental authority.

Yet even among girls and young women who needed to employ subterfuge in order to circumvent familial disapproval, there appeared not only a willingness to so, but a collective sense of approval. Former strikers spoke of the many excuses girls formulated to keep appointments with friends on picket lines and at meetings. Noting the large numbers of young women attending late-night meetings, one editor explained a popular tactic used by young strikers. "Telling their parents they were going to the Starr, girls went out to strike meetings, many of which were in fact held at the Starr." Some, like 14-year-old Consiglia Teutonica, kept in touch with strike activities by accompanying her mother as she made her daily rounds to grocery stores. "She'd be in heated debates herself, you know getting more food for the strikers, plannin' all the things that had to be done. I'd be around too, with my friends and we'd figure out things to do."[138]

Husbands and wives occasionally found themselves divided over the strike. Participation in the strike challenged patriarchal authority as women adhered to traditions of reciprocity and organized along gender specific networks. Leaving Lawrence to find work in Lowell until the strike ended, the husband of Mary Sullivan returned when he learned that his wife had joined strikers and was sending the children on the exodus. Furious, he marched down to the station and demanded that the children be returned. In most cases, however, women tended to hold other women responsible for familial backsliding. Typical was the situation described by Mary Gunkawitch, who, although a striker herself and a member of the IWW, was nevertheless threatened by her neighbors "because her husband was working."[139] That Mary's husband didn't interfere with her participation in the strike seemed less important to her neighbors than Mary's failure to exercise her influence over a recalcitrant husband. Just how much influence wives had over scabbing husbands (or over husbands on strike) is difficult to know, yet at the very least Mary's neighbors believed that she held a voice in the matter and that she could and should convince her husband to join the strike.

For the most part, however, men and women supported each other, and families provided essential resources for strikers. This was especially true in the Plains where "new" immigrant groups relied on principles of collectivity and traditions of reciprocity. "The Poles," reported the papers in the early days of the strike, "have begun to 'double up' in the tenements."[140] Italians owned forty-two tenements in the city and relied on "sympathetic" landlords as well as on communal living to survive the payless weeks of the strike. But here, too, when dissension threatened to weaken collective efforts, neighbors utilized whatever would work to maintain support, no matter how violent or how important the offender. Thus, when local padrone and prominent landlord Jeremiah Campopiano refused to wait on rent payments, his popularity in the community did not protect him from his neighbors' "stones and shots."[141]

The use of violence underscored the dependence of strikers who, without paychecks, had to rely more than ever before on others for essential support. Families were thus a critical factor in the outcome of the strike as ethnic differences in household structure and familial sentiment established patterns of mutuality and obligation. Recalling the extensive help from kin during the strike, one activist remembered, "They [lots of family] help with everything. They give ya a piece of bread or two."[142]

Many immigrants found help from kin or former neighbors who had moved to the outskirts of town or who, like the Brocks, had numerous kin on family-owned farms. The "egg women" was typical of this kind of extended aid, and throughout the strike hundreds of Syrians, Jews, and Lithuanians turned to rural kin for support. Believing it a right and not charity, immigrant women also hounded the city for relief. What the IWW and the soup kitchens couldn't provide, strikers demanded from city agencies and private institutions, including the YWCA, where Protestant women outraged Father O'Reily by serving food to hungry strikers regardless of race or religion.

While "new" immigrants readily turned to families and institutions for aid, Anglo workers were reluctant to do so. According to the newspapers, "the greatest distress was to be found among English speaking" groups who "will not ask for aid from the Overseers of the Poor."[143] For many Irish and English workers who had come to see themselves as Americanized, public aid symbolized a form of personal failure, "a badge of shame," and only the most desperate came to the city for help. Differing attitudes toward the family also separated English-speaking operatives from southern and eastern European immigrants. While the latter assumed a network of reciprocity, the former seldom expected aid from relatives or kin who lived outside the household. "Everyone had a hard time," explained one British operative whose relatives lived nearby, "so why should they even have bothered asking for aid?"[144] Lacking traditions of reciprocity and adhering to a more privatized notion of family life, the English and Irish communities were less able to endure payless paydays. Not surprisingly, these groups accounted for a large proportion of the scab population, especially at the Arlington, a traditionally "all-English" mill. "We just wanted to get our wages," confessed one Anglo operative who refused to strike. "What were we to do without money coming into the house? You expect us to live without wages? Those were hard times."[145] Without the networks of support and socialized arrangements typical of "new" immigrant neighborhoods, Anglo and Irish dependence on the mills was difficult to offset. "I didn't mind that they were striking, but they couldn't expect me to live without my wages."[146]

Many other factors, of course, worked to separate English-speaking workers from the "new" immigrants. By 1912, the Irish had secured a significant degree of influence in the city, and in the mills they joined the English and Yankees as the most skilled group of workers. Sympathetic to the AFL, many of the city's Irish and English operatives opposed the introduction of "greenhorns" into the ranks of American labor, fearing that immigrants from southern and eastern Europe would be used to undermine the labor movement. When the AFL pulled out of Lawrence, they did so with the firm support of the city's Irish/English population. The strike was simply not their own.

Yet even for those groups most in support of the strike, pressure was occasionally needed to maintain solidarity and worker discipline. Women's collective duty was vigorously expressed in the daily attempts to discipline their neighborhoods and prevent community dissension. Both soldiers and scabs knew from personal experience that these networks could be transformed into effective sources of resistance and militancy. Of the 130 women formally arrested during the strike, almost 90 percent were charged with intimidation or assault on an officer.[147]

Women guarded the streets from third- and fourth-floor windows, pouring insults if not scalding water on work-bound neighbors from these makeshift watchtowers. Often others joined in, throwing stones along with heated insults. Shrewdly taking advantage of these opportunities to prevent scabbing, the IWW provided several women with cameras so that they could follow neighborhood traitors and photograph them. Hiding the cameras in cloaks and under skirts, the photographers shadowed their victims and then, amid great hissing and hooting, ceremoniously hung his or her picture in the grocery store.[148]

In most cases, however, sisterhood and communal unity was maintained in the household, where traditions of reciprocity and sharing were now systematized for political struggle. Among activist households, 23 percent were headed by women dependent on a striker's wages. Privileging the future, women worked to transcend immediate financial losses. Mothers often converted their homes into soup kitchens for hungry strikers or provided child care while younger women picketed or paraded. One former striker recalled how her mother would open up the kitchen "to all the kids on the block. She'd make bread or pizza and everybody would be there—all during the strike. My brother was very active, so we didn't see too much of him, you know he was in jail or at the I.W.W. So my mother make so no one goes hungry or cold, not on our block."[149]

Those with fewer resources served at soup kitchens or organized fund-raising drives at stores, restaurants, and other businesses, asking for money or food. "If they don't help you now in your hour of need," proclaimed a popular Wobbly, "you know how to treat them."[150] And most women did. Unsympathetic stores were boycotted and others, who refused credit or food, found red scab signs or "black hands" on their front doors. On the whole, however, local shops contributed to the effort, running soup kitchens as well as supplying food to strikers and their families.

The composition and structure of women's networks had an important bearing on the character and effectiveness of the strike as well. A majority of female activists (54 percent) spoke English, including just under half (47 percent) of those whose birthplace was outside the United States. Born in Russia, Dora Weinbaum's command of English helped convince fellow twisters at the Arlington to join the general strike. Walking out on January 17, Dora was quickly elected to the strike committee and on the following day joined the IWW.[151] While Josephine Lis helped out as a translator for jailed pickets, French-born Emma Poulain taught the "Internationale," the most popular song of the strike, to multinational groups during strike meetings.[152] Numerous others translated speeches as well as strike minutes for circulation in the neighborhoods.

Alliances between generations of women, formed in the performance of customary tasks, were activated and made visible throughout the strike. The ages of female activists ranged widely and included women as young as thirteen and as old as forty-eight. Most, however, were young adults in their twenties.[153] By marching together, however, older women and young girls called attention to issues not specifically defined as wage related. Like all theatrical dramas, marches and parades were arranged with great care and specificity. Children and younger girls made up the center of long waves of horizontal lines while older women took the sides. In this way women sought to both protect young strikers from the soldiers who lined the sidewalks and at the same time expose the abuses of child labor, poor health care, and the general inadequacy of workers' lives. In Lawrence, fully one-half of the city's children worked in the mills, and their high accident rate and poor survival was a constant source of complaint among women. In the years immediately preceding the strike, 169 children out of 1000 died each year while the number of pauper burials was proportionately higher than in New York

City.[154] By placing children in the center of their parades, women pushed the boundaries of the strikers' cause and made clear the connections between wage cuts and youthful mortality.

Indeed, what often appeared to outside observers as spontaneous and largely uncontrolled outbursts or riots were generally events that contained their own internal logic and organizational structure. Women typically branched out from large parades and organized themselves into waves of human chains by linking their arms together and encouraging others to join them. They would then weave through the neighborhoods and business sections jeering, hooting, and singing. At this point, wrote one careful observer, "They would rush out, as if on cue, and attack their enemy." Police militia, unsympathetic priests and nuns, the houses of mill management and unfriendly city officials were all booed, humiliated, and occasionally physically attacked. Several women hid scissors under their long cloaks and when troopers came into their ranks trying to separate them, they drew out these domestic sabers and cut the backs of the soldiers uniforms, exposing their "yellow insides." At other times, female demonstrators would cut suspenders and collectively strip offenders while groups of women pointed and hooted as the victim made his escape from the streets. Always linking arms and moving in groups, women were able to protect each other and avoid arrest. They created chaotic scenes and made constant noises in the hope of confusing officers and camouflaging the identity of individual attackers.[155] Relying on local custom and developing strategies to maximize their collective impact, working-class women used the sources at hand, and in so doing gave meaning, coherence, and unity where contemporaries saw only confusion and disorder.

While almost twenty-four nationalities were represented in the strike, the vast majority of female activists came from "new" immigrant groups, especially Lithuania, Poland, Russia, Italy, and Syria (see table 9). Most worked in the mills, yet each national group contained small proportions of unpaid housewives who battled along side working neighbors, their offspring frequently in tow. Describing one day in his court when forty cases came before him, Judge George Roewer, Jr. told a congressional committee that "most of them were women, and most of the women had little babies in their arms nursing them."[156]

Temporary employment, however, did not seem to detract from women's militancy. Appolina Nowak, a former Lowell operative now home with her children, brought her baby to picket duty. When Julia Blacuda

Table 9. Ethnicity of Female Activists

Ethnicity	N	Percentage[a]
Austrian Polish	18	20.0
Lithuanian	15	17.0
Italian	13	15.0
Syrian	10	11.0
Native-born, foreign-born parent	9	10.0
Russian-Polish	7	8.0
Yiddish	6	7.0
French-Canada	3	4.0
Franco-Belge	1	—
Irish	1	—
Other	5	—
Total	88	

a. Based on those activists whose ethnicity could be traced.

was arrested for "unpeaceful picketing," she calmly nursed her seven-month-old child throughout the court proceedings. "Perplexed" as to "what course to take with the women who carried a child," Judge Mahoney finally settled on thirty days in jail.[157] Unemployed before the strike, Stacia Idipoli "rose early to see the children off." Neither she nor her husband worked in the mills at present, but the exodus provided both an opportunity to demonstrate support for the workers' cause and a chance to feed their own hungry children. Joining the massive processional of women and children that headed toward the train station, Idipoli, kicked by soldiers who "pulled off her shawl," stood firm with the others and fought back when police attempted to interfere with their mission.[158] During such events the boundaries between work and community grew dim and meaningless.

Bread and Roses: The Totality of Female Militancy

The adverse publicity generated by the children's exodus and the government investigations that immediately followed put additional pressure on the American Woolen Company to settle with the "unorganized" immigrant operatives. Unable to fracture the solidarity of the strikers and powerless in the neighborhoods where store owners, shopkeepers, and even landlords now lent support to the rebellious workers, company officials agreed in early March to meet with a committee of strikers. On March 12, men, women, and children collected on the common and overwhelmingly voted to endorse management's offer: no cut in pay, a two-week payment period for premiums instead of the usual four, and no discrimination against any striker.[159] When the Pacific and the Arlington Mills balked at settling with their competitor the American Woolen, a "woman stockholder" who, according to the local press, "is said to be able to swing many more votes," successfully pressured the reluctant Board of Directors to join the negotiations.[160] Three months after it had "exploded," the tumultuous strike was officially over, and every mill in the city reduced working hours without a proportionate drop in wages.

While the vast majority of strikers cheered the results of the three-month struggle, over five hundred Polish and Syrian women refused to return to the mills, voting instead to "stay on strike until their demands were met."[161] Congregating on the steps of the Holy Rosary Church, the women agreed to maintain scab watches at the Pemberton, the Arlington, and the Everett Mills, and to continue scolding and harassing returning workers. "The most talked of subject," reported one observer, was "will they return?"[162] When Annie Welzenbach returned to work at the Washington Mill on March 18, she found that many of the strikers' jobs had been taken over by scabs. Furious, she led "200 menders, burlers, and speckers," out of the mill and back into the streets. Many women talked of a 7 1/2 percent increase while others simply felt that the settlement fell far short of expectations. "It was a victory sure," commented one former militant, "but what really did we get? So much misery, so much, so much hope—My brother he still die the next year—we all still hungry."[163] As an earlier leaflet had argued, "The present problem is not to settle the strike but to settle it right or not at all."[164]

Both the fierce militancy of the female strikers as well as the gnawing disappointment that lead hundreds of women to denounce the settlement calls attention to the "totality" that working-class women typically bring to collective protest.[165] Straddling both the demands of wage labor and the challenges of womanhood, laboring women were less apt than male workers to see their situations as divided into two spheres, between "home and community" and "work," a dichotomy more typical of craft and middle-class women, or even male compatriots. For those whose primary concern was familial survival and welfare, issues of the shop floor were difficult to separate from home and neighborhood. Many female strikers remembered the industrial war of 1912 as "the strike for three loaves" and recalled a variety of issues for which they fought. "We resented you know abuse by the soldiers, and at work the bosses always men, and they's get smart." Recalling the mandatory evening classes for men and women unable to read or write in English, Consiglia Teutonica's rage returned when she described the treatment of women by the male teachers. "They [put] us over in one corner, you know, all the women, and then he ignored us! I want to learn! I want the English!, oh, I gave him words."[166] Others complained about overcharges for city services such as water and hospital rates. During the strike women voiced anger over the Board of Health who refused to provide eyeglasses to poor kids. Others demanded changes in school sanitary conditions and in neighborhood playgrounds that had become fly infested dumps.[167] One woman simply was amazed by "America, everywhere people not healthy, no milk, bad water, and so much sadness."[168] Unable to separate wage reductions, speedups, and pay schedules from the everyday struggle to maintain familial health, feed children, and protect the young, women supplied the strike with a completeness of vision that they themselves described as a "fight for bread and roses."

Throughout the strike, yet often below the surface of official policy, women brought the issues of daily life into the public arena. Socializing child care, food preparation, and living space for the exigencies of the strike, activists confronted the nature of the dual oppression of their lives as women and as members of an exploited class. Called out by friends and neighbors, women utilized the strike to publicize the brutish conditions of their lives, both inside and outside the mill gates. In marches and in protests they directed attention to a broad range of issues, from child labor and mortality to food prices, increasingly broadening their understanding of the roots of their own exploitation, as well the vision of their emancipation. Victims of female abuse reflected the extent to which women held more than one employer or city official accountable for their situation. Violence was directed not only at scabs and "soldier boys," but notorious overchargers, including a doctor as well as several grocers, unpopular city officials, and the board of health, which was painted red by the strikers.[169]

The totality of vision expressed by female militancy and strike participation gave the strike an enthusiasm unique to worker struggles at the time and helped make this struggle "an incipient revolution." As one reporter remarked, "It was the first strike I ever saw which sang!"[170]

Parades, crowds, and singing pickets mirrored female collaborative activities, providing both emotional strength and a consciousness of kind that further encouraged participation and solidarity. "I saw a group of women strikers who were peeling potatoes at a relief station suddenly break into the swing of 'The Internationale.' " Music, a critical vehicle of propaganda among illiterate populations, became in the heterogeneous neighborhoods of Lawrence an important vehicle for collaboration among disparate populations. Revolutionary songs like "The Eight Hour Day," "Workers Shall The Masters Rule Us?" and the popular "Internationale," held important messages of global unity, and, although familiar to many of the Franco-Belge who sang songs at local wobbly meetings, they were for the most part new to women (who were denied membership in the all-male Franco-Belge club, which hosted Local 20) and to many others recently converted to radical activism. Throughout the strike women exchanged verses and, like Emma Poulain, became the song leaders at meetings. According to transcripts made during the trial of Joe Ettor, Mary Stuka "carried her red book of IWW songs" with her everywhere, even to court. "At meetings, soup kitchens, and streets," old tunes were given new and revolutionary meanings. Songs make visible the often hidden process of movement building. In Lawrence they revealed to workers and mill owners alike, "a new obscure enthusiasm, a new halting self-confidence breaking through the mists of apathy."[171] In the same way that women grafted new words onto old tunes, participation in the strike gave new meaning to old injustices. High rents and food prices, dirty parks and sick children, appeared not as isolated events but as somehow connected to wages, to "the powers that prey."

Participating in the strike, women radicalized daily life allowing many who might otherwise have endured their "bad luck" alone to join in the struggle and politicize hard times. Like a pageant, neighborhood women staged dozens of dramatic clashes with authorities, turning "sudden bubblings of riot," into effective tools of unity unmatched in the labor movement. "The sudden gathering and disappearance of the throng," commented one flying reporter from Boston, "indicates perhaps better than any other single element the growth of a strange community of interest among the races."[172] Everywhere women used well-worn networks to promote cooperation and solidify alliances among neighbors. "What impressed me most," recalled a visiting female investigator, "was the force that could have wedded those peoples together. Here were Portuguese, Syrians, Germans, Russians, Franco-Belge, Canadians, Letts, Italians, English, Americans, Jews, Poles, Greeks, all working in perfect harmony."[173] Even the social worker Robert Wood, an ardent critic of the strike, was moved by the ability of the workers to overcome ethnic hostilities and maintain unity. "There is here the most tangible recognition of a crude power of collective formation among previously unorganized babels of laborers."[174] Despite the patronizing, even racist, tone of Wood's remarks, his observation alludes to what many historians of the strike have failed to see: ethnic solidarity was "crude" because it was rooted not in formal institutions like the IWW, but rather in the obscure nooks and crannies of neighborhood life. As a source of authority, these unformalized arenas provided critical support for worker militancy, but as we shall see, associational life would prove impermanent and inconsistent—a crude, unreliable basis for lasting forms of labor organization.

Like Wood, most contemporaries noted with surprise the ability of "new" immigrants to organize and maintain an effective strike. Viewed as greenhorns, "babels of laborers," Lawrence workers were seen as being new, not only to America, but to industrial labor as well. Reconstructing the work lives of female activists, however, challenges assumptions that collective action and worker resistance to modern industrial conditions was the result of worker inexperience and a general unfamiliarity with factory routine and discipline. Many historians, for example, have conceptualized labor unrest as a product of successive waves of "green" immigrant hands, who, while initially active in labor militancy, eventually conform once adjusted to modern industrial patterns and habits.[175] An analysis of Lawrence's female militants shows that although the mean number of years in the United States among activist women was just over eight years, the range was from one to twenty-two years, and a significant minority (17 percent) were native-born children of immigrants (table 10). Just as nonwage earners and property holders joined wage dependent operatives in a cross class demonstration of hostility toward the corporation, long-term residents united with "greenhorns" to protest conditions made intolerable, not by worker inexperience, but by the exploitative practices and conditions of capitalism.

Furthermore, "greenhorns" were not always inexperienced factory workers. As in the case of Sara Axelrod, many rural women had worked in the protoindustrialized countries of Poland, Russia, and Lithuania

Table 10. Years in the United States for Foreign-born Female Activists

	N	%	1-4	5-9	10-14	15-19	20-24
			\<td colspan=5>Number of Years				
Foreign	54	83.0[a]	16	21	8	6	3
Mean = 8.37 years							

a. Eleven female activists (17 percent) were native-born.

(see chapter three). Although her exact occupation in England is not known, Wobbly activist Jeannie Bateman probably learned some of her skills as a worsted winder in her hometown of Bradford, England, Lawrence's major rival in the woolen textile manufacturing industry. A fierce activist during the strike, Jeannie helped organize the "scab" Arlington in the early months of the struggle and took an active role in the IWW.[176]

Like the English, the Franco-Belgians, most of whom were recent arrivals to Lawrence, were also highly experienced textile operatives with almost 90 percent of the men and 95 percent of women former textile workers.[177] Local leaders like Joseph Bedard, Louis Picavet, Samuel Lipson, Cyrille De Tollenaere, and Angelo Rocco were all "green" and all experienced industrial workers.

Even among immigrant groups from predominately rural areas, veteran factory hands and mill operatives could be found in Lawrence. Both Anna Ricci, "on picket duty every day," and Sara Axelrod, "the egg woman," had worked in factories—Anna in a textile mill just outside of Naples and Sara in a paper factory in her native village near Kiev. Angelo Rocco, the "student agitator," similarly had extensive experience in European glass and textile factories.

Furthermore, native-born men and women frequently lived along side immigrants providing, as in the case of Pearl Shinberg and Josephine Lis, links to past struggles in the city. Throughout the strike, Lis's tenement served as a gathering place for a core of male and female militants and her neighborhood saw more arrests and housed more activists than any other district in the city. Living in one of the most cosmopolitan sections of the Plains, Lis was fluent in English and Polish but also knew a smattering of Yiddish and Lithuanian. When her downstairs Yiddish neighbor was arrested, Lis was asked to intervene. A few houses away, Italian-born housewife Pettinella joined wage earners obstructing sidewalks, and again Lis could be counted on to go down and make arrangements. While close living arrangements did not necessarily generate cross-ethnic contacts nor forge bonds between native-born veterans and green horns, the exigencies of the strike supported such efforts and opened new possibilities for mutual cooperation.

The strident and militant behavior that characterized female activists throughout the strike emerged out of women's unique social and sexual position in the working-class communities of Lawrence. Primarily caretakers of the home and family, women were also essential members of the city's textile labor force, and although not all militants actively participated in wage labor, the evidence suggests that for most activists, political consciousness emerged from women's dual roles as both reproducers and producers of labor. It was not the separation of these spheres that contributed to militancy but the exact opposite. Militants did not understand their lives as divided between "work" and "home," nor could they easily separate issues of the community from those of the workplace. The interconnectedness of women's lives, as caretakers of home and family and as essential breadgivers, expanded the issues of wage reductions to include a critique of the "powers that prey." The attitude of "an all or nothing" that dominated female militancy and shocked city officials emerged from such a totality of vision.

Few strikes have had as great an impact on American labor history than the Lawrence strike of 1912. Coming on the heels of the 1909 strike at Mckees Rocks and the "uprising of the 30,000" shirtwaist makers in the Lower East Side, the strike at Lawrence climaxed a series of proletarian revolts. Contemporaries wrote extensively about the "Revolutionary Strike," the "Industrial War," the "Revolt of the Masses," and the "Boiling Over of the Melting Pot."[178] Its success altered wages throughout the New England textile industry and crystallized Lawrence's reputation as a center for labor militancy.

The solidarity and democratic nature of the strike, in which over thirty thousand men, women, and children, from approximately forty different nationalities took part, also gave renewed legitimacy to the class conscious factions in the labor movement and demonstrated an alternative to the craft union strategy of the American Federation of Labor. As David Montgomery has suggested, these mass industrial strikes made skilled workers, increasingly under attack from scientific management and technological change, more willing to align themselves with the unskilled, providing a strong fillip for the "new unionism" which characterized the years between 1909 and 1922.[179]

The revolutionary nature of the struggle also gave leverage to more conservative forms of trade unionism as well. What had become a moribund movement in the New England textile industry was transformed following the successful conclusion of the strike into an energetic organizing campaign. "I have been speaking from the street corners of Lawrence for years," admitted James Duball of the AF of L, "and this is the first time I ever got a crowd."[180] Mill management especially understood the seriousness of the Lawrence crisis and began to view trade unionism as a more moderate and acceptable alternative to the revolutionary forms of organization suggested by the Lawrence struggle for "bread and roses." "I found some mill masters in Lawrence," remarked a visiting reporter, "almost shivering with the astonishing new idea that it might now be good policy to tie up with trade unionism in order to fight the encroachments of this new and revolutionary unionism."[181] Inspired by the victory in Lawrence, grass roots radicals in Lowell, Passaic, and Little Falls orchestrated similar walkouts, making the year 1912 a watershed in the history of worker militancy. "Beware that movement," wrote one sympathetic journalist, "that generates its own songs."

CONCLUSION

Ladies against Women: Americanization and the Lawrence Strike

God made Women, Rockefeller Made Ladies.

—Mother Jones

I cannot imagine anything that would affect better the moral health of any country than something which would blast the greatest number of that indecent, immoral institution—the perfect lady—out of doors and set them smashing and rioting.

—Mary Heaton Vorse

The focus of international attention, the strike of 1912 provided not only a fillip to class-conscious members of the working classes but a new boost as well to those voices seeking to restrict immigration. Convinced that the "Old Yankee stock" was in decline, New England Brahmins worried that the fecundity of "new" immigrants would rapidly overwhelm and crowd out the "glorious old state."[1] Pointing to studies that claimed a declining birth rate in "our most intelligent communities," national leaders like Theodore Roosevelt, Henry Cabot Lodge, and Edward A. Ross raised the specter of "race suicide." A 1922 cartoon in *Life Magazine* reflected fears that the foreign-born and their descendants would outbreed native stock. Entitled "The Last American in Captivity," the sketch shows a "Yankee gentlemen" displayed in a glass case, an apparent relic from a previous generation. "In 1975," reads the caption, "crowds swarmed like bees 'round a hive,' to see in a tent an American gent—the very last Yankee alive."[2]

As Linda Gordon points out, the idea of race suicide was a tangle of fears that "unified in the minds of believers," a "belief in large families, women's domesticity, nativism, and racism."[3] Denouncing women who left their sphere to pursue "newfangled" notions of economic independence, ambition, and wealth, critics exhorted the woman of "superior stock" to "have as many children as they can care for and properly rear," or else prepare "to turn the region over to the irreligious or ignorant foreigner."[4] Railing against woman who refused to do their duty to the country and pursued instead "selfish" notions of independence and careers, President Roosevelt spoke for a generation of male elites when he called on women to take up their rightful places as wives and mothers. The whole fabric of society," he argued, "rests upon the home."[5]

In Lawrence and other manufacturing centers that were fast becoming "immigrant cities," fears of race suicide were tempered by the reality of industrialists' dependence on the cheap labor of immigrants and their children. Yet in the conservative ideology of domesticity and motherhood, manufacturers found an alternative to the growing demand for restriction. Adopting traditional notions of motherhood—the bearing and rearing of the race—industrialists defined immigrant women as forces that could either propel family members forward toward modern, industrial life, or hinder their productive participation in the social and economic future of America.[6] Upholding mother power, they threw their weight behind programs that would "educate" the foreign-born woman in the areas of domestic hygiene, food preparation, and child rearing.

As Caroline Rowan has argued in her study of working-class women in England, programs directed at educating poor mothers necessitated the construction of a new "subject." In prewar England writes Rowan, "This was the ignorant but well-meaning working-class mother who would now be addressed directly by state agencies and not, as before, indirectly via the male head of the family."[7]

In the United States, where immigrants from southern and eastern Europe most vividly dramatized the problems of worker poverty, congestion, and poor health, it was the ignorant foreign-born women, the "oxen without horns," that provided a similarly constructed "subject" of national concern. Widely photographed in her *Babuska* with the families' possessions tied around her back or balanced on her head, the foreign-born woman increasingly symbolized the challenge of assimilation and the importance of Americanization efforts.[8]

In New England, where foreign-born populations swelled the operative districts, town fathers feared the breakdown of local patterns of control and accommodation as workers developed and expanded their own forms of leisure, politics, and heterosociability.[9] Fears over the growth of a permanent and self-conscious working-class intensified anxieties among industrialists, reformers, and restrictionists, whose warring images over immigrant women frequently centered on their ability or inability to "arouse and cultivate the economic instincts of working-class family life."[10] Progressive theorists argued that because immigrant mothers tended to eschew the factory, they hampered the development of a "modern consciousness," for "they are not yet co-ordinated with the industrial civilization which is penetrating their home and sifting through their activities."[11] Because they viewed immigrant women as lagging "behind the man in a slough of confusion and dejection"[12] Americanizers alternately blamed immigrant women for "the decline in family life, . . . juvenile delinquency," urban squalor and poor health, and fertility rates that threatened to "crowd out the superior races."[13] In the deeply gendered rhetoric of Americanization, women from Poland, Lithuania, Russia, Southern Italy, and Syria, were increasingly associated with ignorance, backwardness, and low evolutionary development and frequently portrayed as "loose women, poor housekeepers, and bad mothers."[14]

In Lawrence, fears over the rise of a separate and permanent class of immigrant workers took on new immediacy as the fight for bread and roses brought into focus the widespread poverty and ill-health of the nations industrial workers. As the "melting pot boiled over," a startled nation evaluated the peasant masses of unskilled workers with new intensity, leading many who were once indifferent to conclude now that the "new" immigrants were dangerously alienated from American life.[15] "Bewildered by the Lawrence terror," even "enlightened" reformers asked, "What have we done that a pack of ignorant foreigners should hold us by the throat?"[16] To many, the extreme militancy that characterized the strike was the result of outside agitators, who manipulated ignorant foreigners. Others, however, put the blame not on the IWW, but on what one judge called "unruly female elements." Weaving through city streets in defiance of the National Guard, immigrant women startled public officials, but it was their refusal to obey the law, to submit to rules of public deference and decorum, that awakened many to the messages of those who saw in the female immigrant the dangers of the "untrained woman whose only companion is as unfortunate as herself."[17] In the aftermath of the "Revolutionary Strike," the "oxen without horns" generated new concern over female rebelliousness and disorder, a growing theme in the popular press to which Americanizers both responded and helped to create. Acting neither confused nor dejected, female strikers displayed a sense of themselves and an understanding of their cause that ruptured images of passivity and industrial indifference. By defying authorities and taking part in acts of violence, female strikers challenged the economic order as well as the sexual labeling upon which it was based. As one Lawrence official reminded his audience, "Just as soon as women disregard constituted authority by catching and tearing officers' coats, why, then you have the foundation for all that follows."[18] At least some women operatives agreed. Explaining why half of the menders at the Wood refused to go out, a women told reporters that "when we have trouble we go to our overseer like ladies and try to show the breeding that we have received, not like Turks, smashing and destroying everything in our way."[19]

Such attitudes deepened the conviction among city authorities that education was the path to economic as well as social harmony between the classes. Like their English counterparts, they sought "not the abolition of poverty, overcrowding and insanitary conditions," but the education of poor women whose behavior in the streets was interpreted as a challenge to industrial as well as patriarchal order.[20] Noting that many of the most militant women were the mothers and wives of operatives, manufacturers accepted the view that immigrant women were more resistant to industrial labor than their male counterparts. Convinced that ignorance and tradition, not radical politics, informed their actions, manufacturers directed their efforts to the immigrant home and neighborhood. "We can make contact" wrote one Lawrence industrialist, "with men in clubs and other organizations," but women, he argued, "were difficult to reach."[21] In hopes of bringing a more "modern consciousness" to immigrant women, manufacturers agreed to finance the International Institute For Women, an organization whose primary function would be to "quickly Americanize" the "ignorant foreign women" of the city.

Located in the heart of the Plains, the Institute operated like many turn-of-the-century settlement houses, providing "services to families" and acting as local advocates for immigrants and their neighbors.[22] Dedicated to educating immigrant mothers, the founders hoped to concentrate on the problems of "cleanliness, overcrowding, and overcharging." The issues of "labor reform, suffrage," and in 1920, "the Equal Rights Amendment to the Constitution," which had infiltrated the Young Women's Christian Association, were to be countered with American ideas of domesticity, motherhood, and patriotism.[23]

Hoping to dilute the influence of the "Y" and establish a bridge into the obscure world of immigrant women, manufacturers gave generously to the institute, whose fenced in yards and neat interiors helped translate the values of private family life and the principles of domestic order to the foreign-born.[24]

Like many companies seeking ways to reduce labor conflict and secure a loyal work force, Lawrence's mill men saw the benefits of local welfare programs and encouraged the city to organize an Association for Welfare Work. As founders noted, "It establishes justice in industrial relations so as to forestall anarchy";[25] it also helped direct public attention away from the shop floor and onto the homelife of immigrant operatives.[26] Having located the source of worker unrest in the "domestic life of the workers," reformers joined with Lawrence's manufacturers in the campaign to eradicate ignorance and modernize the immigrant home.[27]

Forced to acknowledge the extent of poverty in the city, authorities were nevertheless reluctant to explore the role of manufacturers in its creation. While mill work was regarded as difficult, Clark Carter, director of the Lawrence City Mission, and a staunch opponent of the strike, provided an alternative explanation for the ill-health of the mill worker: "Incompetency on the part of the mother, poor cooking and bad housekeeping," argued Carter, "may impair the health of the whole family." Positioning women in the center of reform efforts, Carter noted as well that "discouraged and deserting husbands, undernourished and wayward children, and unhappy wives have been traced to the inability of the home maker."[28] Calling for "a doctor of domestic difficulties, one who can visit almost daily and direct the home making of the family,"[29] city officials caused the problem of worker poverty, malnutrition, and social unrest, to be redefined as a problem of maternal ignorance; the result of a poor home environment.

Male administrators of welfare programs thus paid special attention to the education and training of immigrant women. "Doubly anxious about the children and defective girls, the potential mothers in our midst,"[30] local authorities established a citywide network of "clubs for mothers" and a school program that promoted "mothercraft," a set of courses that included "diet, recreation, vocation, morals, and baby care."[31] Concerned that private agencies lacked the authority of the state to involve themselves in the immigrant home, local officials sought to place the visiting nurse program under the direction of the Lawrence Board of Health. Welfare administrators argued that "the visiting nurse has access only to the families that welcome her, while under the board of Health she can render her services wherever need summons her."[32]

While manufacturers and city officials funded Lawrence's Americanization programs and directed their operations, it was often their sisters and wives who assumed positions on the front line.[33] Calling upon the city's middle-class women to help sweep working-class poverty away, officials drew on the arguments of social housekeepers to promote the reform of immigrant women. "One of the greatest influences for good in the world today," observed one Lawrence missionary, "is the personal contact of the woman trained in brain and heart for her work with the untrained woman."[34] Working as volunteers and paid staff, the wives and daughters of Lawrence's business and professional class comprised the bulk of the city's "domestic doctors" bringing food, medicine, and the skills of "mothercraft" to the most remote kitchens in the city. A tendency among these reformers was to view immigrant women as victims of poverty and ignorance. When striker Annie LoPizzo was killed during a street meeting of neighborhood women, members of the Woman's Progressive Club joined with Wobbly leaders to denounce the "treatment of innocent women whose only crime was being in the wrong place at the wrong time." Like many of their male counterparts, club members refused to see women as active participants in the strike and LoPizzo became a favorite symbol for the victimization of the city's laboring women.

Steeped in the language of social housekeeping, the campaign to educate Lawrence's foreign-born women supported the belief that class differences could be narrowed by programs aimed at assimilation. In this sense national unity itself appeared to be at stake in reforming the immigrant population. As if to announce the new role that "home managers" would play in solidifying national unity, city leaders organized an elaborate pageant in the heart of the city that proclaimed the "natural" bonds between "Maternal Love and Patriotism."[35] Hoping to reseal social harmony and reclaim the hermetic world they imagined to be their heritage, city officials found in the trilogy of domesticity, motherhood, and Americanism, a powerful symbol for the constancy and certainty that eluded them in the turbulent decades of the new century.

Figure 20. Sewing class at the International Institute, Lawrence, c. 1914. Courtesy of Immigrant City Archives.

Like most Americanization campaigns, of course, efforts on the part of city reformers to "educate" immigrant mothers and daughters probably had their greatest impact on those who organized them. Yet in the competing discourses that constituted the responses of manufacturers and reformers to immigrant women, the veterans of 1912 located both the limits and the possibilities of female identity. "Words," one scholar reminds us, "are actions; outsider's labels help create the fund of interpretive possibilities from which identity can be drawn."[36] In the feverish aftermath of the 1912 strike, that fund contained a number of competing images that for strikers and their children, had multiple and often ambiguous meanings. At times, such contests surfaced in local struggles over women's proper dress and spending habits. During the strike red, white, and blue clothing along with large American flags provided legitimacy to immigrant actions and helped establish the logic of their struggle. By investing Old Glory with extraordinary emotional and symbolic significance, immigrant strikers sought to link their struggle with American ideals of justice and fair play. Representing themselves as patriots they simultaneously confirmed their allegiance to their cause and to each other. Yet among strikers there was disagreement too over the meaning of those American objects most clearly associated

Figure 21. Maternal Love and Patriotism in a pageant at Lawrence. One of a dozen pageants held in Lawrence between 1910-17 to promote "Civic Pride" and to "Americanize" the city's immigrant population. Typically "Progress" and America were represented as women who were mothers of workers and the nation.

with a materialistic and consumer culture. Hats, stylish dresses, and the wearing of cosmetics could thus divide women strikers as much as the violent "Turkish" behavior of female militants. In those neighborhoods, for example, where shawled women kept watch for scabs, hats and "powered faces" were initially interpreted as signs of disloyal neighbors and kin, for such things represented not simply a new demand on thin family budgets but also a new source of division among the immigrant community.[37] Only after Annie Welzenbach popularized the stylish American hat during strike meetings and street demonstrations did girls and women feel completely free to coordinate American fashions with their IWW ribbons.

In the attempt to "modernize" immigrant women, the city's Americanization programs further propelled women, especially young women

Figure 22. Wearing American hats, immigrant women show their support for the strike and the IWW. Courtesy of Immigrant City Archives.

and girls, further into the world of American fashion and style, combining lessons on mothercraft with modern techniques of food preparation, shopping, and personal dress. In the "land of dollars" Americanizers represented women workers as eager consumers earning pin money for themselves and their family. They constituted, of course, only the most formalized versions of the American working girl. As Kathy Peiss has shown, the intensive commercialization of leisure in the early 1900s "consciously encouraged the participation of women . . . altering traditional patterns of sociability."[38] In newspapers, magazines, and especially in movies, Lawrence's immigrant daughters caught a glimpse of an urban culture that encouraged experimentation, "flamboyant fashion," "personal freedom," and "unsupervised fun."

Lacking the big dance palaces and amusement parks available to workers in larger cities, Lawrence's men and women found opportunities to socialize in clubs, dances, and outings organized by the socialist immigrant community as well as by both the International Institute for Women and the "Y." Following the strike, the Star Theater continued to be one of the most popular spots for women and girls who now came

Figure 23. Dressed for the "God and Country Parade." Employers sponsored displays of patriotism following the strike of 1912. Courtesy of Immigrant City Archives.

Figure 24. Polish woman in her first American clothes. International Institute. Courtesy of the Immigrant City Archives.

together over "candy nights, grocery nights and chicken nights," to watch Theda Bara and Rudolf Valentino.[39] In the cultural ferment that surrounded them, Americanization was less a monologue than a polyglot babel of competing voices and visions.

As administrators like Clark Carter were also to discover, Americanization, even in the controlled hands of the International Institute, could expand the boundaries of domesticity when, as one outraged official noted, "nice wasp ladies taught not so nice ideas of reform."[40] Along side classes in home crafts, program directors like Ethel Miller, Miss Church, and Elizabeth Glendower Evans set up sessions on "home justice" and encouraged their clients to report landlord overcharges, poor heat, and both police and domestic brutality. At both the "Y" and the International Institute social workers also established investigative committees composed of staff members as well as clients. Dubbed the "angel of the strikers," for her tireless efforts on behalf of workers during the 1919 strike, Evans later became a leading figure on the Sacco-Venzetti Defense Committee.[41]

It was in the everyday operations of the "Y" and the Institute, however, where activists like Miller and Church made their deepest impact on the lives of immigrants. Classes in English, math, and history, as well as summer programs in "labor reform, suffrage, and social reform," supplemented those in "mothercraft" where, reported a disappointed Trustee, there was "not a large attendance."[42] Former strikers recalled with a note of pride their participation in classes at the "Y" and at least a few took advantage of national scholarships sponsored by the organization to attend the American International College in Springfield, Massachusetts. For some former strikers, however, like Josephine Lis and Paula Nowak, the struggle for autonomy led to estrangement from the old neighborhood world of family and friends. Dependent on the labor of their children and fearful of the attractions that the New World held for them, not a few immigrant parents were skeptical of female reformers—"meddlers"—who they believed disrupted the values and cohesion of the immigrant community. "The people ridiculed parents for sending daughters to college," explained the daughter of striking parents, "they saw it as a class situation."[43] Still others feared not only the loosening of community and family loyalty but also the undermining of parental authority as young women and girls attended the many "socials" organized by the reformers. At the "Y" women sponsored summer outings to the shore, picnics at socialist inspired Maple Park, dances, and at the institute summer camps, hikes, and lectures on suffrage and the ERA. "Everyone went," recalled one former striker, "socialist "stinkers" (like us)—the smarties—even Catholics would go."[44]

Parents were not the only ones who feared the influence of reformers on the city's immigrant community. Resenting the popular appeal of the "Y," where immigrant girls readily accepted free showers and cheap meals, neighborhood priests railed over the ecumenicalism preached by its executive director, Ethel Miller. To the local priesthood at the Holy Rosary Church, it was the "Devil's House" not simply because the "Y" was a Protestant organization, but because they saw it as encouraging anticlerical sentiments already widespread among the city's immigrant groups.[45] At the International Institute a similar policy of secularism existed, "No hymns or services" were to be provided, just "counseling and classes."[46]

In the minds of conservatives, the "ecumenical way" rekindled anarchist strike slogans of "No God, No Master." Three groups in particular—the Lithuanians, the Austrian Poles, and the Franco-Belgian—harbored deep suspicions of clerics who traditionally represented the landed classes in the Old World. The daughter of one former striker explained her mothers' antipathy towards the Lithuanian Roman Catholic church by pointing out what "every one knows: Over there all the priests spoke Polish—they saw themselves above all the people but especially above Lithuanians."[47] For many Russian Jews, radicalized by the Revolution of 1905 and by their participation in the Bund, organized religion stood in the way of democratic principles and the socialist revolution. "Actively anti-clerical," former Jewish strikers organized an "Ideal Club," which sponsored leftist speakers as well as social events for the radical community. "I couldn't go to public dances—no way. But the private dances at the Ideal, there we could all go. So these socialist meetings, well they were for me!"[48]

Distancing themselves from the religious and civic culture of the Americanizers, radical immigrant groups also geographically separated themselves from the city controlled land used for military parades and patriotic pageants. Joining together shortly after the strike, a group of Lithuanians purchased a large track of land on the outskirts of town where they could hold their own cultural events. Opened in 1915, the Park also meant that socialists would not have to depend on city authorities for permits to hold mass meetings. A place where "everyone came together over cabbage soup and beer," Maple Park organized lectures on pacifism, socialism, and cooperation as well as concerts featuring folk music and opera.[49] To the dismay of Father Virmauskis, who sought funds from manufacturers to buy land for religious Lithuanians, people of all creeds went to Maple Park, because "they feel they are at home, nobody is bothering them."[50]

Such spaces provided possibilities for contestation and change. "I believe," recalled Amelia Olenio, "that it is correct to say that the YW fought no battles (that I know of) for the working women—but the YW did give us a greater awareness of our own worth, added self-confidence and strength as we compared notes and shared ideas and learned to take action for ourselves as individuals and as part of a larger group."[51] This was especially important in the years immediately following the strike when city authorities launched bitter campaigns against the Wobblies and all other forms of radicalism, including feminism, which in the minds of conservatives stood for "non-motherhood, free love, easy divorce, economic independence for all women, and other demoralizing and destructive theories."[52] Father O'Reilly, who had enormous influence in the Irish and French-Canadian communities encouraged parishioners to guard their daughters against such "Devils ideas" and encouraged the local Knights of Columbus to sponsor various pageants and exhibitions on American motherhood and the role of women in the "patriotic home." During the "For God and Country Parade," which was held on Columbus Day 1912, contests were held throughout the city challenging women employees and parishioners to create patriotic dresses and costumes. Highlighting the contested meaning of both the strike and women's militant participation in it, almost thirty thousand Lawrence residents turned out to cheer the marchers and applaud the patriotism of the costumed women.[53]

The desire of Americanizers to transform Lawrence's "unruly female elements," into "competent mothers," "happy wives," and "good housekeepers," was, of course, part of a growing national project organized by conservative elites and middle-class business and professional leaders to articulate a new collective identity that had at its core "the belief that there was such a thing as an American inheritance."[54] By defining, characterizing, and identifying working-class and immigrant women as a special group of strangers in the land, they defined, characterized, and identified themselves as the custodians of American tradition. The American "lady" was thus "traditionalized" to both secure the boundaries of "Americanness" and to prevent its corruption from below, what could now be defined as a deviation from the past, a rupture with the national heritage. To the guardians of tradition, the Lawrence strike thus served as a clarion call for a cultural offensive in which "no kitchen in the land would be immune."[55]

The power of categorization—of pigeonholing—is far from external to the construed realities of laboring women whose ability to shape what John Tagg calls "the command of meaning" diminished in an industrial world increasingly defined and shaped by dialogue and image, by male words and a "male gaze."[56] In its ability to speak for women—to claim, that is, the right to do so—language itself became an expression of power as the voices of mill owners, craftsmen, Americanizers, and reformers both reflected and helped to construct the world of the laboring woman and her place in it.[57] The eclipse of the self-supporting woman, like the invention of the "ignorant but well-meaning immigrant mother," remind us that the politics of representation, wryly captured in the title of a recent feminist theater group, "Ladies Against Women," are often central terrains upon which power is both exercised and contested.

So, too, can we see in the strikes of 1882 and 1912 the agency of working women whose actions and gestures challenged notions of a monolithic worker identity. Indeed, both strikes brought to public attention the vitality of women in action—their ability to create their own forms of social and sexual life—and it was this as much as their participation in the strike that stood at the center of conservative anxieties. Establishing autonomous social spaces in their neighborhoods and work places, laboring women came into political consciousness as members of particular communities of women. Drawn by the exigencies of industrial life into reciprocal acts of exchange, the strikers of 1882 and 1912 experienced themselves as women and as workers in ways that were collectively thought out, not up, as they exchanged gossip, compared prices, shared advice, offered aid, nursed kin and neighbor, made friends, and built alliances. In everyday acts of collaboration, they secured for themselves and their community a consciousness of kind that in both 1882 and 1912 brought them into confrontation with an industrial order they saw as undermining their efforts as women and as women who needed to work. "Women in motion" also make it clear to historians that contests over the meaning of womanhood did not simply run parallel to or reflect the events of 1882 and 1912; but rather that the formation and reformation of identity was integral to the political process as a whole. As Elizabeth Stuart Phelps so clearly understood, womanhood lies "deep in the tangled roots of things."

Written history, as Carolyn Steedman has argued, is the most impermanent of written forms. As a story, "it can only be told by the implicit understanding that *things are not over,* that the story isn't finished, can never be finished, for some new item of information may alter the account that has been given."[58] Many have told the story of the Lawrence strike of 1912 and like this book, they stand as evidence that it is a tale far from over. For some historians the strike was an anomaly, a matter of outside agitators leading misguided greenhorns while for others it demonstrated the strength and political acumen of the Wobblies as well as the ability of immigrant and unskilled workers to organize. For those who lived through the story, the strike had different meanings as labor radicals, unionists, social activists and the participants themselves sought to define strikers political goals and aspirations. Even before the strike was settled, debates over its name and objectives were integral to the shaping of the struggle and how the story itself would be preserved. But even these debates took place within a deeper context of struggle as strikers sorted out in their lives and then again in their memories the meaning of their involvement in radical politics and militant collective action. That we continue to write their story and remember their struggle as a fight for Bread and Roses, is perhaps the best evidence of all that things truly are not over. In many ways, therefore, the Lawrence strike is still in the making and its meaning for the future will depend in large part on the construction of that history and the place of laboring women in such struggles.

Notes

Preface

1. *New York Times,* Jan. 12, 1860.

2. Table 17, "Standard of Living of Selected Pemberton Workers," in Clarisse A. Poirier, "Pemberton Mills, 1852–1938: A Case Study of the Industrial and Labor History of Lawrence, Massachusetts" (Ph.D. diss., Boston University, 1978).

3. Alice Kessler-Harris, *Out to Work: A History of Wage-Earning Women in the United States* (New York: Oxford University Press, 1982), 71.

4. Quoted in Hannah Josephson, *The Golden Threads: New England's Mill Girls and Magnates* (New York: Russell & Russell, 1949), 8.

5. Elizabeth Stuart Phelps, *Chapters from a Life* (Boston: Houghton & Mifflin Co. 1896), 89.

6. Thomas Dublin, *Women at Work: The Transformation of Work and Community in Lowell, Massachusetts, 1826–1890* (New York: Columbia University Press, 1979), 92; Caroline Ware, *The Early New England Cotton Manufacture: A Study in Industrial Beginnings* (New York: Russell & Russell, 1966), 278.

7. "A Working Woman's Statement," *Nation* (Feb. 21, 1867): 155–56.

8. Amos Lawrence to Abbott Lawrence, Oct. 8, 1848, MS Amos A. Lawrence Papers, folder misc., *Massachusetts Historical Society* (hereafter *MHS*).

9. Steve Dunwell, *The Run of the Mill: A Pictorial Narrative of the Expansion, Dominion, Decline and Enduring Impact of the New England Textile Industry* (Boston: David R. Godine, 1987), 85; Jonathan F. C. Hayes, *History of the City of Lawrence, Massachusetts* (Lawrence, 1868), 35.

10. Hayes, *History,* 37; see also Philip Scranton, *Proprietary Capitalism: The Textile Manufacture at Philadelphia, 1800–1885* (Cambridge: Cambridge University Press, 1983), 42–71.

11. Quoted in Kessler-Harris, *Out to Work,* 65.

12. Victor Turner, *Ritual Process* (Chicago: Aldine Pub., 1969), 125, 108–30.

13. Denise Riley, *"Am I That Name?": Feminism and the Category of "Women" in History* (Minneapolis: University of Minnesota Press, 1988), 16.

Introduction

1. *Lawrence Evening Tribune* (hereafter *Tribune*), May 14, 1902. For information on the loom fixers during the strike of 1912, see *Tribune,* Jan. 14, 1912; on mule spinners, see Jan. 11, 1912. See also Edwin Fenton *Immigrants and Unions: A Case Study, Italians and American Labor, 1870–1920,* (New York: Arno Press, 1975), 332–33; *Lawrence Sun* (hereafter *Sun*), Jan. 12, 1912; Transcript of the Trial of *Commonwealth vs. Joseph Caruso, Joseph Ettor, Arturo Giovannitti, alias,* Superior Court, Essex County, Massachusetts, 20–4, courtesy of Kimbal Mahoney.

2. *Tribune,* Feb. 23, 26, 28, 1912.

3. Essex Co., Samuel Lawrence to Charles Storrow, Mar. 6, 1847, MS 306, Museum of American Textile History, (hereafter MATH).

4. Jacquelyn Dowd Hall, "Disorderly Women: Gender and Labor Militancy in the Appalachian South," *Journal of American History* 73, no. 2 (Sept. 1986): 355. Important exceptions to this early historiography include Ware, *Early New England Cotton Manufacture;* Josephson, *The Golden Threads;* Dublin, *Women at Work.*

5. The clearest argument for this position is in David Brody, "The Old Labor History and the New: In Search of the American Working Class," *Labor History* 20 (Winter 1979): 11–26. Here, Brody urges labor historians to study "men and women *at work.*" See also Mary H. Blewett, *Men, Women, and Work: Class, Gender, and Protest in the New England Shoe Industry, 1780–1910* (Urbana: University of Illinois Press, 1988), xv. Quote from Daniel J. Walkowitz, *Worker City, Company Town: Iron and Cotton Worker Protest in Troy and Cohoes, New York, 1855–1884* (Chicago: University of Illinois Press, 1978), 119. He concluded that the lack of militancy in one nineteenth-century cotton town resulted from a heavily feminized population that lacked both "a male leadership cadre" and "a distinctive work subculture" (pp. 249–52). For a different perspective on family, community, and worker militancy in Troy, see Carole Turbin, "Reconceptualizing Family, Work and Labor Organizing: Working Women in Troy, 1860–1890," *Review of Radical Political Economics* 16 (1984): 1–16.

6. See, for example, " 'Where Are the Organized Women Workers?' " *Feminist Studies* 3 (Fall 1975): 92–110; June Nash, *We Eat the Mines and the Mines Eat Us: Dependency and Exploitation in Bolivian Tin Mines* (New York: Columbia University Press, 1979); Elizabeth Jameson, "Imperfect Unions: Class and Gender in Cripple Creek, 1894–1904," in *Class, Sex and the Woman Worker,* ed. Milton Cantor and Bruce Laurie (Westport, Conn: Greenwood Press, 1977), 166–202; Meredith Tax, *The Rising of the Women: Feminist Sol-*

idarity and Class Conflict, 1880–1917 (New York: Monthly Review Press, 1981); Temma Kaplan, "Female Consciousness and Collective Action: The Case of Barcelona, 1910–1918," *Signs* 7 (Spring 1982): 545–66; Kaplan, "Class Consciousness and Community in Nineteenth Century Andalusia," *Political Power and Social Theory* 2 (1982): 21–57; Martha Ackelsberg, *Free Women of Spain: Anarchism and the Struggle for the Emancipation of Women* (Bloomington: Indiana University Press, 1991) and Ackelsberg, "Mujeres Libres: Individuality and Community: Organizing Women during the Spanish Civil War," *Radical America* 18, no. 4 (1984): 7–21; Nancy Hewitt, *Women's Activism and Social Change: Rochester, New York, 1822–1872* (Ithaca, N.Y.: Cornell University Press, 1984); Ruth Milkman, ed., *Women, Work and Protest: A Century of U.S. Women's Labor History* (Boston: Routledge, 1985); Louise Tilly, "Paths of Proletarianization: Organization of Production, Sexual Division of Labor and Women's Collective Action," *Signs* 7 (1978): 400–417; Turbin, "Reconceptualizing Family"; Hall, "Disorderly Women"; Linda Jean Frankel, "Women, Paternalism, and Protest in a Southern Textile Community: Henderson, North Carolina, 1900–1960" (Ph.D. diss., Harvard University, 1986).

7. See also Vicky Ruiz, *Cannery Women, Cannery Lives: Mexican Women, Unionization, and the California Food Processing Industry, 1930–1950* (Albuquerque: University of New Mexico Press, 1987); Louise Lamphere, *From Working Daughters to Working Mothers: Immigrant Women in a New England Industrial Community* (Ithaca, N.Y.: Cornell University Press, 1987); Sharon Harley and Rosalyn Terborg-Penn, *The Afro-American Woman: Struggles and Images* (Port Washington, N.Y.: National University Publications, 1978); Carol Groneman and Mary Beth Norton, eds., *"To Toil the Livelong Day": America's Women at Work, 1780–1980* (Ithaca, N.Y.: Cornell University Press, 1987); Jacqueline Jones, *Labor of Love, Labor of Sorrow: Black Women, Work, and the Family from Slavery to the Present* (New York: Basic Books, 1985).

8. See especially Jeanne Boydston, "To Earn Her Daily Bread: Housework and Antebellum Working-Class Subsistence," *Radical History Review* 35 (1986): 8; Christine Stansell, "Women, Children, and the Uses of the Streets: Class and Gender Conflicts in New York City, 1850–1860," *Feminist Studies* 8 (Summer 1982): 309–37; Stansell, *City of Women: Sex and Class in New York, 1789–1860* (Urbana: University of Illinois Press, 1987); Judith Smith, *Family Connections: A History of Italian and Jewish Immigrant Lives in Providence, Rhode Island, 1900–1940,* (Albany: State University of New York Press, 1985), esp. 35–82; and Nancy Hewitt, " 'The Voice of Virile Labor': Labor Militancy, Community Solidarity, and Gender Identity among Tampa's Latin Workers," *Work Engendered: Toward New Understandings of Men, Women, and Work,* ed. Ava Baron (Ithaca, N.Y.:Cornell University Press, 1991).

9. Susan Levine, "Workers' Wives: Gender, Class, and Consumerism in the 1920s," *Gender and History* 3:1 (Spring 1991): 45–64; on consumer protest, see Dana Frank, "At the Point of Consumption: Seattle Labor and the Politics

of Consumption, 1919–1927" (Ph.D. diss., Yale University, 1988); Steven M. Cohen and Paula E. Hyman, eds., *The Jewish Family; Myths and Reality* (New York: Holmes and Meyer, 1986); and Hewitt, " 'The Voice of Virile Labor.' "

10. Mary Heaton Vorse, *A Footnote to Folly: Reminiscences of Mary Heaton Vorse* (New York: Farrar & Rinehart, 1935), 13–14.

11. Herbert Gutman, *Work, Culture, and Society in Industrializing America: Essays in American Working-Class and Social History* (New York: Vintage Books, 1977), esp. chap. 5.

12. Ackelsberg, "Communities, Resistance, and Women's Activism: Some Implications for a Democratic Polity," in *Women and the Politics of Empowerment,* ed. Ann Bookman and Sandra Morgan (Philadelphia: Temple University Press, 1988).

13. Ibid., 301. These ideas are also developed extensively in Ackelsberg, *Free Women.*

14. Michel Foucault, *The Order of Things: An Archaeology of the Human Sciences* (New York: Pantheon Books, 1970), 387. The search for approaches to the past that expand the boundaries of history has been especially important to historians of women and other oppressed groups who have frequently been marginalized by the *de facto* nature of traditional categories of analysis. Two works that have been especially influential in widening definitions of history and that question the search for order are Hayden White, *Tropics of Discourse: Essays in Cultural Criticism* (Baltimore: Johns Hopkins University Press, 1978) and Dominick LaCapra, *Rethinking Intellectual History; Texts, Contexts, Language* (Ithaca, N.Y.: Cornell University Press, 1983).

15. David Lowenthal, *The Past Is a Foreign Country* (Cambridge, Mass.: Cambridge University Press, 1985), 218.

16. Robert Frost, quote by Dinesen from Anthony Kronman, "Comments on 'Narrative as Knowing' " (Paper delivered at the Tenth Anniversary Symposium, *Constructing Traditions: Renovation and Continuity in the Humanities,* Whitney Humanities Center, Yale University, Feb. 1991).

17. Among the "classic" early texts that sought to restore women to history, are: Renate Bridenthal and Clausia Koonz, *Becoming Visible: Women in European History* (Boston: Houghton Mifflin, 1977); Sheila Rowbotham, *Hidden From History: Rediscovering Women in History from the 17th Century to the Present* (New York: Vintage Books, 1976); Gerda Lerner, *The Majority Finds Its Past: Placing Women in History* (Oxford: Oxford University Press, 1979). For recent works that especially question the concept of marginality, see bell hooks, *Feminist Theory from Margin to Center* (Boston: South End Press, 1985).

18. For a concise explanation of poststructuralist ideas and their usefulness to historians, see Joan Wallach Scott, *Gender and the Politics of History* (New York; Columbia University Press, 1988), esp. 1–50; see also, James Clifford,

"Introduction: Partial Truths," in *Writing Culture: The Poetics and Politics of Ethnography,* ed. James Clifford and George Marcus (Berkeley: University of California Press, 1986), 1–26; Jacquelyn Dowd Hall, "Partial Truths," *Signs* 14, no. 4 (Summer 1989): esp. 907; and Edward M. Bruner, "Ethnography as Narrative," in *The Anthropology of Experience,* ed. Victor W. Turner and Edward M. Bruner (Urbana: University of Illinois Press, 1986), 144.

19. Clifford Geertz, *The Interpretation of Cultures* (New York: Basic Books 1973), 316. While the literature that charts the paradigm shift in history from questions of causality and the search for origins is extensive and growing, the following are particularly helpful in linking recent trends to gender and labor history: Scott, "On Language, Gender, and Working-Class History," *International Labor and Working Class History* 31 (Spring 1987): 1–13; Mari Jo Buhle and Paul Buhle, "The New Labor History at the Cultural Crossroads," *Journal of American History* 75 (June 1988): 151–57; Lynn Hunt, ed., *The New Cultural History* (Berkeley: University of California Press, 1989), see esp. chaps. 1, 2; Susan Porter Benson, *Presenting the Past: Essays on History and the Public* (Philadelphia: Temple University Press, 1986), 424; Hewitt, " 'The Voice of Virile Labor.' "

20. Robert Darnton, *The Great Cat Massacre and Other Episodes in French Cultural History* (New York: Vintage Books, 1985), 192–93. For the most important figure in the rethinking of historical categories and analyses of power, see Michel Foucault, *Power/Knowledge: Selected Interviews & Other Writings, 1972–1977,* trans. and ed. Colin Gordon (New York: Pantheon Books, 1980), 82. Among the many essays on Foucault, I have relied most heavily on Patricia O'Brien, "Michel Foucault's History of Culture," in *The New Cultural History,* ed. Lynn Hunt (Berkeley: University of California Press, 1989): 25–46; Mark Poster, "The Tyranny of Greece," in *Foucault: A Critical Reader,* ed. David C. Hoy (New York: B. Blackwell, 1986): 205–20; White, *Tropics of Discourse,* chap. 11; Poster, "Foucault and History," *Social Research* 49 (1982): 116–42.

21. Scott, in Elaine Abelson, David Abraham, and Marjorie Murphy, "Interview with Joan Scott," *Radical History Review* 45 (Fall 1989): 52. See also Riley, *"Am I That Name?";* John Tagg, *The Burden of Representation: Essays on Photographies and Histories* (Amherst: University of Massachusetts Press, 1988).

22. For a discussion of the relationship between periods of social stress and conservative fears over the decline of "the family," see Linda Gordon, *Heroes of Their Own Lives: The Politics and History of Family Violence* (New York: Viking Penguin, 1988), 3–7.

23. Mary Ryan, *Womanhood in America: From Colonial Times to the Present* (New York: New Viewpoints, 1975), 164, chap. 6 generally; and Carroll Smith-Rosenberg, *Disorderly Conduct: Visions of Gender in Victorian America* (New York: Oxford University Press, 1985), 245–96.

24. Smith-Rosenberg, *Disorderly Conduct,* 283.

25. John F. W. Meagher, "Homosexuality: Its Psychobiological and Psycho-pathological Significance," *Urologic and Cutaneous Review* 33 (1929): 511, cited in Smith-Rosenberg, *Disorderly Conduct,* 283.

26. Hall, "Partial Truths," p. 909. For a more detailed discussion of these ideas and their usefulness for historians, see Scott, "Gender: A Useful Category of Historical Analysis," *American Historical Review* 91, no. 5 (Dec. 1986): 1053–75; Leslie Wahl Rabine, "A Feminist Politics of Non-Identity," *Feminist Studies* 14, no. 1 (Spring 1988): 11–32; "Why Gender and History?" *Gender and History* 1, no. 1 (Spring 1989): 1–6.

27. American examples of those changes are found most clearly in Alice Kessler-Harris, "Gender Ideology in Historical Reconstruction; A Case Study from the 1930s," *Gender and History* 1, no. 1 (Spring 1989): 31–49; Blewett, *Men, Women,* 124–31, 137–41, 189–90; Stansell, *City of Women.* See also, Dublin, *Women at Work;* Carol Karlsen, *The Devil in the Shape of a Woman: Witchcraft in Colonial New England* (New York: Vintage Books, 1989), 75; J. Meyerowitz, *Women Adrift: Independent Wage Earners in Chicago, 1880–1930* (Chicago: University of Chicago Press, 1988).

28. Tagg, *Burden,* 171; Michel Foucault, *Order of Things* and *Power/Knowledge.*

29. Abelson et al, "Interview with Joan Scott," 52.

30. Teresa de Lauretis, *Alice Doesn't: Feminism, Semiotics, Cinema,* (Bloomington: Indiana University Press, 1984), 5.

31. Margaret Mead, *Blackberry Winter: My Earlier Years* (New York: Morrow, 1972), 305; Foucault, *Power/Knowledge,* 81–83.

32. Scott, *Gender,* 61;

33. "Working Woman's Statement," 156.

34. Culled from newspaper accounts, hospital files, government reports, arrest records, and oral histories, the names of striking women were first traced for correct spellings and for place of birth, names of parents and, if married, husband's last name, in Records of Vital Statistics, Massachusetts Department of Vital Statistics. Names were then traced in the federal Manuscript Census Schedules for 1910, where information on age, ethnicity, household structure, family structure, occupation, length of residency, marital status, and birth place was added to create an "activist file" for women strikers.

35. "A Working Woman's Statement," also quoted in Ardis Cameron, "Bread and Roses Revisited: Women's Culture and Working-Class Activism in the Lawrence Strike of 1912," in *Women, Work and Protest,* ed. Ruth Milkman (Boston: Routledge, 1985).

Chapter 1: The "Woman Question" and Self-supporting Women

1. The most complete history of the Pemberton Mill is found in Clarisse A. Poirier, "Pemberton Mills."

2. Phelps, "The Tenth of January," in *The Silent Partner: A Novel and "The Tenth of January: A Short Story"* (New York: Feminist Press, 1983), reprint edition with an afterword by Mari Jo Buhle and Florence Howe, 306.

3. Donald B. Cole, "The Fall of the Pemberton," *Essex Institute* 96 (1960): 47–55.

4. For descriptions of the collapse see Poirier, "Pemberton Mills," and Cole, "The Fall of the Pemberton," 31. For a contemporary fictional account see, Phelps, "The Tenth of January," 306.

5. Poirier, "Pemberton Mills," 243–44.

6. *Boston Journal,* Jan. 19, 1860; Poirier, "Pemberton Mills," 96; "Third Annual Report of the Patrons of Lawrence City Mission," *Lawrence City Mission,* 13–14; Charles S. Storrow to Amos A. Lawrence, Jan. 21, 1860, MS MATH; Committee of Relief for the Sufferers by the Fall of the Pemberton Mill, *Records,* Box C, MATH.

7. Ware, *Early New England Cotton Manufacture,* 278.

8. Phelps, *Chapters from a Life,* 89.

9. *Vanity Fair,* Jan. 21, 1860.

10. Mari Jo Buhle, *Women and American Socialism, 1870–1920* (Urbana: University of Illinois Press, 1981).

11. "The myth that 'all men support all women,' " was, according to Mary Rice Livermore, "long known to be false." Buhle, *Women and American Socialism,* 51. The gender consciousness of the "Woman's Movement" is best explored in Buhle, Ibid., 49–94.

12. "Working Woman's Statement," 155.

13. Ibid.

14. Buhle, *Women and American Socialism,* 50.

15. Virginia Penny, *Employments of Women: A Cyclopaedia of Woman's Work* (Boston: Walker, Wise, & Co., 1863), v.

16. The only exception was the Catholic Friends Society, established in 1856 by the "Grey Nuns," the Sisters of Charity. Katherine O'Keefe, *Sketch of Catholicity in Lawrence and Vicinity* (Lawrence, Massachusetts, 1882), 44–45.

17. "First Annual Report," Ladies Union Charitable Society of Lawrence, (hereafter LUCS), 1875, Archives of the Lawrence General Hospital.

18. "Twelfth Annual Report to the Patrons of Lawrence City Mission," Lawrence City Mission, 1871, 13–14; "Report of the President," LUCS, 1881.

19. Harriet Beecher Stowe, *Pink and White Tyranny: A Society Novel* (Boston: Roberts Brothers, 1871).

20. *Andover Advertiser,* Feb. 25, 1858.

21. Stowe, *Pink and White,* 47.

22. Buhle, *Women and American Socialism,* 57.

23. Quoted in Poirier, "Pemberton Mills," 201; Caroline Dall, *Woman's Right to Labor; Or, Low Wages and Hard Work* (Boston, 1860), vii.

24. Dolores Hayden, *The Grand Domestic Revolution; A History of Feminist Design for American Homes, Neighborhoods, and Cities* (Cambridge, Mass.: MIT Press, 1981), 152.

25. Elizabeth Stuart Phelps, "The Higher Claim," *Independent* (Oct. 5, 1871): 1.

26. The best single source for an overview of the Gilded Age Woman's Movement is Buhle, *Women and American Socialism,* esp. chaps. 2, 3. On the political aspirations of the antebellum woman's rights movement, see Ellen Carol DuBois, *Feminism and Suffrage: The Emergence of an Independent Women's Movement in America, 1848–1869* (Ithaca, N.Y.: Cornell University Press, 1978). A community study that offers a full and insightful analysis of antebellum women's activism is Nancy Hewitt, *Women's Activism.* Nancy Cott, *The Grounding of Modern Feminism* (New Haven: Yale University Press, 1987), provides a useful and illuminating interpretation of feminism in the early decades of the twentieth century.

27. Phelps, "Higher Claim," 1.

28. Mary Rice Livermore, *What Shall We Do with Our Daughters* (Boston, 1883), 204–5.

29. Phelps, "Higher Claim," 1.

30. Dolores Hayden, *Grand Domestic Revolution,* 77–113.

31. "Reports," LUCS, Oct. 1, 1885.

32. Ibid., 1881, 1885.

33. *Lawrence Daily American* (hereafter *American*), Sept. 11, 1869.

34. *Lawrence Sentinel,* (hereafter *Sentinel*), July 31, Sept. 9, 1868; Aug. 1, Sept. 4, 9, 1869; Feb. 17, Apr. 7, 1882; *Lawrence Daily Eagle* (hereafter *Eagle*), June 18, 1877; Mar. 6, 13, 1882; Spring, 1895. Poirier, "Pemberton Mills," 201.

35. *Eagle,* Mar. 2, 1882; Apr. 28, 1877.

36. *Eagle,* Sept. 11, 1869.

37. Ellen DuBois, *Feminism and Suffrage,* 66.

38. *American,* Sept. 11, 1869.

39. Buhle, *Women and American Socialism,* 55.

40. Descriptions of Pemberton victims from *Order Book . . . Ward Inspectors' Lists of Victims to Visit,* (hereafter *Order Book*), Jan. 16, 1860, MS, 117.10, MATH.

41. Cole, "The Fall of the Pemberton," 51.

42. Dorgan, *History of Lawrence,* 147.

43. Horace A. Wadsworth, *History of Lawrence, Massachusetts* (Lawrence, Mass., 1880), 93.

44. Kessler-Harris, *Out to Work,* 144.

45. Ware, *Early New England Cotton,* 234–35.

46. Kessler-Harris, *Out to Work,* 64.

47. Cole, *Immigrant City: Lawrence, Massachusetts, 1845–1921* (Chapel Hill: University of North Carolina Press, 1963); table 4, p. 210.

48. Poirier, "Pemberton Mills," 126, 132–33. Irish newcomers increasingly entered the city's mills, although native girls from economically depressed sections of New England continued to enter the mills in sizable numbers.

49. Poirier, "Pemberton Mills" tables 7, 10, 11, pp. 128–35. Throughout the state, male participation in the cotton work force increased by an annual rate of almost 5 percent. For the state as a whole, 38 percent of cotton workers in 1860 were men, as opposed to 34 percent in 1850. As Poirier has demonstrated, Lawrence reflected this trend, so that while women continued to dominate the shop floor, (by 2–1 in the Pemberton Mill), male operatives increasingly took over jobs once held solely by women and girls.

50. Quoted in Massachusetts Bureau of Statistics of Labor, *Thirteenth Annual Report* (1882), 220. (Hereafter BSL.)

51. By this I do not mean to deny the possibility that women might choose to be single. In fact, many Anglo, middle-class women did exactly that in the decades both before and after the Civil War. However, whenever poor women in general, and Irish women in particular, lived in cities where sex ratios were more equal, they did marry. Often they married late, at times reluctantly, but in a world of constrained possibilities, marriage offered what factories could not: the promise of a better life. See Hasia R. Diner, *Erin's Daughters in America: Irish Immigrant Women in the Nineteenth Century* (Baltimore: Johns Hopkins University Press, 1983), 99–103; Barbara Taylor, *Eve and the New Jerusalem: Socialism and Feminism in the Nineteenth Century* (New York: Pantheon Books, 1983), 110–12.

52. *Eagle*, Apr. 12, 1882.

53. "Population and Sex," *Massachusetts Census of 1875*, 4.

54. Poirier, "Pemberton Mills," 226.

55. BSL, *Thirteenth Annual Report* (1882), 202.

56. Carroll D. Wright, *Massachusetts Census of 1875*, vols. 1, 2, Boston, 1876–77, 57–70. In his study of Polish immigrants to Lawrence, Siergiej notes that as late as 1910, "the Commonwealth was the only state in the country with an excess of females in the foreign element of the population." Native women typically outnumbered males in New England and in urban areas in general. Dania L. Siergiej, "Early Polish Immigrants to Lawrence, Massachusetts: European Background and Statistical Profile" (Master's thesis, Tufts University, 1977), 48–49. A report in 1816 listed 66,000 women, 24,000 boys, and 10,000 men employed in the nation's cotton mills. See Ryan, *Womanhood*, 54. See also Frank L. Mott, "Portrait of an American Mill Town: Demographic Responses in Mid-Nineteenth Century Warren, Rhode Island," *Population Studies* (Mar. 1972): 156; Daniel Walkowitz, "Working-Class Women in the Gilded Age: Factory, Community and Family Life in Cohoes, New York, Cotton Workers,"

Journal of Social History 5, no, 49 (Summer 1972): 464–90; Turbin, "Reconceptualizing Family," 1–16; Edith Abbott, *Women in Industry: A Study in American Economic History* (New York, 1919), 46, 85, 275; and Dublin, *Women at Work*, 26, 29, 141–42, 198.

57. Charles Elliott, "Work and Wages of Women," *North American Review*, 135:146.

58. *Massachusetts Census of 1875*, 57–70, xxviii–xxxv.

59. Elliott, "Work and Wages of Women," 146.

60. Occupations are derived from a street analysis of three neighborhoods: the Plains Central, the Everett, and the Corporate Reserve.

61. Orchard Street, for example, was composed almost entirely of skilled mill men, overseers, craftsmen, and their families. As one moves closer to the Everett, however, operatives dominate the households.

62. Fifteen years after the war, over 80 percent of the female operatives living in the Plains were of Irish ancestry, many of them boarding with widows or families not their own. BSL, *Thirteenth Annual Report* (1882), 285, table 1; Poirier, "Pemberton Mills," 155–56; Cole, "The Collapse of the Pemberton Mill," 27–28.

63. Poirier, "Pemberton Mills," 293. The 1880 federal manuscript schedules further suggest the transition to the Plains and suggest the mixed nature of boarding houses. While corporate houses continued to provide for single women, few were segregated and many included married women, some without husbands present. One house at 22 Orchard St. rented only to German men, but this was the exception, most containing more heterogeneous populations. More typically, however, female operatives lived in houses beyond the Corporate Reserve.

64. The number of males per 100 females by ward and ethnicity are as follows for 1875:

	Ethnicity			
Ward	English	Irish	Scots	Canada
1	102	66	48	69
2	112	67	60	49
3	103	63	42	60
4	94	70	84	75
5	94	92	95	90
6	100	85	104	87

Based on *Massachusetts Census of 1875*, 287–339. See also Donald B. Cole, *Immigrant City*. See table 5, p. 211, for general population statistics in Lawrence. Estimates of the ethnicity of the labor force are derived from Wadsworth, *History of Lawrence*, 88. In 1875, Wards 1, 2, and 3, began at the Merrimac River and radiated outward towards Methuan, including the Plains, the Arlington, and the suburban neighborhoods north of the Spicket River. The Arlington district was almost exclusively English and Scottish, as the mills there consistently preferred these groups to the Irish. French Canadians predominated in Wards 4 and 5, beyond the Plains, while Irish dominated in the Plains along with a sprinkling of Scots and French Canadians. Ethnic figures from the *1875 Census,* therefore, are fairly reliable in reflecting neighborhood data. The influx of "new" immigrants in the 1890's as well as the gerrymandering of wards would change this, making neighborhoods less reflective of ward statistics.

65. *Massachusetts Census of 1875.*

66. Based on Manuscript Census schedules for Lawrence, 1880. Neighborhoods sampled include the following: Everett, Corporate Reserve, and Plains. All households containing a female mill operative were recorded for the following streets: Newbury, Garden, Orchard, Jackson, Essex, Methuen, Canal, Maple, Chestnut, Elm, Oak, Short, Lincoln, White and Turner.

67. Poirier, "Pemberton Mills," 139. See table 2 for 1880 figures. Percentages here represent the number of married women combined with widows from all three neighborhoods, a total of 56 out of 230, or 24.3 percent. Ages are also compiled from neighborhood data, Table 2.

68. "Order Book . . . January 16, 1860. Ward Inspectors Lists of Victims to Visit," MS MATH 117.10. Pemberton. Letter by George P. Wilson to "Gentleman of the Committee," *Reports of Inspectors of the Pemberton Relief Committee* MATH, MS, 1.2.

69. Of the 116 victims listed in the "Order Book of January 16, 1860," 88 cases contained information concerning the living arrangements of victims. Ten lived with husbands, eleven with both parents, while the remaining 66 lived in boarding situations that included 29 households headed by women. In Buffalo, New York, almost 1 in 5 Irish households was headed by a woman. Ellen Horgan Biddle, "The American Catholic Irish Family," in *Ethnic Families in America: Patterns and Variations,* ed. Charles H. Mindel and Robert W. Habenstein (New York: Elsever, 1976), 101.

70. Blewett, *Men, Women and Work,* see esp. 208, 213, 292; Kessler-Harris, *Out to Work;* Turbin, "Reconceptualizing Family."

71. For a detailed analysis of lodgers and boarders in late nineteenth century, see Mark Peel, "On the Margins: Lodgers and Boarders in Boston, 1860–1900," *Journal of American History,* 72, no.4 (Mar. 1986): 813–34. For a discussion of the strolling poor, see Bruce C. Daniels, *The Fragmentation of New England: Comparative Perspectives on Economic, Political, and Social Divisions in the Eighteenth Century* (New York: Greenwood Press, 1988), 47.

72. Aggravated by the depression of 1873, the situation was only slightly more dramatic than in 1860 when fully one-third of the Pemberton victims investigated lived in female-headed households, and a scant 10 percent occupied

homes where two parents were in residence. The 1880 figures are derived from "Sample of Female Millhands," compiled from *U.S. Manuscript Census Schedules, Lawrence, Mass., 1880.* For statistics on the Pemberton, see "Order Book," MS 117.10.

73. Meyerowitz, *Women Adrift,* xvii; Katz, *People of Hamilton,* 60; Kessler-Harris, *Out to Work,* 77.

74. Meyerowitz, *Adrift,* chaps. 4, 5.

75. Statistics on sisters from "Sample of Female Mill Hands, 1880."

76. *Sentinel,* June 16, 1882. Several recent studies illustrate the importance and widespread influence of these debates in the Gilded Age. For the importance of the home to populists, socialists, and women reformers, see Buhle, *Women and American Socialism,* 87, 117–18, 134, 167–68, 220; Dolores Hayden, *Grand Domestic Revolution,* provides a full and insightful analysis of the place of the home in Gilded Age politics.

77. *Sentinel,* June 16, 1882. The Boston Co-Operative Building Company, organized in 1871 by reformers Abby W. May and Anna Cabot Lodge, sought "to hold and improve real estate in said city as homes for working people." Recognizing the need for houses that freed laboring women from domestic duties, they also made plans for a set of model houses in Lawrence. That same year, The Women's Economical Garden Homestead League organized to "establish industrial homestead settlements in or near the city" of Boston. One scheme involved buying a tract of three hundred house-lots in Lawrence "with a view of aiding the factory-women of that city." The land was purchased, but like the model houses of the Boston Building Company, the goals were never reached after a fire in 1872 depleted the funds of both groups. BSL *Eighth Annual Report* (1877), 91; BSL *Fourth Annual Report* (1874), 263–65.

78. BSL, *Thirteenth Annual Report* (1877), 202.

79. Descriptions of individual women from "Order Book." Lawrence families consistently outnumbered buildings in the years following the war. *Lawrence City Directory,* 1870, 1875, 1880.

80. *Lawrence Courier* (hereafter *Courier*), Jan. 19, 1860.

81. For a detailed discussion of the importance of neighbors and friends in Italian and Jewish immigrant communities, see Smith, *Family Connections,* 106–7. For the role of "fictive" kin in black neighborhoods, see Carol Stack, *All Our Kin* (New York: Harper and Row, 1975), and Jacqueline Jones, *Labor of Love, Labor of Sorrow: Black Women, Work, and the Family from Slavery to the Present* (New York: Basic Books, c1992), 30–31.

82. Hasia R. Diner, *Erin's Daughters,* 102–3.

83. *American,* Oct. 13, 1865.

84. Stansell, *City of Women,* esp. 138. For more detailed studies that explore the history of the family wage as a class strategy, see Martha May, "Bread and Roses: American Workingmen, Labor Unions, and the Family

Wage," in Milkman, *Women, Work and Protest,* 1–21; May, "The Historical Problem of the Family Wage; The Ford Motor Company and the Five Dollar Day," *Feminist Studies* 8, no. 2 (Summer 1982).

85. Barbara Taylor, *Eve and the New Jerusalem,* 112. Debates over the development and form of working-class domesticity are discussed in Stansell, *City of Women,* esp. 22, 64, 138; Susan Levine, "Labor's True Women," *Journal of American History* 2 (Sept. 1983): 322–39; Sean Wilentz, *Chants Democratic: New York City and the Rise of the American Working Class, 1788–1850* (New York: Oxford University Press, 1984), 248–49; Blewett, *Men, Women and Work.*

86. Geertz, *The Interpretation of Cultures,* 220.

87. The classic work that first called attention to the disputed authority of the manufacturer in the late nineteenth century is Gutman's, *Work, Culture and Society,* 262–72.

88. *Eagle,* Apr. 3, 1877. For an insightful analysis of domestic violence and working-class family life, see Linda Gordon, *Heroes of Their Own Lives;* Barbara Taylor, *Eve and the New Jerusalem;* Nancy Tomes, "A 'Torrent of Abuse': Crimes of Violence Between Working-Class Men and Women in London, 1840–75," *Journal of Social History* 11 (1978): 332.

89. Geertz, *The Interpretation of Cultures,* 221.

90. *Courier,* Apr. 10, 1855.

91. Ibid.

92. *Sentinel,* July 31, 1868.

93. Ibid., July 31, 1868.

94. Ibid., Mar. 24, 1882.

95. BSL, *Thirteenth Annual Report* (1882), 203.

96. Ibid., 203.

97. "Working Women's Statement," 156.

98. *Eagle,* Jan. 27, 1882.

99. Turbin, "Reconceptualizing Family."

100. *Sentinel,* Jan. 14, 1860; *Courier,* Jan. 14, 21, 28, 1860; *New York Times,* Jan. 11–17, 19, Feb. 4, 1860.

101. Women's attitudes toward textile labor varied, of course, according to a number of factors including race, region, and both the type of textile product produced and the character of the textile industry during the time of employment. Woolens, for example, required more highly skilled workers than did cotton, and the Pemberton, whose products included fancy cottonades that resembled wool, required large numbers of semiskilled and skilled women. Similar findings among Gilded Age textile workers in Cohoes, New York, are discussed in Turbin, "Reconceptualizing Family." Oral histories support studies that argue for greater complexity among women workers and confirm that for many women, especially those in skilled positions, textile labor was a point of

pride and status among operatives. For studies of Southern mill women, see Jacquelyn Dowd Hall, et al., *Like a Family: The Making of a Southern Cotton Mill World* (Chapel Hill: University of North Carolina Press, 1987), esp. 74–77, 154; Victoria Morris Byerly, *Hard Times Cotton Mill Girls: Personal Histories of Womanhood and Poverty in the South* (Ithaca, N.Y.: ILR Press, New York State School of Industrial and Labor Relations, Cornell University, 1986).

102. Christine Stansell, "The Origins of the Sweatshop: Women and Early Industrialization in New York City," in *Working-Class America: Essays on Labor, Community, and American Society,* ed. Michael H. Frisch and Daniel J. Walkowitz (Urbana: University of Illinois Press, 1983), 95.

103. Myrna M. Breitbart and Martha A. Ackelsberg, "Terrains of Protest: Reappropriation of Space and Transformation of Consciousness in Urban Struggle" (Paper in author's possession). See also Ackelsberg, "Women's Collaborative Activities and City Life: Politics and Policy," in *Political Women: Current Roles in State and Local Government,* ed. Janet Flamming, vol. 8 of *Sage Yearbooks in Women's Policy Studies* (Beverly Hills, Calif.: Sage Publications, 1984), 242–59.

Chapter 2: Women, Consciousness, and Militancy

1. *Eagle,* Mar. 14, 1882. No name was given at the time of this speech. Later references imply that it was given by Halley.

2. *Lawrence Journal,* May 27, 1882.

3. *Eagle,* Mar. 21, 1882.

4. BSL, *Thirteenth Annual Report* (1882), iii.

5. *Lawrence Journal,* Apr. 1, 1882.

6. *Eagle,* Mar. 17, 1882.

7. *Eagle,* Mar. 22; *New York Times,* Mar. 27, 1882.

8. *Eagle,* Mar. 22, 1882.

9. Ibid.

10. *Lawrence Journal,* May 6, 1882.

11. *Lawrence Journal.* Mar. 18, 1882.

12. *Eagle,* Mar. 14; *Lawrence Journal,* Mar. 17, 18, 22, 1882.

13. *Eagle,* Mar. 16, 1882.

14. *Eagle,* Mar. 14, 1992.

15. *Lawrence Journal,* June 3, 1882.

16. "A Working Woman's Statement," *Nation* (Feb. 21, 1867): 156.

17. *Boston Evening Voice,* Feb. 27, 1867.

18. *Lawrence Journal,* Apr. 1, 1882.

19. *Lawrence Journal,* Apr. 29, May 6, 1882; *Eagle,* Apr. 2, 1882.

20. For descriptions of the shop floor intimidation, see *Eagle,* Mar. 14, 1882; *Tribune,* May 14, 1902.

21. To rural New Englanders "calico," a plain muslin, was more than a cloth. Harking back to revolutionary days, when it was synonymous with homespun, calico conjured up a set of images rooted in republican virtue. In the decades following the Civil War, "dress" took on new and more complex meanings as small town residents and old families suddenly found themselves confronted by both a growing population of factory workers and a status-hungry class of factory owners, managers, and business associates. For an increasingly class-conscious middle class, clothing worked to distinguish the boundaries between "the good, orderly, and respectable" and "the loud or noisy or pretentious." Calico—plain, simple, and practical—connoted the former, while silk, makeup, and lace, signified the latter. In her "society novel" *Pink and White Tyranny,* Stowe uses a plethora of material objects to show how the "true blue"—those New England families of "ancestral reputation"—differentiated themselves from "the vulgar, pushing class." Food, furniture, gardens, art, decoration, as well as dress, were vehicles that marked boundaries and revealed inner character. Like many rural Americans who sought to come to terms with the "topsy-turvy" world of post–Civil War America, Stowe represents differences between these groups, not in terms of class—that is, according to categories of ownership—but rather according to "genial qualities" of dress, especially women's fashions. The parvenue industrialist whose wife appeared overly adorned in French silks and bonnets was as "shoddy" as any overdressed mill girl. There may be no accounting for taste, but in rural New England there was a way to measure it. See Stowe, *Pink and White Tyranny,* 185, 188.

22. BSL, *Thirteenth Annual Report* (1882), 216.

23. *Eagle,* Mar. 13, 20, 21, 1882.

24. *Eagle,* Mar. 18, 1882.

25. *Sentinel,* Mar. 17, 1882.

26. *Eagle,* Apr. 24, 1882.

27. *Eagle,* Mar. 14, 16, 1882.

28. *Eagle,* Apr. 1, Mar. 18, 1882.

29. *Eagle,* Apr. 24; *Lawrence Journal,* June 3, 1882.

30. *Eagle,* Mar. 17, 1882.

31. *Eagle,* Mar. 16, 17, 1882.

32. *Eagle,* Mar. 20, 1882.

33. *Sentinel,* Mar. 31; Apr. 21, 1882.

34. *Journal,* Apr. 1, 1882.

35. Ibid. July 22, 1882.

36. Ibid. Apr. 8, 1882.

37. Ibid. May, 6, 1882.

38. A number of studies now chronicle women's as well as men's resistance to the degradation of work. See Patricia Cooper, *Once a Cigar Maker: Men,*

Women and Work Culture in American Cigar Factories, 1900–1919, (Urbana: University of Illinois Press, 1988); Blewett, *Men, Women, and Work;* Kessler-Harris, *Out to Work.*

39. *Eagle,* Apr. 24, 1882.

40. *Sentinel,* Apr. 21, 1882.

41. *Sentinel,* Apr. 6, 1967.

42. *Lawrence Journal,* May 27, 1882.

43. *Eagle,* Mar. 25, 1882.

44. *Eagle,* Apr. 17, 1882.

45. *Lawrence Journal,* Mar. 25, 1882.

46. *Sentinel,* Mar. 25, 1882.

47. *Lawrence Journal,* Mar. 21, 1882.

48. Cole, *Immigrant City,* 120.

49. Ibid., 120–21.

50. BSL, *Thirteenth Annual Report* (1882), 349.

51. Jean-Claude G. Simon, "Textile Workers, Trade Unions and Politics: Comparative Case Studies, France and the United States, 1885–1914" (Ph.D. diss., Tufts University, 1983,) 24.

52. Ibid., 22; Cole, "The Collapse of the Pemberton Mill," 103.

53. BSL, *Thirteenth Annual Report* (1882), 293. On information concerning mill banks, see *Pacific Corporation,* 10; Fred Kiami, "Early Industrial Relations in Lawrence, Massachusetts" (Master's thesis, Boston University, 1951), 45.

54. "27th item of the will of Abbott Lawrence," Sept. 10, 1855, Baker Library, Harvard University.

55. *Eagle,* Mar. 11, 1882.

56. Cole, *Immigrant City,* 54.

57. Sean Wilentz, *Chants Democratic; New York City and the Rise of the American Working Class, 1788–1850* (New York: Oxford University Press, 1984), 249–48.

58. *Eagle,* Apr. 25, 1882.

59. Kiami, "Early Industrial Relations," 32.

60. *Eagle,* Mar. 22, 1882.

61. *Sentinel,* Mar. 24, 31, 1882.

62. *Lawrence Journal,* Apr. 8, 1882; *Sentinel,* Apr. 7, 1882.

63. *Sentinel,* Mar. 31, 1882.

64. *Sentinel,* June 16, 1882; *Lawrence Journal,* May 27, June 3, 17, 24, 1882.

65. *Lawrence Journal,* July 1, 1882.

66. *Lawrence Journal,* Mar. 25, 1882.

67. *Eagle,* Apr. 10, 11, 1882.

68. *Eagle,* Mar. 21, 1882.

69. *Lawrence Journal,* Apr. 8, 1882.

70. *Lawrence Evening Tribune,* Jan. 16, 1902.

71. *Journal*, July 22, 1885.

72. Harry Braverman, *Labor and Monopoly Capital: The Degradation of Work in the Twentieth Century* (New York: Monthly Review Press, 1975); David Montgomery, *Workers Control in America: Studies in the History of Work, Technology, and Labor Struggle* (New York: Cambridge University Press, 1979).

73. *Eagle*, Mar. 17, 1882.

74. *Eagle*, Mar. 18, 1882.

75. *New York Times*, Mar. 27, 1882.

76. *Eagle*, Mar. 25, 1882.

77. For a general discussion of deskilling and the responses of male craftsmen and skilled workers, see David Montgomery, "Worker's Control of Machine Production in the Nineteenth Century," *Labor History* 17 (Fall 1976): 485–509; Ava Baron, "Questions of Gender: Deskilling and Demasculinization in the United States Printing Industry, 1830–1915," *Gender and History* 1 (Summer 1989): 178–99.

78. BSL, *Thirteenth Annual Report* (1882), 202–3.

79. Ibid., 202.

80. Ibid.

81. For a similar reaffirmation, see Blewett, *Men, Women*, 116.

82. *Sentinel*, Apr. 7, 1882; *Journal*, Oct. 30, 1886. For a discussion on the uses of the past as a element in the construction of class solidarity, see Francis Hearn, *Domination, Legitimation, and Resistance: The Incorporation of the Nineteenth Century English Working Class* (Westport, Conn.: Greenwood Press, 1978), chap. 1. As a form of resistance to change and as a way to "deplore the present," see James C. Scott, *Weapons of the Weak: Everyday Forms of Peasant Resistance* (New Haven: Yale University Press, 1985), 178.

83. *Lawrence Journal*, Aug. 12, Sept. 23, Oct. 30, 1882.

84. On the role of tradition as an active participant in the construction of the "folk," see Dell Hymes, "Folklore's Nature and the Sun's Myth," *Journal of American Folklore* 88 (Oct.–Dec. 1975): 353–54.

85. *Lawrence Journal*, Oct. 30, 1886.

86. This discussion draws on Joan Scott, "On Language, Gender, and Working-Class History," 1–14. On the concept of gender, see Scott, "Gender: A Useful Category," 1053–75.

87. See, for example, the arguments of suffrage leader Anna Howard Shaw who argued that the labor of married women in the home was true work, the mainstay of home and husband: "Women Debate Wife's Economic Relation," *New York Evening Call*, 8 Jan. 1909.

88. *New York Call*, Jan. 23, 1912.

89. "Sixth Annual Report to the Patrons and Families of the Lawrence City Mission," *Lawrence City Mission*, 1865, 15–16. *Lawrence City Documents, 1865–1985*.

90. *Eagle,* Apr. 28, 1887.

91. Gerald N. Grob, "The Political System and Social Policy in the Nineteenth Century: Legacy of the Revolution," *Mid-America* 58 (1976): 5–19.

92. *Journal,* Apr. 29, 1882.

93. Ibid., Apr. 2, 1877.

94. *Lawrence Journal,* Apr. 29, 1882.

95. Smith-Rosenberg, *Disorderly Conduct,* esp. 217–44; Linda Gordon, *Woman's Body, Woman's Right: A Social History of Birth Control in America* (New York: Penguin Books, 1977).

96. "Records," Lawrence Medical Club, Oct. 27, Dec. 22, 1879; Jan. 26, 1880. Archives Lawrence General Hospital.

97. Smith-Rosenberg, *Disorderly Conduct,* 181.

98. Ibid., 245.

99. Nathan Allen, *Journal of Psychological Medicine,* quoted in Mary Rice Livermore, "Superfluous Women," *Chautauguan* (Dec. 7, 1886): 216.

100. Ibid.

101. Elenor Flexner, *Century of Struggle: The Woman's Rights Movement in the United States* (New York: Atheneum, 1973), 175.

102. Foucault, *Order of Things,* xvii.

103. Senator Vest, quoted in Flexner, *Century of Struggle* 174.

104. "The Wild Woman As Social Insurgent," *Eclectic Magazine* 117 (Nov. 1981): 667–73.

105. A number of studies delineate the outlines of this history. See especially, Paula Baker, "The Domestication of Politics: Women and American Political Society, 1780–1920," *American Historical Review,* 89 (June 1984): 620–47; Barbara Epstein, *The Politics of Domesticity: Women, Evangelism, and Temperance in Nineteenth-Century America* (Middletown, Conn.: Wesleyan University Press, 1981); Wortman, *Domesticating the Nineteenth-Century City.*

106. Baker, "The Domestication of Politics," 647.

107. Ryan, *Womanhood,* 136–37.

108. Jane Addams, *Twenty Years At Hull House,* (New York, 1960), 93. Ryan, *Womanhood,* 136–37.

109. Ryan, *Womanhood,* 136–37.

110. For the best single account of independent wage women in the years before the war, see Meyerowitz, *Women Adrift.* Quote from p. 43.

111. Mark Connelly, *The Response to Prostitution in the Progressive Era* (Chapel Hill; University of North Carolina Press, 1980), 145. See also Stansell, *City of Women,* chap. 4, for an earlier portrait of middle-class images of working women.

112. Ira Stuart, *Boston Evening Voice,* Oct. 13, 1865. See also Stansell, 138; John Commons, et al, *A Documentary History of American Industrial Society*

(New York: Russell & Russell, 1958), 6:282–84; Sean Wilentz, *Chants Democratic*, 364–86; May, "Bread and Roses," 1–21.

113. Buhle, *Women and American Socialism*, 52. For a discussion of the work ethnic in the turn-of-the century woman's movement, see Daniel T. Rogers, *The Work Ethic in Industrial America, 1850–1920* (Chicago: University of Chicago Press, 1974), chapter 7.

114. Gilman's central arguments are contained in Charlotte Perkins Gilman, *Women and Economics: A Study of the Economic Relation between Men and Women As a Factor in Social Evolution* (1898; reprint ed., New York: Harper and Row, 1966). Her definition of work is found in Gilman, "What Work Is," *Cosmopolitan* 27 (1899): 678–82. See also "Women Debate," for the poor reception of her ideas among working-class women.

115. Kessler-Harris, *Out to Work*. See Poster, "Foucault and History," 116–42, for a discussion of the role of "discursive practice" in the construction of hegemony.

116. Robert Tewksbury, *History of Lawrence, Massachusetts*, MS. MATH, 1905. For a detailed discussion of the movement to create a Yankee heritage, see Michael Wallace, "Visiting the Past: History Museums in the United States," in Benson *Presenting the Past*, 140–55.

117. *New York Call*, Jan. 4, 1912.

118. Robert Tewksbury, *History of Lawrence, Massachusetts*, MS. Typescript, chap.19, unnumbered pages. MATH.

119. I adapt this interpretation of remembrance from Scott, chap. 5, "History According to Winners and Losers," *Weapons of the Weak*, 178. Both this chapter and chapter eight, "Hegemony and Consciousness," have shaped the concerns expressed here.

120. *New York Call*, Jan. 4, 1912.

Chapter 3: Immigrant Women and Textile Culture

1. Dorgan, *History of Lawrence*, 145–46; Cole, *Immigrant City*, 68–69. For French-Canadian migration into Lawrence, see Ralph Dominic Vicero, "Immigration of French Canadians to New England, 1840–1900: A Geographical Analysis" (Ph.D. diss., University of Wisconsin, 1968). Jacques Ducharme, *The Shadows of the Trees: The Story of French Canadians in New England* (New York, 1943) and George Theriault, "The Franco-Americans of New England," in *Canadian-American Dualism: Studies of French-English Relations*, ed. Mason Wade (Toronto: University of Toronto Press, 1960), 392–418, also provide valuable information on the role of *la survivance* in Franco-American culture and on Irish-Franco relations in industrial towns.

2. Cole, *Immigrant City*, 11; United States Census Bureau, *Thirteenth Census of the United States . . . 1910: Abstract of the Census . . . with Supplement*

for Massachusetts . . . (Washington, D.C.: GPO, 1913) 596, 609; *Boston Evening Transcript,* Jan. 12, 1912.

3. "The American Woolen Company," *Fortune* 3 (Apr. 1931): 71–112; Arthur Harison Cole, *The American Wool Manufacture,* vol. 2 (Cambridge, Mass., 1926): 239–41. See Edward G. Roddy, *Mills, Mansions and Mergers: The Life of William M. Wood* (North Andover, Mass.: MATH 1982): 33–43, 62–67.

4. Dorgan, *History of Lawrence,* 146. For detailed description of the American Wool Company, see Bulletin of The National Association of Wool Manufacturers, (Boston, Massachusetts), vol. 30, Mar. 1900; p. 16, vol. 35, 1905, p. 258; vol. 36, 1906, p. 136; David J. Goldberg, *A Tale of Three Cities: Labor Organization and Protest in Paterson, Passaic, and Lawrence, 1916–1921,* (New Brunswick: Rutgers University Press, 1989), 84–85. Although the Wood's enormous size and productive capacity was not typical of most textile plants, the American Woolen Company's commitment to expansion was shared by cotton and wool manufacturers throughout the country. In the boom year of 1906, fifty-six new woolen mills were constructed, yet even this represented only three mills more than the annual average for the decade.

5. Immigration Commission, "Woolen and Worsted Goods in Representative Community A," *Immigrants in Industries,* Part 4: Woolen and Worsted Goods Manufacturing, Immigration Commission, *Reports,* X, 61 Congress, 2 Session, Doc. 633. (Washington, D.C.: GPO, 1911) (hereafter, Immigration Commission).

6. Immigration Commission, 771.

7. *Tribune,* Aug. 29, 1903.

8. *Tribune,* Oct. 4, Dec. 15, 1905.

9. Interview with Angelo Rocco, Aug. 11, 1981.

10. Immigration Commission, 741–56.

11. Martha Brown, interview with author, Aug. 12, 1981.

12. Immigration Commission, 795; W. J. Lauck, "Investigations of the United States Immigration Commission," *Survey,* 27 (Mar. 1912): 1773.

13. The only exception to this pattern was among the Polish between 1910–20, Siergiej, "Early Polish Immigrants," 186.

14. Ibid., table 22, pp. 186–95.

15. Louise Seymore Houghton, "Syrians in the United States," *Survey* 26 (1908): 484, 486, 487–88.

16. See Smith, *Family Connections,* chap. 1.

17. Lauck, "Investigations," 1773.

18. Immigration Commission, 756.

19. Donna Gabaccia, "Sicilians in Space: Environmental Change and Family Geography," *Journal of Social History* 16 (1983): 21–22.

20. Typically women used their skills in the cottage industry to convert income into luxury items such as "pots, silver buckles, or coral earrings. Others

were skilled as "midwives, shopkeepers, seamstresses, or at the least, as field workers who could sew, make brooms, straw articles, or embroidery." Gabaccia, "Sicilians in Space," 53.

21. Immigration Commission, 771.

22. Ibid., 656.

23. "Detailed Expenditures for Food of Two Families and of Three Lodgers, by Race, Aug. and Oct. 1911," table B, pp. 82–83. Charles P. Neill, *Report on Strike of Textile Workers in Lawrence, Massachusetts in 1912*, 62 Congress, 2 Session, Senate Doc. 870 (Washington, D.C.: GPO, 1912). In a city plagued by the overproduction of woolen cloth, it would take her between three and six weeks to buy her husband a woolen suit, two to three weeks to buy herself a dress, and three to five weeks to secure a new suit. Ibid., 179e.

24. Ibid., 82–83.

25. John Bodner, *Immigration and Industrialization: Ethnicity in an American Mill Town, 1870–1940* (Pittsburgh: University of Pittsburgh Press, 1977).

26. Immigration Commission, 770.

27. Nagib Abdou, *Dr. Abdou's Travels in America* (Washington, 1907), 68, 80; *Tribune*, Aug. 3, 1900, Nov. 7, 1901; Cole, *Immigrant City*, 69–70; Houghton, "Syrians in the U.S.," 495.

28. Houghton, "Syrians in the U.S.," 487.

29. W. J. Lauck, "The Significance of the Situation at Lawrence: The Condition of the New England Worsted Operative," *Survey*, Mar. 1912, 1773; Houghton, "Syrians in the U.S.," 489; Chief of the Bureau of Statistics of Labor, *Massachusetts Census of 1905*, 1 (Boston, 1909), 109. Like the Jews in Russia who found their traditional relationships between Nobles and peasants undermined by the abolition of serfdom and their livelihoods eroded by international competition and industrialization, Syrian Christians increasingly found themselves destitute in a hostile land. For many, emigration to America seemed the only solution, and villagers educated in local church schools founded by Wolcot's father responded to the son's encouraging reports from Lawrence. Between 1900 and 1910, Syrians migrated to Lawrence in a chain that steadily drew more than three thousand Christians from the Mt. Lebanon sections, making it the largest Syrian community in America outside New York City. Cole, *Immigrant City*, 12, 20; Houghton, "Syrians in the U.S.," 492.

30. Cole, *Immigrant City*, 71; Todd and Sanborn, *Report of the Lawrence Survey*, 54–60, 87.

31. Cole, *Immigrant City*, 72; Todd and Sanborn, *Report of the Lawrence Survey*.

32. Cole, *Immigrant City*, 11; *Boston Evening Transcript*, Jan. 12, 1912; United States Census Bureau, *Thirteenth Census of the United States . . . 1910: Abstract of the Census . . . with Supplement for Massachusetts* (Washington, D.C.: GPO, 1913), 596, 609.

33. Todd and Sanborn, *Report of the Lawrence Survey,* 87; BSL, *Forty-Third Annual Report* (1912), 18.

34. Amelia Stundza, Oral History Project (hereafter OHP), Immigrant City Archives, (hereafter ICA), interviewed by Jonas Stundza, June 7, 1979, folder #24.

35. Ezilda Murphy, OHP, ICA, Interviewed by Clarisse A. Poirier, June 27, 1979, folder #48.

36. Manuscript Census Schedules, United States Census Bureau. *Thirteenth Census...*1910. Lawrence, Massachusetts.

37. Todd and Sanborn, *Report of the Lawrence Survey,* 57–58, 90.

38. Interview with Rose Angelotti (Capriolo), June 22, 1981.

39. Murphy, OHP, ICA.

40. "Report of Inspector of Buildings," *Lawrence City Documents,* 1906–1907, 8.

41. Todd and Sanborn, *Report of the Lawrence Survey,* 32–33, "Report of Building Inspector," 6–8, 24.

42. Lowell, fearing congestion and "conflagration," prohibited this type of housing in 1906, so that the city contained only 140 such structures. Fall River had 95; Salem, 90; Lynn, 50; New Bedford, 55. Worcester, 60 percent larger than Lawrence, had only 120. Alexander Johnson, ed., *Proceedings of the National Conference of Charities and Correction, 38th Annual Session,* June, 1912, ed. (Fort Wayne, Ind.: Fort Wayne Printing Company).

43. Interview with Anna Marino, Aug. 8, 1881.

44. Todd and Sanborn, *Report of the Lawrence Survey,* 57–58, 90.

45. Elizabeth Vilkaite, interview with author, Oct. 1981.

46. Louise Sciuto, OHP, ICA, Feb. 1982, tape #80, interviewed by Theresa De Pippo.

47. Roger Aziz, OHP, ICA, folder #46.

48. Dora Swartz, interview with author, Aug. 12, 1981; Murphy, OHP.

49. Neill, *Report on Strike,* 182.

50. Anna Marino, interview with author, Aug. 1981.

51. Antonietta Carpinone, interview with author, Oct. 25, 1981.

52. Consiglia Teutonica, interview with author, Sept. 6, 1981.

53. Ibid.

54. Anna Marino, interview with author, June 1981.

55. Eugene R. Declercq and Richard Lacroix, "The Politics and Sociology of the Practice of Immigrant Midwives in Lawrence, Massachusetts, 1890–1920" (Paper presented at the Seventy-Sixth Annual Meeting of the Organization of American Historians, Cincinnati, Ohio, Apr. 6–9, 1983), 2. According to Declercq and Lacroix, midwives attended 19.6 percent of all recorded births in the city in 1900, 38 percent in 1907, and 40.9 percent in 1913. In all, 93 percent of all recorded midwife assisted deliveries were to immigrant mothers. Ibid., 14.

56. My thanks to Eartha Dengler, Immigrant City Archives, for pointing this out.

57. Declerq and Lacroix, "Politics and Sociology."

58. Ibid., 15, table 4. German midwives maintained especially mixed clientele on the average attending "at least 10 births to mothers from a half dozen different ethnic groups."

59. Ibid., 8–13.

60. Charles Dickens, *Hard Times for These Times,* ed. David Craig (New York: Penguin Books, 1969), 102, 65. For descriptions of Lawrence's Plains, see *Lawrence City Documents,* 1899–1912. Newspapers continually complained over the constant "stench between Lawrence and Short Street" and the "slime" that clinged to the surface of the city's streams and canals. *Evening Tribune,* July 11, 1910.

61. Dorgan, *History of Lawrence,* 145–46; *Tribune,* Aug. 29, 1903; Lauck, "Significance," 773.

62. Neill, *Report on Strike,* 19.

63. Cole, *Immigrant City,* 72–74; Mary Kenney O'Sullivan, "The Labor War At Lawrence," *Survey,* Apr. 16, 1912, 72–74; food prices, see *Massachusetts Report on the Cost of Living, 1910, Commonwealth of Massachusetts,* 21; "Average Prices Paid," 1860, 1872, 1881,1902, 1904, 1906, 1907, 1910," 64, 67, 68–69; Cole, *Immigrant City,* 74; Neill, *Report on Strike,* 26, 165–78; Alice O'Connor, "A Study of the Immigration Problem in Lawrence, Massachusetts" (Social Worker's thesis, Lawrence, 1914), 30–32.

64. *New York Call,* Feb. 6, 1912.

65. Tentler, *Wage-Earning Women,* 17; *Massachusetts Report of Commission on Minimum Wage Boards, 1912,* 222.

66. Statistics on foreign-born women from, "Immigration Commission," table 102, p. 784; "Sources of Family Income in Detail," "Immigration Commission," table 21, p. 824.

67. Cole, *Immigrant City,* 72; Todd and Sanborn, *Report of the Lawrence Survey,* 54–60; Siergiej, "Early Polish Immigrants," 69; "Immigration Commission," table 102, p. 784.

68. *New York Call,* Jan. 15, 1912.

69. Lorin F. Deland, "The Lawrence Strike: A Study," *Atlantic Monthly,* 109 (1912), 699.

70. Elizabeth Gurley Flynn, *Rebel Girl* (1955; reprint, New York 1986), 132–35.

71. Elizabeth Shapleigh, "Occupational Disease in the Textile Industry," *New York Call,* Dec. 29, 1912; Cole, *Immigrant City,* 105–8; Charles Harrington, "Report on Sanitary Conditions of Factories, Workshops, and Other Establishments," Massachusetts Board of Health, *Report,* 38 (1906): 475–79; *City Documents,* 1899–1900, esp. 123, 184.

72. Shapleigh, "Occupational Disease"; Cole, *Immigrant City,* 76; *Evening Tribune,* Aug. 8, 1902.

73. *Evening Tribune,* July 10, 1910.

74. *The Strike at Lawrence, Massachusetts, Hearings before the House of Representatives . . . 1912,* 62 Congress, 2 Session House Doc. No. 671, Washington, 1912, 170.

75. Cole, *Immigrant City,* 75.

76. *New York Call,* Jan. 18, 1912.

77. Hayes, *History,* 33, 35; *Tribune,* Jan. 24, 1912; *New York Call,* Jan. 18, 1912; Cole, *Immigrant City,* rents, 118–19; BSL, *Forty-third Annual Report* (1912), 33; *Tribune,* May 6, 1912.

78. Dickens, *Hard Times,* 102.

79. Todd and Sanborn, *Report of the Lawrence Survey,* 32, 58.

80. Todd and Sanborn, *Report of the Lawrence Survey,* 58, 32; Cole, *Immigrant City,* 72; "Cost of Living," Massachusetts Commission, 68–69; Neill, *Report on Strike,* 25.

81. Paul U. Kellogg, "The Minimum Wage and Immigrant Labor," Proceedings, 177.

82. Todd and Sanborn, "The Housing Problem in Industrial Communities," in Proceedings, 1912, 154.

83. For a detailed discussion of antebellum reform and middle-class conceptions of domestic life, see Stansell, "Women and Children."

84. *Tribune,* July 5, 1908, 1910, 1911.

85. Loom fixers also "pushed" for more enforcement of existing laws on the ages of women and children employed in the mills. Threatened by the rapid increase in unskilled labor and the constant threat of deskilling practices, they organized around enforcement. See *Tribune,* Sept. 16, 1903. For child labor "discoveries," see *City Documents,* 1904–5; *Tribune,* June 6, 1904. Liquor dealers, who serviced the larger establishments often led the fight to close down kitchen barrooms. See *Tribune,* Jan. 10, 1905, Oct. 2, 1905, Oct. 4, 1905. Midnight inspections intended to root out overcrowding and collective living arrangements occurred throughout the decade, see *Tribune,* Feb. 17, 1906. Consiglia Teutonica, interview with author, July 1981.

86. Jeremiah Carey, "Report of the Building Inspector," *City Documents,* 1906–07, 8.

87. *Tribune,* Oct. 8, 10, 1905. Angelo Rocco, interview, June 1981.

88. Mary Simkhovitch, *The City Worker's World* (New York: Henry Holt & Co., 1917), 79–80, quoted in Elizabeth Ewing, *City Lights: Immigrant Women and the Rise of the Movies.*

89. Ruth Rosen and Sue Davidson, eds., *The Maimie Papers* (Old Westbury, N.Y.: Feminist Press, 1977), 20.

90. Mrs. Rose Angelotti (nee Capriola), interview with author, July 1981,

91. *Tribune*, July 26, 1905.

92. *City Documents*, 1904–5.

93. High fees and expensive halls meant that most new immigrants continued to socialize in more public spaces. See especially *Tribune*, July 5, 1910.

94. *Tribune*, Aug. 29, 1903.

95. Ibid., Oct. 4, 1905, July 10, 1910.

96. *Public Documents of Massachusetts*, 1897–1912; *Records*, Clerks Office, City of Lawrence.

97. Stansell, *Women, Children*, 330.

98. *Tribune*, June 6, 1904.

99. Charles E. Persons, Mabel Parton, Mabelle Moses, and "Three Fellows," *Labor Laws and Their Enforcement* (New York: Arno and the New York Times, Reprint Series, 1971), 198.

100. Stansell, *Women, Children*, 313.

101. *City Documents*, 1904–12; *Tribune*, June 4, 1904, Jan. 2, 1906. Role of loom fixers, see *Tribune*, Sept. 16, 1903.

102. *Tribune*, June 4, 1904.

103. Lithuanian, this expression literally refers to policemen but was used by several Lithuanian and Russian women to mean "official outsiders," those responsible for alien laws and "troubles." Translation courtesy of William Wolkovich.

104. Marino Interview.

105. Lillian Rosenberg Shosberg, OHP, May 20, 1979 tape #10.

106. Capriola Interview. There is some evidence to suggest that such schemes of "swapping" persisted in female efforts on the shop floor. Among weavers, for example, women seem to have consistently received higher average amounts of premiums or bonuses than did their male counterparts. Among weavers who received premiums in the month of Nov., for example, 54.3 percent were male and 62.7 percent were female. Neill, *Report on Strike*, 82.

107. Marino Interview.

108. See especially Smith, *Family Connections*.

109. Brown Interview; Interview with Olga Veckys, Oct. 18, 1981.

110. Activist file, no. 023. In possession of author.

111. Quoted in Cameron, "Bread and Roses Revisited"; "Immigrant Commission," 785.

112. Michael Gold, *Jews without Money* (New York: Avon Books, 1930), 49.

113. Todd and Sanborn, *Report of the Lawrence Survey*, 67, 68, 88.

114. Ibid. The average number of persons per apartment in Lawrence was 7, or 1 1/2 persons per room. *Massachusetts Statistics of Labor, 1912*, 33. In 1910, there were 1.6 families per house and 8.2 persons per house, placing Lawrence 4th and 6th in the state for families per household. See Cole, *Immigrant City*, 73.

115. Smith, *Family Connections.*

116. Murphy, OHP, ICA.

117. Consiglia Teutonica, interview with author, July 1981.

118. Dora Swartz, interview with author, May 1981.

119. William Wolkovich, interview with author, Oct. 1981.

120. Elizabeth Vilkaite, interview with author, Oct. 18, 1981.

121. Interview with anonymous striker. June 1982.

122. Brown Interview.

123. Ezilda Murphy Interview.

124. For information concerning Lithuanian girls and such practices see Jonitis, 71. For Italian and Greek patterns for male children see Frank Thistlewaite. For Lawrence practices, see *New York Call,* Feb. 1, 1912; Neill, *Report on Strike,* 13, 41, 67; *Tribune,* Feb. 19, 27, 1912; interviews with Amelia Stundza.

125. Sandra Morgan and Ann Bookman, "Rethinking Women and Politics: An Introductory Essay," in *Women and the Politics of Empowerment,* ed. Bookman and Morgan, 3–29.

126. See especially, Nash, *We Eat the Mines;* Louise A. Tilly, "Paths," 400–417. The term comes from Michelle Perrot who writes that strikes in the mines of France were "an affair of the tribe." Quoted in Tilly, "Paths," 411.

127. Tilly, "Paths," 415.

128. The idea that women develop and sustain a separate gender-defined consciousness has been suggested in a variety of recent studies by social scientists concerned with sexual asymmetry and cultural constructions of gender. See especially, Louise Lamphere, Carol Gilligan, Nancy Choderow. In a classic discussion of women's separate emotional world in the nineteenth century, see Carol Smith-Rosenberg, "The Female World of Love and Ritual," in Disorderly Conduct, 53–76, which suggests that middle-class women developed worlds of visions and values, even "symbolic and cosmological systems" that differed in "highly significant ways" from that of men. For women of the popular classes, such differences have been located in the division of labor by sex whereby female obligations and responsibilities, revolving around women's role as caretakers of the home and family, create a sense of rights that, according to Temma Kaplan, "provides motive force for actions different from those of Marxist or feminist theory generally try to explain." Kaplan, "Female Consciousness," 545. Kaplan argues that the scope of female consciousness among popular women focuses on female duties as "gatherers and distributors of scarce resources in the community." See also Kaplan, "Class Consciousness," 21–57.

129. Ackelsberg, "Terrains of Protest," 11.

130. Nancy Hewitt, "Feminist Friends," Feminist Studies 12 (Spring, 1986), 43.

131. Anna Marino, interview with author.

132. *Tribune,* Jan. 17, 1912.

133. Interview with Consiglia Teutonica, Aug. 1981.

134. Averaging roughly 90 mealers a week. "Records" YWCA Feb. 1907–Mar. 1913, 138, 137; Sept. 25, 1911. ICA, Lawrence, Massachusetts.

Chapter 4: Neighborhoods in Revolt

1. Cole *Immigrant City,* 74; Neill, *Report on Strike,* 26, 165–78.

3. *Strike at Lawrence,* 32, 154–55, 244, 380–86.

4. Cole, *Immigrant City,* 32, 74.

5. Dexter Arnold, "You Can't Weave Cloth with Bayonets!" (Ph.D. diss., University of Wisconsin, 1976), 13.

6. Ray Stannard Baker, "The Revolutionary Strike," *American Magazine* (May 1912): 18–30C.

7. Oliver Christen, "Wages," *Boston Globe,* Jan. 28, 1912.

8. Myles Jackson, ed., "Anonymous Strike: The Lawrence Textile Strike," *Viewpoints on American Labor Series* (New York: Random House Records, 1972).

9. Michael Seddon, "Provocation: Why the Lawrence Strike of 1912 Happened" (Honors thesis, University of Massachusetts, 1972), 58.

10. *Strike at Lawrence,* 33.

11. Jeanne Davis, "Undercover in a Textile Factory," *The Survey,* Aug. 10, 1918, Vol. 40, 540.

12. *Globe,* Jan. 28, 1912.

13. Neill, *Report on Strike,* 452.

14. Ibid., 10; Seddon, "Provocation," 78.

15. In Nov. 1911, for example, female weavers received lower average earnings than their male counterparts, but the "amount of premium received by females was greater than that received by males." To make this possible the female weavers needed to outproduce the men so that the base upon which the premium was derived would exceed that of the men. See Neill, *Report on Strike,* 82.

16. *Strike at Lawrence,* 164.

17. Arnold, "Can't Weave Cloth," 7.

18. Ibid., 6.

19. Table from Arnold, "Can't Weave Cloth," 265; Immigration Commission, 758.

20. Neill, *Report on Strike,* 23, 80, 86.; Arnold, "Can't Weave Cloth," 17–18.

21. *Tribune,* Feb. 12, 1912.

22. Neill, *Report on Strike,* 33, 452.

23. Seddon, "Provocation," 57–58.

24. Raymond Swing, "Blame for Lawrence," *Nation,* vol. CVIII, No. 2808, 26 Apr. 1919.

25. Baker, "Revolutionary Strike," 25.

26. BSL, *Report of 1912*, 22–23; Melvyn Dubofsky, *We Shall Be All: A History of the Industrial Workers of the World* (Chicago: Quadrangle Books, 1969), 233–35.

27. *Tribune*, Jan. 19, 1912.

28. *Tribune*, Jan. 1, 2, 3, 1912; *Boston Herald*, Jan. 28, 1912. Records of the Franco-Belge Club, courtesy of Loren Velke, Lawrence, Mass. Translations of the Flemish, courtesy of Loren Velke.

29. *Tribune*, Jan. 1–15, 1912.

30. James R. Green, *The World of the Worker: Labor in Twentieth-Century America* (New York: Hill and Wang, 1980), 33.

31. *Sun*, Jan. 4, 1912.

32. *Tribune*, Jan. 11, 1912.

33. Geertz, *Interpretation of Cultures*, 316.

34. *Tribune*, Jan. 12, 13, 1912. *Lawrence Telegram*, Jan. 10, 1912. For information on the loom fixers during the first days of the strike, see *Tribune*, Jan. 14; mulespinners, Jan. 11; back boys, Jan. 9, 11. See also Fenton, *Immigrants and Unions*, 332–33; *Lawrence Sun*, Jan. 11, 12. Transcript of the *Trial of Commonwealth vs. Joseph Caruso*.

35. A cotton manufacturing establishment, the Everett employed mostly Lithuanians and Poles, 80 percent of whom were women. *Complete History of the Lawrence Strike*, vol. 4, Lawrence Public Library.

36. Approximately 80 percent of the weavers in the Everett Mill were of Polish origin. According to government testimony, the female weavers stopped almost two thousand looms when they found "not enough pay." Neill, *Report on Strike*, 25; see also, *Tribune*, Jan. 12, 13, 15, 1912. For the best general description of the strike, see Barbara Mayer Wertheimer, *We Were There: The Story of Working Women in America*, (New York: Pantheon Books, 1977), 358–68; Neill, *Report on Strike*, 11–25. For a conservative analysis of the strike, see Cole, *Immigrant City*, "Part Three," 179–81. The most comprehensive study of the strike is in Dexter Arnold, "Can't Weave Cloth." For an insightful discussion of prestrike conditions and workers lives, see Seddon, "Provocation." One of the best studies that investigates family life and female participation in the strike is by Caroline Shoemaker, "Families Through Crisis: The Lawrence Textile Workers Strike of 1912" (Senior essay, Yale University, 1977).

37. *Tribune*, Jan. 12, 1912; *Sun*, Jan. 12, 1912.

38. Baker, "Revolutionary Strike," 22. *New York Call*, Jan. 12, 1912. Representatives to the General Committee were elected at large by ethnic group. Embracing all (twenty-eight) major nationalities except the Germans, who delayed their approval until the following Friday, the committee became the official negotiators for the strikers. Like the local organizations, both men and women were elected by their communities, and although almost all committee mem-

bers wore the white ribbons of the IWW, all committees remained independent of Wobbly affiliation.

39. *Tribune*, Jan. 29, 1912.

40. Dubofsky, *We Shall Be All*, 241.

41. This distinction is made by Geertz who argues that the "politics of meaning is anarchic in the literal sense of unruled, not in the popular one of unordered." It is this concept of politics as the "struggle for the real," that calls attention to the different meanings of organization and leadership. Geertz, *Interpretation of Cultures*, 316.

42. The strike in Lawrence is probably the most well documented and intensely studied labor conflict in American history. Those that focus on the role of the IWW include: Paul Brissenden, *The I.W.W.: A Study of American Syndicalism* (New York: Columbia University Press, 1920), esp. chap. 12; Dubofsky, *We Shall Be All*, chap. 10; Joseph R. Conlin, *Bread and Roses Too: Studies of the Wobblies*, 101; Patrick Renshaw, *The Wobblies: The Story of Syndicalism in the United States* (Garden City; Doubleday, 1968), chap. 5. See also Nick Salvatore, *Eugene v. Debs* (Urbana: University of Illinois Press, 1982), 251–61, for a discussion on the effect of the strike, and IWW participation, on the socialist movement in America. One of the few studies to explore the aftermath of the strike on Lawrence's labor movement is David J. Goldberg, *A Tale of Three Cities*, chaps. 5, 7. For more general studies see, Justus Ebert, *The Trial of the New Society* (Cleveland, 1913), 33, 36, 49; Edwin Fenton, *Immigrants and Unions;* Cole, *Immigrant City,* "Part Three," 178–205.

43. For a detailed study of ethnic national organizations, see Goldberg, *A Tale of Three Cities*, chaps. 5, 7.

44. *New York Call*, Jan. 16, 1912.

45. *Tribune*, Jan. 12, 13, 14, 1912; *Sun*, Jan. 14, 1912.

46. *Boston Herald*, 28 Jan. 1912.

47. Goldberg, *A Tale of Three Cities*, 93–94.

48. Quote from Goldberg, *A Tale of Three Cities*, 91.

49. *Tribune*, Feb. 24, 1912, in Maurice B. Dorgan, *Complete History of the Industrial Upheaval in Lawrence, 1912*, vol. 3; Testimony, 241, *Strike at Lawrence.*

50. *Tribune*, Jan. 17, 1912; *Sun*, Jan. 13, 14, 1912.

51. Although the exact occupation or mill in which Rurak worked is not known, it's very possible that she also worked at the Everett Mill. What is known, however, is her home address and the occupations of several of her neighbors, many of whom worked in the nearby Everett. Activist File, no. 71; *Tribune*, Jan. 13; *Sun*, Jan. 14, 1912.

52. *Sun*, Jan. 27, 1912.

53. *Tribune*, Feb. 1, 1912.

54. Mary K. O'Sullivan, "Labor War," 73.

55. *Sun,* Jan. 14, 1912.

56. *Tribune,* Jan. 13, 14, 15, 1912.

57. *Tribune,* Mar. 17, 1912; *Sun,* Jan. 13, 1912.

58. Quoted in Paul Buhle, "Debsian Socialism and the 'New Immigrant' Worker," in *Insights and Parallels,* ed. William O'Neill (Minneapolis: University of Minnesota Press, 1973), 280; Goldberg, *A Tale of Three Cities,* 91.

59. In Nov. of 1912, the IWW would attempt to break up the language federations although their efforts were resisted. See Goldberg, *A Tale of Three Cities,* 92.

60. This position is especially well formulated by Dubofsky, who overemphasizes the role of Wobbly leadership in the strike. In his view, Ettor "taught the inexperienced immigrants the nature of industrial warfare," and put them "in an aggressive mood." *We Shall Be All,* see especially 228, 242, 248. See also Brissenden, *The I.W.W.,* 286, 291; "Strike of Textile Workers in Lawrence," *Strike Literature* 496–505, Lawrence Public Library.

61. *Records,* Franco-Belgian Club; Goldberg, *A Tale of Three Cities,* 93; Dubofsky, *We Shall Be All,* 256; Conlin, *Bread and Roses,* 114.

62. Anna Marino, interview with author, Aug. 1981.

63. *Strike at Lawrence,* 440.

64. *Tribune,* Jan. 17; Cameron, "Bread and Roses Revisited," 43.

65. Alfred Schutz, quoted in Geertz, *Interpretation of Cultures,* 365.

66. Based on Activist file. Even among older women, workers outnumbered housewives. Among women 30 and over, for example, 47.3 percent were at home while a majority worked.

67. The breakdown for occupations given in table 7 is as follows:

At home	20
Clerk	3
Grocery store	1
Midwife	1
Teacher	1
Operative, cotton	3
Mender, woolen	3
Weaver, woolen	1
Spinner, worsted	4
Mender, worsted	2
Weaver, cotton	6
Operative, worsted	1
Carding room, cotton	2
Spinner, cotton	5
Weaver, worsted	2
Winder, worsted	1

Spooler, cotton	1
Basking	1
Burler	1
Bakery	1
Winder, cotton	1
Jack spooler	1
Timekeeper, cotton	1
Dressing room	1
Mill operative	16
Bookkeeper	2
Twister, woolen	1

68. Shoemaker, "Families through Crisis," 26.

69. *Tribune*, Feb. 28, 1912.

70. *Tribune*, Jan. 17, 1912.

71. *Boston Globe*, Mar. 6, 1912.

72. Cameron, "Bread and Roses Revisited," 51–55. Martha Brown, interview with author Aug. 1981; Dora Swartz, Aug. 1981; Consiglia Teutonica, July and Sept. 1981.

73. *Boston Herald*, Jan. 28, 1912; *Tribune*, Jan. 29, 1912; *Lawrence Telegram*, Feb. 1, 1912.

74. *Lawrence Telegram*, Jan. 28, 1912.

75. John Bruce McPherson, "The Lawrence Strike of 1912," National Association of Woolen Manufacturers, *Bulletin*, vol. 4, 1912, 243; *Tribune*, Jan. 29, 1912.

76. *Tribune*, Feb. 17, 1912. For details of the militia, see *New York Call*, Jan. 31, 1912; *Tribune*, Feb. 13, 1912.

77. *Tribune*, Jan. 20, 1912; Activist file, no. 097; *Tribune*, Jan. 31, Feb. 29, 1912.

78. *Tribune*, Feb. 26, 1912.

79. Troops, called into Lawrence almost from the first day, were costing the already bankrupt city four thousand dollars a day, and the mills threatened to hold the city financially accountable for damage to their property. *Tribune*, Feb. 12, 9, 1912.

80. The Starr was a vaudeville house but showed "stand pictures" for a nickel. See Seddon, "Provocation," 97–98.

81. Cameron, "Bread and Roses Revisited," 44.

82. *New York Call*, Jan. 23, 1912; Wertheimer, *We Were There*, 362.

83. *Tribune*, Feb. 22, 1912.

84. *Tribune*, Feb. 16, 1912.

85. *Tribune*, Feb. 23, 1912.

86. Wertheimer, *We Were There*, 362.

87. Flynn, *Rebel Girl,* 130; Dubofsky, *We Shall Be All,* 240; William D. Haywood, *Bill Haywood's Book: The Autobiography of Big Bill Haywood* (New York: International Publishers, 1929).

88. Fred Beal, *A Proletarian's Journey* (New York: 1937), 39.

89. Dora Swartz, interview with author, Sept. 1981.

90. Martha Brown, interview with author, July 1981.

91. *Tribune,* Feb. 17, 1912.

92. *New York Call,* Feb. 1, 1912; Neill, *Report on Strike,* 13, 41, 67; *Tribune,* Feb. 19, 22; Angelo Rocco interviewed by author May, June 1980; Mary Sullivan, interviewed June 1980; Swartz, interviewed Sept. 1981; Ben Axelrod, interviewed June 1983; Wertheimer, *We Were There,* 365.

93. *Tribune,* Feb. 12, 1912; Wertheimer, *We Were There,* 366.

94. *Tribune,* Feb. 13, 16, 1912.

95. *Strike At Lawrence,* 162. Writing of the incident, a nationally known "race theorist" observed, "The scene at the depot was repulsive and nauseating but no more revolting to witness than a surgical operation." Lorin F. Deland, "The Lawrence Strike," 696.

96. Elizabeth Gurley Flynn, quoted in the *Tribune,* Feb. 19, 1912. For contemporary critics of the plan, see *Anzeiger und Post,* Jan. 20, 1912. Translation courtesy of Eartha Dengler. See also C. C. Carstens, "The Children's Exodus From Lawrence," *Survey,* Apr. 6, 1912, 70–71. For workers' explanations of the exodus idea, see *New York Call,* Feb. 8, 1912.

97. *Tribune,* Feb. 19, 1912.

98. Ibid.

99. *Lawrence Telegram,* Feb. 1, 1912.

100. *Boston Globe,* Jan. 23, 1912.

101. Ibid.

102. *Sun,* Mar. 11, 1912.

103. *Tribune,* Feb. 2, 1912.

104. Ibid., Jan. 30, 1912; *Lawrence Telegram,* Feb. 1, 1912.

105. *Tribune,* Jan. 30, 1912; *Lawrence Telegram,* Feb. 1, 1912.

106. Ackelsberg, "Communities, Resistance, and Women's Activism," 300–301.

107. *Tribune,* Feb. 15, 1912.

108. *Lawrence Sun,* Feb. 22, 1912.

109. Haywood, *Bill Haywood's Book,* 249.

110. *Lawrence Sun,* Mar. 1, 1912.

111. Ibid., Mar. 6, 1912; *Tribune,* Mar. 6, 7, 1912.

112. Helen Marot, *American Labor Unions* (New York: Henry Holt & Company, 1914), 68.

113. *Sun,* Feb. 20, 1912.

114. *Sun,* Mar. 6, 1912.

115. *Tribune,* Feb. 23, 1912.

116. Dora Swartz, interview with author, Sept. 1981.

117. Marino, interview with author, Aug. 1981.

118. Teutonica, interview with author, Aug. 1981.

119. Ibid.

120. For a detailed study of ethnic networks and female association, see Judith Smith, "Our Own Kind: Family and Community in Providence, Rhode Island," in Nancy Cott and Elizabeth Pleck, *A Heritage of Our Own,* (New York: Simon & Schuster: 1979), 393–412; Smith, *Family Connections;* Stack, *All Our Kin.*

121. Located near the old well, this was a traditional meeting spot for women both before and during the strike. *Tribune,* Feb. 20, 1912; Teutonica, Marino, Veckys—interviews with author.

122. Brown, interview with author, May 1980; Swartz interview with author Aug. 1981; *Tribune,* Feb. 22, 1912.

123. *Tribune,* Feb. 20, 1912; Interview with Teutonica.

124. *Tribune,* Feb. 22, 1912; *Vienybe Liebuninku,* Feb. 28, 1912. Translation courtesy of William Lawrence Wolkovich-Valkavicius.

125. *Tribune,* Jan. 15, Mar. 2, 1912.

126. *Tribune,* Feb. 23, 1912; *Sun,* Feb. 22, 24, 1912.

127. *Sun,* Feb. 24, 1912.

128. *Sun,* Feb. 24, 1912.

129. Baker, "Revolutionary Strike," 30. Interview, Brown; interview with Ben Axelrod, June 1982 and Hymie Axelrod, Aug. 1981.

130. "The Lawrence Strike from Various Angles," *Survey,* 73.

131. *Tribune,* Jan. 27, 1912; O'Sullivan, "Labor War," 73.

132. *Tribune,* Mar. 4, 1912.

133. *Tribune,* Feb. 16, 20, 1912, Mar. 6, 1912.

134. For a detailed discussion of the Lithuanian church in Lawrence see Arunas Alisauskas, "Changing Patterns of Religious Behavior, Organization, and Belief in Immigrant Subcultures: The Lithuanian Settlements at Lawrence, Massachusetts, 1890–1930" (Paper dated 1980, courtesy of Immigrant City Archives, Lawrence, Mass).

135. Activist file, no. 004; *Tribune,* Mar. 7, 1912.

136. Thomas Chalmers, "Some Problems Presented By The Lawrence Strike," *The Protectionist,* Apr. 1912, vol. 23, 681.

137. *Tribune,* Feb. 24, 1912.

138. Interview with Teutonica.

139. Activist file, no. 117; *Tribune,* Mar. 13, 1912.

140. *Boston Globe,* Jan. 23, 1912.

141. Seddon, "Provocation," 45, 86; *Tribune,* Mar. 13, 1912.

142. Shoemaker, "Families through Crisis," 21.

143. *Tribune,* Feb. 23, 1912.

144. Shoemaker, "Families through Crisis," 21.

145. Ibid.

146. Ibid.; *Tribune,* Feb. 23, 1912; *Boston Globe,* Feb. 23, 1912.

147. One Polish woman, Pauline Nowak, was arrested three weeks after giving birth. Massachusetts Vital Statistics.

148. *Tribune,* Jan. 19, 25, Feb. 22; Interview with Angelo Rocco, June, Aug. 1981.

149. Teutonica, interview with author, Aug. 1981.

150. *Tribune,* Feb. 19, 1912.

151. Activist file, no. 079.

152. Activist file, no. 055, *Tribune,* Feb. 28, 1912.

153. The mean age for activists was 26 years with the 20–24 and 25–29 categories containing the highest concentrations. Activist File.

154. Baker, "Revolutionary Strike," 26; accident rates are difficult to assess as company records do not exist. Government reports, however, provide some evidence of the unusually high accident rates at various mills. One report, for example, claims over 1,000 significant accidents at the Pacific alone between 1900–1905. Charles Harrington, "Report on Sanitary Conditions," 477–79. Dr. Elizabeth Shapleigh also commented on the "considerable number of boys and girls who die the first two or three years after beginning work. . ." Elizabeth Shapleigh, "Occupational Disease." In 1910, deaths under 1 year of age reached 346 per 1000, deaths under 5, soared to 467 per 1000. See Cole, *Immigrant City,* table 30, p. 419. *Le Courrier de Lawrence,* Feb. 15, 22, 1912.

155. For details of female strike tactics, see *Tribune,* Feb. 12, 19, 24, 26, 1912; Cameron, "Bread and Roses Revisited," 45–49.

156. *The Strike at Lawrence,* 251.

157. Activist file, nos. 12, 111, *Tribune,* Feb. 26; *Lawrence Telegram,* Feb. 26, 1912.

158. Activist file, no. 035.

159. Cole, *Immigrant City,* 183–84; Wertheimer, *We Were There,* 366.

160. *Tribune,* Mar. 14, 1912.

161. *Tribune,* Mar. 16, 1912.

162. "The Complete History of The Lawrence Strike," Scrapbook, Lawrence Public Library, vol. 4, Mar. 17, 1912.

163. Antonietta Capriola, interview with author, Oct. 1981.

164. *Tribune,* Feb. 13, 1912.

165. Ackelsberg, "Female Collaborative Activity."

166. Interview with Teutonica.

167. *Tribune,* Jan. 31, 1912; *Lawrence City Documents,* 1899–1900, 37.

168. Interview with Swartz.

169. *Tribune,* Mar. 13, 1912. Interviews: Angelo Rocco, Consiglia Teutonica, Lithuanian by Studza.

170. Baker, "Revolutionary Strike," 19, 30A.

171. Walter E. Weyl, "It is Time to Know," in "The Lawrence Strike From Various Angles," *Survey*, v. 28, 1912, 65–66.

172. *Boston Herald*, Jan. 28, 1912.

173. "Complete History," Lawrence Public Library.

174. Robert A. Woods, "The Various Angles," 66.

175. Gutman, *Work, Culture and Society*. For a critique of this approach, see David Montgomery, "The 'New Unionism' and the Transformation of Worker's Consciousness in America, 1909–1922," *Journal of Social History*, vol. 7, 1974, 509–29.

176. Activist file, no. 052

177. This contrasts sharply with the nonstriking French Canadians who had little experience in textile manufacturing before emigrating to Lawrence. Only 9.0 percent of French Canadian men and 32.5 percent of French Canadian women who reported past occupations, had worked in a textile mill. Immigration Commission, 756.

178. See especially, Walter M. Pratt, "The Lawrence Revolution," *New England Magazine*, vol. 46, 1912, 7–16; Richard W. Child, "The Industrial Revolt in Lawrence," *Colliers*, vol. 48 (1911–12): 13–15; Robert W. Beers, "Our Country's Greatest Danger," Lawrence, 1912; Baker, "Revolutionary Strike," 30A–30B; Robert Woods, "Breadth and Depth of the Lawrence Strike," *Survey*, Apr. 1912, 67; Al Priddy, "Controlling the Passions of Men in Lawrence," *Outlook*, Oct. 1912, 344; "Real Labor War Now in Lawrence," *New York Times*, Jan. 30, 1912.

179. David Montgomery, "New Unionism." See also James R. Green, *The World of the Worker, Labor in Twentieth Century America* (New York: Hill and Wang, 1980), 67–99, and Montgomery, "The Past and Future of Worker's Control," *Radical America*, (May–June, l982): 92–95.

180. *Tribune*, Jan. 29, 1912.

181. Baker, "Revolutionary Strike," 30A–30B.

Conclusion

1. Thomas F. Gossett, *Race: The History of an Idea in America* (New York: Shocken Books, 1965), 300.

2. *Life Magazine*, June, 1922. The idea of race suicide is discussed in detail in Gossett, Ibid. The implications of race suicide theories for women's reproductive freedom are explored in Linda Gordon, *Woman's Body, Woman's Right*, 140–45.

3. Gordon, *Woman's Body, Woman's Right*, 141.

4. Gossett, *Race*, 300.

5. Gordon, *Woman's Body, Woman's Right*, 140.

6. In their efforts to target immigrant women, Lawrence's manufacturers mirrored national drives aimed at Chicano families, where women allegedly

maintained a "fortress against alien values." George F. Sanchez, " 'Go After the Women': Americanization and the Mexican Immigrant Women, 1915–1929," in Ellen Carol DuBois and Vicki L. Ruiz, eds., *Unequal Sisters: A Multi-Cultural Reader in U.S. Women's History,* ed. Ellen Carol DuBois and Vicki L. Ruiz (New York: Routledge, 1990), 250–63.

7. Caroline Rowan, "For the Duration Only: Motherhood and the Nation in the First World War," in *Formations of Nation and People* (London: Routledge, 1984), 152–53. Unwilling to abolish "poverty, overcrowding and insanitary conditions," state concern, argues Rowan, focused instead on the "education of working-class mothers in the areas of domestic hygiene and infant management." In a similar discussion of the reconstructed working-class woman in the years that followed WWI, see Gordon, *Heroes,* p. 221. "The absence of a feminist interpretation," notes Gordon, "conditioned the disappearance of incest and the 'discovery' of female sexual delinquency." Gordon, Ibid.

8. This theme has been explored most fully for Jewish women, see Charlotte Baum, Paula Hyman, Sonya Michel, *The Jewish Woman in America* (New York: Dial Press, 1976).

9. Roy Rosenzweig, *Eight Hours for What We Will: Workers & Leisure in an Industrial City, 1870–1920* (Cambridge: Cambridge University Press, 1983); Kathy Peiss, " 'Charity Girls' and City Pleasures; Historical Notes on Working-Class Sexuality, 1880–1920," in *Powers of Desire: The Politics of Sexuality,* ed. Ann Snitow, Christine Stansell, and Sharon Thompson, (New York: Monthly Review Press, 1983): 74–87.

10. Ewen, "Immigrant Women in the Land of Dollars," 242.

11. Simon Patten, *The New Basis of Civilization* (New York, 1907), 59.

12. Ibid.

13. Maxine Seller, ed., *Immigrant Women* (Philadelphia: Temple University Press, 1981), 7–8.

14. Ibid.

15. Solomon, *Ancestors,* 199.

16. John Graham Brooks, quoted in Solomon, *Ancestors,* 199.

17. Records of the Lawrence City Mission, 1916, 13–14, ICA.

18. Quoted in Cameron, "Bread and Roses," 44.

19. *Lawrence Sun,* Jan. 27, 1912.

20. Rowan, "For the Duration," 153.

21. *Records,* International Institute, 1912–1913.

22. *Records,* 1900–1910, I.C.A.

23. Amelia Olenio, interview "Recollections of the YMCA," Immigrant City Archives, Lawrence, Massachusetts.

24. For exact amounts given to Institute and Welfare Work, see Yearly Reports, City Mission, 1912, 1915, International Institute, 1912.

25. City Mission, Yearly Reports, 1913, 7.

26. Ibid, 1913–17.

27. T. O. Marvin, "Handling the Lawrence Strike," *Protectionist*, Apr. 1912, 658.

28. City Mission, Yearly Reports, 1921, 4.

29. *Yearly Reports*, 1921, 4.

30. Ibid., 4–5.

31. Ibid., 1917, 14–15. Annual Report Commission of Immigration, Bureau of Immigration, International Institute, misc records, Immigrant City Archives.

32. *Yearly reports*, Ibid, 8.

33. With the exception of two "foreign visitors," bourgeois women, many of whom had influential husbands comprised the governing board of the International Institute. Several husbands sat on the Board of Trade and were involved in the North American Civic League for Immigrants. City Documents, 1910, 1912.

34. *Yearly Reports*, 1916, 13–14.

35. Hayden, Ibid, 284. Ryan, Ibid.

36. Jacquelyn Dowd Hall, "Private Eyes, Public Women: Images of Class and Sex in the Urban South, Atlanta, Georgia, 1913–1915," in *Work Engendered: Toward a New History of American Labor*, ed. Ava Baron, (Ithaca, N.Y.; Cornell University Press, 1991): 272.

37. *Sunday Advertiser*, Jan. 27, 1912.

38. Peiss, *Cheap Amusements*, 186.

39. Elizabeth Ewen, *Immigrant Women in the Land of Dollars*, 217.

40. *Records*, International Institute (hereafter II), ICA, 1912–14.

41. Goldberg, *A Tale of Three Cities*, 105.

42. *Records*, II, ICA.

43. Olga Veckys, Ibid.

44. Anonymous striker, Interviewed by author Oct. 18, 1981.

45. Amelia Olenio, "Recollections of the YWCA," unpublished paper, MS, ICA.

46. *Records*, II. Ibid. ICA

47. Olga Veckys, Oct. 10, 1981.

48. Dora Swartz (nee Glassman), interviewed by author, Aug. 12, 1981.

49. Olga Veckys, interviewed by author, Oct. 18, 1981, Nov. 2, 1981.

50. Quoted in Goldberg, *A Tale of Three Cities*, 94–5.

51. Amelia Olenio, "Recollections."

52. Cott, *The Grounding of Modern Feminism*, 3; Eleanor Flexnor, *Century of Struggle: The Woman's Rights Movement in the United States*

53. Goldberg, *A Tale of Three Cities*, 93.

54. Wallace, "Visiting the Past," 140.

55. Records of the Lawrence City Mission, Mar. 1913. Kathy Peiss, *Cheap Amusements: Working Women and Leisure in Turn-of-the-Century New York* (Philadelphia: Temple University Press, 1986), 178.

56. John Tagg, *The Burden of Representation.*

57. As one of the central notions of poststructuralist theory, this idea has been expressed in a number of studies. Here I am referring most specifically to Lynn Hunt, *Politics, Culture, and Class in the French Revolution* (Berkeley: University of California Press, 1984), 23.

58. Carolyn Steedman, "Culture, Cultural Studies, and the Historians," in *Cultural Studies,* ed. Lawrence Grossberg, Cary Nelson, Paula Treicher (New York: Routledge, 1992), 614.

Index

Abortion, campaign to eliminate, 67–68
Addams, Jane, 8, 70
American Federation of Labor (AFL), 140, 159, 168
American Woolen Company (AWC), 59, 75–77, 162–63
Americanization, 171–74; and immigrant women, 176–79, 182–83; and Americanizers as custodians of tradition, 184–85
Anglo-American, 158
Anarchy, 126, 140
Architecture: to affirm social hierarchy, 58–59; of Pemberton, 17–18; and female exchange, 89, 91; and urban landscape, 32–34, 38, 83–84, 97, 99–101
Arlington Mill, 28, 59, 63, 123, 148, 158, 163, 167
Association for Welfare Work, 175
Atlantic Mill, 122
Axelrod, Sara, 79–81, 108, 110, 141, 153, 154, 166–67
Ayer Mill, 59, 76

Barthes, Roland, 12
Bavaria, textile district of, 77. See also Immigrants

Blacklisting, 57–58, 62, 80
Board of Health, 54, 66, 164, 176
Boston, Massachusetts, 42, 55, 60
Bower, William, 59; activist wife, 26
Brox, Faris, 94

Cameras, 159
Canadians, French: sex ratio, 33; role in strike of 1882, 52–53; population, 28, 33, 75, 84; wages, 120; role in strike of 1912, 127; Anglo, 36. See also Immigrants
Capitalism, 1, 40, 47, 51, 56, 65
Carter, Clark, 106, 115, 175
Catholic church, 52–53, 77, 82, 100, 101, 107, 127, 134, 139, 141, 144, 155, 158, 163, 183–84
Central Labor Union, 65, 98, 122, 123, 149
Chicago, 37
Child care: and children's boarding houses, 110–11; exchange of, 93, 109; older women and, 109; role in strikes, 3, 142, 164, 52; as strike issue, 114, 164, 107
Children's exodus, 142–43, 145, 154
Child labor, 30, 100, 105–7
Civil War, 12, 20, 28–29

Class, 2–4, 8–9, 20, 41, 66, 95, 141, 173, 176, 182, 184
Collectivism, 4–5, 45, 61, 109, 137, 150, 158
Command of meaning, 7, 10, 65, 185
Community, 4–5, 12, 26, 57, 91, 95–97, 107–8, 113, 126, 135, 158, 163, 177, 185
Corporate power, 1, 49, 54, 59, 61
Cotton Spinners Association, 57
Crocker, Dr. Susan, 20–21, 68

Darnton, Robert, 7
Davis, Natalie, 11
Democracy, 4, 127, 149, 168
Dickens, Charles, 97, 100
Difference, 58, 66, 133
Domesticity: as artisan ideal, 40, 60, 64, 66; as Progressive strategy, 66, 69–70, 101, 104, 171, 175, 182
Dress: as "Tyranny," 21; role in strike of 1882, 50–51, 54; F.N., 201; role in strike of 1912, 139, 142, 148–49, 161; as self-representation, 177–79, 181

Education, 3, 50, 62, 174, 182
Elliott, Charles, 31
English, 17, 52, 57, 59, 76, 81, 148, 158–59
Entrepreneurism, 100
Equal Rights Amendment, 174, 183
Essex Savings Bank, 48, 60
Ethnicity, 2, 9–10, 20, 33, 52, 57, 59, 75, 79, 81–84, 89, 91, 95–97, 99, 102–5, 108–11, 121, 123–28, 133, 138, 154, 158, 160, 165–66, 174, 183; as permeable, 93–95, 109; as form of strike organization, 121, 123
Everett Mills, 28, 59, 163
Ettor, Joe, 124, 126, 128, 133–35, 140–41

Factory girl, 9–10, 22, 30, 32, 72; as social construction, 22

Family economy, 27, 40–42, 45, 65, 70–71, 100
Family life, 8, 40, 41, 65, 78, 81–82, 91, 104, 107, 155, 173–75
Family wage, 40–42; as signifier of sexual difference, 41, 66, 69–71; as invented past, 60, 65–66
Female activists, 2–5, 9–11, 25–26, 34, 39, 41, 44, 47, 66, 68, 70–72, 79–80, 89, 93, 96, 99–100, 103, 105–6, 111, 128, 130, 132–33, 139–41, 149–50, 152, 154–57, 160–63, 165, 167, 176, 178, 182; and construction of gender deviancy, 8–9, 61, 66–72, 171, 175; and cult of motherhood, 69–70, 174–76, 178–79
Female consciousness, 39, 113, 185
Female friendships, 43, 45, 110; and gender consciousness, 51, 114
Feminism, 38, 184; and scholarship, 2; and politics,
Festivals, 55, 60, 91, 101–2
Flynn, Elizabeth Gurley, 99, 141, 143
Folsom, Jeannie, 52, 54, 56, 66, 70
Food: and female collaboration, 89, 91, 93–96, 107; and riots, 111–12, 114–15; high prices of, 97–98, 102, 117–18
Foucault, Michel, 4, 9, 11, 69
Franco-Belge, 81 89; in strike of 1912, 122, 124, 127, 183
Frank Leslie's Illustrated, 19
French Revolution, as fearful image of female militancy, 68–69

Gender, 4, 8, 13, 50–51, 55, 57, 64, 68, 79, 81, 111, 173; and the Woman Question, 7, 17, 25–27; and pay equity, 24, 49, 119; and division of labor, 45, 50–51, 112–13; and skilled men, 44; and ethnicity, 96; and identity, 10, 39, 40, 176, 177; typing, 7, 25, 41, 65–66, 69, 174; deviancy, 8, 69, 104–5, 130, 173; and sexual difference, 41, 57, 176

Germans, 57, 59, 60, 89. *See also* Immigrants
Gilded Age, 21, 26–27, 30, 41, 66
Gilman, Charlotte Perkins, 71
Giovannitti, Arturo, 140–41
Goldman, Emma, 70, 141
Great Industrial War, 122
Greenback Labor Club, 60

Halley, Mary E., 47, 49–50, 52, 54–56, 60, 65–66, 70–72
Hamilton, Mary Ann, 20, 27, 30
Harper's Weekly, 19
Harvard College, 54, 62
Hawthorne, Nathaniel, 72
Haywood, Big Bill, 124, 126, 133–34, 141
History: literary nature of, 6–8, 12, 185–86; and creation of artisanal past, 65–66; and strike memory, 71–72; and strike of 1912, 100, 125–26
Home ownership programs, 58–59
Housewifery, 3, 40
Housing, 3, 32, 38, 51, 58, 83–84, 89, 92–93, 100–101, 107–8, 111, 114, 168, 174
Howard, Robert, 60, 65

Identity: as political, 5, 9–11, 185–86; and female strikers, 177, 185. *See also* Wage labor
Immigrants, 2, 33, 37, 40, 52, 57, 59, 61, 75, 77, 79, 81–84, 89, 91, 93–96, 98–99, 102–10, 113, 115, 119, 127–28, 134–35, 138–40, 148, 154–58, 161, 163, 165–66, 171–72, 175, 178, 182–83; as "new," 75–77, 84; as experienced factory workers, 166–67
Industrial life, 19, 24, 31, 40, 83, 100; and upheaval of 1912, 3, 118, 164
Industrial Workers of the World (IWW), 121–28, 137–38, 140–42, 152, 157–60, 165–66, 173, 178. *See also* Wobblies

Inflation, 98
International Institute for Women, 174, 179, 182
Irish, 28–30; sex ratios, 33; as women outside family economy, 31, 34, 37–40; as skilled operatives, 44; role in strike of 1882, 52–53, 61; involvement in corporate welfare, 59; role in strike of 1912, 127, 158–59; population, 29–30, 32, 35, 84. *See also* Immigrants
Italians, 75, 77, 81, 89, 105; in strike of 1912, 124–25, 128, 130, 157, 161; as "Turks," 131. *See also* Immigrants

Kelly, Florence, 105
Kiev, 79–80, 167
Knights of Columbus, 184
Knights of Labor, 61, 65

Labor unrest, 1, 41, 166
Ladies Soldiers Aid Society, 20
Ladies Union Charitable Society (LUCS), 20, 25–26
Language, 3, 5, 10, 44, 65, 70, 173, 177, 185; and history, 6, 12, 186; and stump speeches, 1; and labor, 66
Lawrence, Abbott, 21
Lawrence City Mission, 175
Lawrence Eagle, 55
Lawrence Journal, 62
Lawrence Short Time Committee, 59
Leisure, 140, 179–82; regulation of kitchen bars, 101–2, 104; and hunting, 102; in ethnic clubs, 103–4
Le Proqres, 52
Lesbian, 8, 31; F.N. 195, 71
Life Magazine, 171
Lis, Josephine, 128, 139, 152–53, 156, 160, 167–68, 182
Lithuanians, 81, 89, 106, 108; in strike of 1912, 127–28, 161, 183. *See also* Immigrants
Livermore, Mary Rice, 25–26, 55, 68

McGill, Pearl, 140–41
McKinley-Dingley tariff, 76
Marino, Anna, 95–96, 114
Marot, Helen, 149
Marriage, 33–34, 37, 39, 43, 45, 50, 68, 72, 81, 103, 110, 157, 184

Race, 9, 20, 26; race suicide, 72, 171–73; as social construction, 173, 175
Radicalism, 80, 184
Reality, construction of, 6–9
Representation, 185
Robinson, Harriet, 72
Rocco, Angelo, 124–26
Rocco, Consiglia, 124. See also Teutonica, Consiglia
Rosenberg, Lillian, 106
Ruskin, John, 60
Russians: as Jewish immigrants, 75, 77, 79–81, 89, 108; in strike, 127, 155, 161, 183; as Polish immigrants, 75, 77, 108; in strike of 1912, 124, 128–30, 155, 157, 161. See also Immigrants
Russian Poland, textile district of, 77

Sabotage, 53–54
Sampson, Bridget, 20, 27, 29–30
Sanger, Margaret, 142
Sanitation, 3, 89, 97, 99, 164
Saxony, textile district of, 77
Scabs, 52, 138–40, 147–50, 155, 159, 163–64, 167, 178
Scientific management, 63, 123, 168
Scottish, 52, 59
Sexual imbalance, 31–33, 42, 78; as labor "problem," 41–42, 61, 65; sex ratios, 32–33, F.N. 64, 196, 78
Sexuality, 2, 8–10, 20
Sexual harassment, 48, 50, 55
Silesia, textile district of, 77
Social conceptualization, 7, 9
Social Darwinism, 70
Social housekeepers, 60, 82, 104–5, 107, 110, 137, 172, 174, 184

Socialism, 8, 25–26, 38, 41, 57, 70, 140, 142, 153, 158, 164, 182–83
Socialist Labor party, 57
Solidarity, 52–53, 55–56, 61, 91, 113, 121, 125, 128, 138, 162, 166, 168
Speedups, 47, 63
Syrians, 75, 79, 82–83, 89, 105; and peddling, 104; in strike of 1912, 125, 134, 156, 158, 161. See also Immigrants
Starr Theater, 140, 143, 179
Steward, Ira, 40, 65
Stowe, Harriet Beecher, 21
Strikes: as sites of conceptual contests, 9, 11–12, 13
Suffrage, 25, 26, 42, 68, 70, 174, 182–83
Surrey Magazine, 79

Tampa, 2
Ten-Hour Movement, 57
Teutonica, Consiglia, 96, 109, 156, 164
Tewksbury, Robert, 71–72
Thompson, E. P., 95
Tresca, Carlo, 141

Unemployment, 43, 77
Unionism, 3–4, 42, 49, 57, 60–61, 121, 169
United Textile Workers, 121, 127

Vanity Fair, 19
Violence, 10, 53–54, 130–31, 133, 134, 138–40, 143, 147, 149, 150, 153, 156–57, 161–62, 164, 174

Wage labor, 19, 27, 43, 51, 69, 72, 77, 81, 97, 115, 163; as social construction 9–10, 40–41; as source of female identity, 43–45, 47, 50, 54, 81–83, 112
Wage reductions, 47, 50, 98, 118
Washington Mill, 55, 63, 76, 100, 123, 163. See also Bay State Mill
Weinbaum, Dora, 160
Welsenback, Annie, 154–55, 163

Wobblies, 121, 124–26, 134, 138, 141, 160, 165, 167, 176, 186. *See also* Industrial Workers of the World

Women: economic indispensability of, 34, 38, 45, 60, 79, 80, 95, 103; employment opportunities for, 78–79, 81; as "ignorant" immigrants, 173, 175; invisibility of in history, 6, 11, 19, 27; solidarity of, 27, 43, 45; without men, 37–39, 44, 68, 70–71; "women in motion," 185; as "scab/muggers," 133, 138, 139, 147, 149, 161; as source of male anxiety, 8, 65, 67–69, 72, 171–73; refuse to settle strike of 1912, 163–64; and social space, 4, 45, 89, 93–96, 107, 113, 135–39, 151, 185; and deskilling, 62–64; as proletariat, 31; as skilled operatives, 44, 49, 54; and respectability, 67, 69; as category, 7, 9–11, 69, 70–71; as pioneer immigrants, 79, 82; older, 109

Women's Trade Union League, 121

Wood, Duncan, 42, 48, 60–61

Wood, Robert, 143, 166

Wood, William, 59, 75–76, 124

Wood Mill, 75, 77, 80, 123, 135, 154

World War I, 75, 83, 97, 99, 107

World War II, 2

Young Women's Christian Association (YWCA), 72, 115, 158, 175, 179, 182–84

Books in the Series
Women in American History

Women Doctors in Gilded-Age Washington: Race,
Gender, and Professionalization
Gloria Moldow

Friends and Sisters: Letters between Lucy Stone and
Antoinette Brown Blackwell, 1846-93
Edited by Carol Lasser and Marlene Deahl Merrill

Reform, Labor, and Feminism: Margaret Dreier Robins and the
Women's Trade Union League
Elizabeth Anne Payne

Private Matters: American Attitudes toward Childbearing and Infant
Nurture in the Urban North, 1800-1860
Sylvia D. Hoffert

Civil Wars: Women and the Crisis of Southern Nationalism
George C. Rable

I Came a Stranger: The Story of a Hull-House Girl
Hilda Satt Polacheck
Edited by Dena J. Polacheck Epstein

Labor's Flaming Youth: Telephone Operators and
Worker Militancy, 1878–1923
Stephen H. Norwood

Winter Friends: Women Growing Old in the New Republic,
1785-1835
Terri L. Premo

Better Than Second Best: Love and Work in
the Life of Helen Magill
Glenn C. Altschuler

Dishing It Out: Waitresses and Their Unions
in the Twentieth Century
Dorothy Sue Cobble

Natural Allies: Women's Associations in American History
Anne Firor Scott

Beyond the Typewriter: Gender, Class, and the Origins of Modern
American Office Work, 1900–1930
Sharon Hartman Strom

The Challenge of Feminist Biography: Writing the Lives of Modern
American Women
*Edited by Sara Alpern, Joyce Antler, Elisabeth Israels Perry, and
Ingrid Winther Scobie*

Working Women of Collar City: Gender, Class, and Community in
Troy, New York, 1864–86
Carole Turbin

Radicals of the Worst Sort: Laboring Women in Lawrence,
Massachusetts, 1860–1912
Ardis Cameron

Books in the Series
The Working Class in American History

Worker City, Company Town: Iron and Cotton-Worker Protest in
Troy and Cohoes, New York, 1855–84
Daniel J. Walkowitz

Life, Work, and Rebellion in the Coal Fields:
The Southern West Virginia Miners, 1880–1922
David Alan Corbin

Women and American Socialism, 1870–1920
Mari Jo Buhle

Lives of Their Own: Blacks, Italians, and Poles in Pittsburgh,
1900–1960
John Bodnar, Roger Simon, and Michael P. Weber

Working-Class America: Essays on Labor, Community,
and American Society
Edited by Michael H. Frisch and Daniel J. Walkowitz

Eugene V. Debs: Citizen and Socialist
Nick Salvatore

American Labor and Immigration History, 1877–1920s:
Recent European Research
Edited by Dirk Hoerder

Workingmen's Democracy: The Knights of Labor
and American Politics
Leon Fink

The Electrical Workers: A History of Labor at General Electric and
Westinghouse, 1923–60
Ronald W. Schatz

The Mechanics of Baltimore: Workers and Politics in the
Age of Revolution, 1763–1812
Charles G. Steffen

The Practice of Solidarity: American Hat Finishers
in the Nineteenth Century
David Bensman

The Labor History Reader
Edited by Daniel J. Leab

Solidarity and Fragmentation: Working People and Class
Consciousness in Detroit, 1875–1900
Richard Oestreicher

Counter Cultures: Saleswomen, Managers, and Customers in
American Department Stores, 1890–1940
Susan Porter Benson

The New England Working Class and the New Labor History
Edited by Herbert G. Gutman and Donald H. Bell

Labor Leaders in America
Edited by Melvyn Dubofsky and Warren Van Tine

Barons of Labor: The San Francisco Building Trades and
Union Power in the Progressive Era
Michael Kazin

Gender at Work: The Dynamics of Job Segregation by Sex
during World War II
Ruth Milkman

Once a Cigar Maker: Men, Women, and Work Culture
in American Cigar Factories, 1900-1919
Patricia A. Cooper

A Generation of Boomers: The Pattern of Railroad Labor Conflict in
Nineteenth-Century America
Shelton Stromquist

Work and Community in the Jungle: Chicago's Packinghouse
Workers, 1894–1922
James R. Barrett

Workers, Managers, and Welfare Capitalism: The Shoeworkers and
Tanners of Endicott Johnson, 1890–1950
Gerald Zahavi

Men, Women, and Work: Class, Gender, and Protest in the
New England Shoe Industry, 1780–1910
Mary Blewett

Workers on the Waterfront: Seamen, Longshoremen,
and Unionism in the 1930s
Bruce Nelson

German Workers in Chicago: A Documentary History of
Working-Class Culture from 1850 to World War I
Edited by Hartmut Keil and John B. Jentz

On the Line: Essays in the History of Auto Work
Edited by Nelson Lichtenstein and Stephen Meyer III

Upheaval in the Quiet Zone: A History of Hospital Workers' Union,
Local 1199
Leon Fink and Brian Greenberg

Labor's Flaming Youth: Telephone Operators and Worker Militancy, 1878–1923
Stephen H. Norwood

Another Civil War: Labor, Capital, and the State in the Anthracite Regions of Pennsylvania, 1840–68
Grace Palladino

Coal, Class, and Color: Blacks in Southern West Virginia, 1915–32
Joe William Trotter, Jr.

For Democracy, Workers, and God: Labor Song-Poems and Labor Protest, 1865–95
Clark D. Halker

Dishing It Out: Waitresses and Their Unions in the Twentieth Century
Dorothy Sue Cobble

The Spirit of 1848: German Immigrants, Labor Conflict, and the Coming of the Civil War
Bruce Levine

Working Women of Collar City: Gender, Class, and Community in Troy, New York, 1864–86
Carole Turbin

Southern Labor and Black Civil Rights: Organizing Memphis Workers
Michael K. Honey

Radicals of the Worst Sort: Laboring Women in Lawrence, Massachusetts, 1860–1912
Ardis Cameron